TEACHING SECONDARY ENGLISH

TEACHING SECONDARY ENGLISH

Mark A. Pike

Paul Chapman Publishing

Paul Chapman Publishing
A SAGE Publications Company
6 Bonhill Street
London EC2A 4PU

SAGE Publications Inc
2455 Teller Road
Thousand Oaks, California 91320

SAGE Publications India Pvt Ltd
B-42 Panchsheel Enclave
Post Box 4109
New Delhi 100 0 17

Library of Congress Control Number: 2002115857

A catalogue record for this book is available from the
British Library

ISBN 0 7619 4163 0
ISBN 0 7619 4164 9 (pbk)

Typeset by Pantek Arts Ltd, Maidstone, Kent

Printed in Great Britain by Cromwell Press, Trowbridge,
Wiltshire

Contents

For Luke and Lydia,
my very own
Keen Readers

Introduction

This book is based on over ten years' recent experience of teaching English at secondary level, finally as Head of English, Communications and Drama in a large comprehensive school. It is also informed by my work with students on the PGCE Secondary English course at the University of Leeds, one of the largest and most successful courses in the country, which I currently lead. Approaches developed during my classroom-based Ph.D research are also drawn upon to help teachers of English foster keen readers, writers and communicators who do more than acquire skills and knowledge: they experience the power of literature and learning to transform lives.

In this book teachers and student-teachers provide their own insights into such topics as how they learnt to plan lessons, match objectives to tasks, mark work and organize classes while maintaining their sanity and social lives in the process. There is reference throughout to the latest requirements for the award of Qualified Teacher Status (QTS) and how these standards can be met but this book also seeks to provide readable, engaging and thought-provoking insights that help English teachers appreciate what they do and also see new possibilities. Anecdotes and illustrations are used to illustrate key points as a deliberate attempt is made here to demystify the art of English teaching.

For the sake of clarity the text is divided into three parts although there is necessarily some overlap between them. Part I ('Principles and practice') considers some foundational principles and practices for the English classroom and applies these to the planning and assessing of teaching. Part II ('Teaching the English curriculum') examines English teaching at Key Stage 3, GCSE and AS/A2 level. Part III ('Challenging English') explores a range of challenges facing English teachers today and provides strategies for rising to them.

In Part I, Chapter 1 considers the aims of English and its nature as an arts subject. Chapter 2 is practical and employs the mnemonic 'Operational' to explain how effective English lessons can be planned. Chapter 3 uses another mnemonic, this time 'Metre', to demonstrate how assessment is an integral element of the art of teaching English. Chapter 4 looks at how English teachers can improve their art and explores the relation between professional development, action research and aesthetic response.

In Part II, Chapter 5 looks at ways of teaching literature and literacy at Key Stage 3 and their relationship. The transformation of English at Key Stage 3 and the impact of the National Literacy Strategy are clearly described and evaluated. Chapter 6 gives guidance on how to teach GCSE English and English literature in an integrated way and provides examples of work with a range of texts and various topics. Chapter 7 is a guide to the new AS and A2 levels in our subject and includes lesson sequences to illustrate the application of literary and learning theory.

In Part III, Chapter 8 describes approaches to teaching the media, drama and ICT and suggests that all three are essentially concerned with reading and how we construct and exchange meanings. Chapter 9 tackles differentiation, an aspect of English teaching which is a constant challenge, and argues that although we should differentiate in response to gender, ethnicity and ability we should also focus on the individual identity of the learner. Chapter 10 provides theoretical perspectives on, and practical strategies for, teaching pre-twentieth-century texts so they are relevant to adolescent readers saturated in twenty-first-century culture. Chapter 11 looks at how motivated and perceptive readers of poetry can be fostered and gives examples of successful and inspiring poetry teaching. Lastly, Chapter 12 explores the spiritual and moral dimension of English and how we can ensure our teaching has significance.

Please note that all names are pseudonyms unless permission to use actual names has been obtained. Readers should also note that details of examination specifications and set text should be obtained from the relevant examination board rather than from this book which should not be relied upon as a definitive guide.

Acknowledgements

It has been my privilege to work with many gifted and talented people in both schools and universities who have informed my thinking about the art of teaching English at secondary level. The PGCE English team at the University of Leeds; especially Andrew Stibbs and Stephen Clarke, commented on ideas as they developed. Nick McGuinn at the University of York identified omissions in an earlier draft and thereby ensured the text became more comprehensive. Much of the material on reading and the reader's response, would not have been possible without the expert guidance of Professor Michael Benton, who supervised my 'Keen Readers' PhD research at Southampton University.

Student-teachers of English whom I taught in the School of Education at the University of Leeds between 2000 and 2003 provided unique insights into the processes at work when learning to teach. While I was writing students gave refreshingly honest and critical feedback on draft chapters. Matt Bromley's thorough reading of the manuscript, while on his first teaching practice, was especially shrewd and Emily Cronin's encouragement was timely. Marian Moodie, Anna Goodall, Liam McNamara, Tara Cooksley and Luisa Graham all commented perceptively.

Hayley Pegg (Ryedale School, North Yorkshire) found time to write entertaining and incisive comments on the manuscript during the Christmas holiday following her first four months as a teacher of English. Halima Alam (formerly Head of English at Monmouth Comprehensive School) read an earlier draft and generously contributed insights from her extensive teaching experience. Bryony Hart (Arnewood School, Hampshire) and Joanne Rathmell (Beckfoot School, Bingley) gave permission to include extracts from their work on the way their experiences as pupils influenced their teaching. Struan Bates (Countesthorpe College) surprised me by writing an article for *The Times Educational Supplement* after attending a workshop I ran on teaching classic poetry and allowed me to include extracts from it here. Danny Fitzsimmons was encouraging throughout and commented helpfully on Chapter 2, Hillary Headey advised me on literacy and Wendy Adeniji was especially helpful with ICT and language teaching. Sue Pearson provided perceptive and also meticulous guidance regarding special needs.

Helmut Heuss, my father-in-law, brought editorial experience from Klett to the text and Ursula Heuss, my mother-in-law, helped to organize the earlier work on which this book is based. They were both the most congenial of hosts in Gomadingen, Baiersbronn and Stuttgart when I was engaged in preparatory reading, often undertaken sitting on a balcony in the sunshine after a long walk. My parents, Norm and Ruth Pike, who are the best teachers I know, encouraged me to carry on studying while showing remarkable stamina and good humour as babysitters although my son, Luke, and daughter, Lydia, still managed to provide the enjoyable interruptions and distractions during writing which puts everything in perspective. My wife, Babs, gave uncompromising advice and consistent support throughout and typed the original Ph.D thesis on which this book is based. Above all these sources, though, I must acknowledge my most significant Source, the Alpha and Omega, as this book emerged from a spiritual transaction as well as an aesthetic and literary one.

Mark A. Pike Ph.D
University of Leeds
September 2003

Part I

Principles and practice

1

The art of teaching English

Teaching English: painting the picture or copying the diagram?

> I think aesthetic teaching is the highest of all teaching because it deals with life in its highest complexity. But if it ceases to be purely aesthetic – if it lapses anywhere from the picture to the diagram – it becomes the most offensive of all teaching. (George Eliot, 1866/1967: 9–10).

In arguing that 'the highest of all teaching' is essentially aesthetic (creative, imaginative, visionary and inspirational), George Eliot strikes a chord with English teachers who currently find their work being increasingly characterized as straightforwardly instructional and more akin to the 'diagram' than the 'picture'. Eliot does not hesitate to designate such educational practice 'the most offensive of all teaching' and nor should we. Consequently, this chapter emphasizes the importance of the 'picture' and of creativity in English teaching. While there are similarities between pictures and diagrams, essential features present in one are conspicuously absent from the other. Diagrams are explicit; pictures, on the other hand, are often most successful if meaning is implicit so that the individual can form a personal interpretation and the work can become personally significant.

Far from being seen as an art, however, English teaching is being increasingly construed as a diagram to follow, a technology to employ or a method to adopt in order to achieve specific ends. It has even been asserted that construing teaching as an art rather than a technology may be responsible for a lack of excellent teachers in our schools because such a view results in attention being devoted to 'personal factors and qualities' (Muijs and Reynold, 2001: vii) which are difficult to manage. Attempts to reduce what should be aesthetic and inspired to the explicitly diagrammatic and instrumental make George Eliot's views especially relevant to English teachers at the start of the twenty-first century who believe in the importance of the 'picture' rather than the 'diagram' in English teaching (Pike, 2003f).

The aims of English teaching

Most handbooks on the teaching of English (Brindley, 1994; Davison and Dowson, 1998; Fleming and Stevens, 1998) prompt the reader to think about the aims of English teaching. The Cox models (DES, 1989) provide a helpful starting point as they describe different emphases within English. Yet these models and the aims they describe cannot be adequately evaluated without reference to the teaching methods generally employed to implement them. An important question to ask is which model or models enable the 'aesthetic teaching' so highly praised by George Eliot to take place. It is important to consider which models allow children to paint pictures and which have a heavy emphasis on getting them to copy diagrams. The models are as follows:

A 'personal growth' view focuses on the child: it emphasizes the relationship between language and learning in the individual and the role of literature in developing children's imaginative and aesthetic lives.

A 'cross-curricular' view focuses on the school: it emphasizes that teachers (of English and of other subjects) have a responsibility to help children with the language demands of different subjects in the school curriculum, otherwise areas of the curriculum may be closed to them. In England, English is different from other school subjects, in that it is both a subject and a medium of instruction in other subjects.

An 'adult needs' view focuses on communication outside the school, it emphasizes the responsibility of English teachers to prepare children for the language demands of adult life, including the workplace, in a fast-changing world. Children need to learn to cope with the day-to-day demands of spoken language and of print, they also need to be able to write clearly, appropriately and effectively.

A 'cultural heritage' view emphasizes the responsibility of schools to lead children to an appreciation of those works of literature that have been widely regarded as amongst the finest in the language.

A 'cultural analysis' view emphasizes the role of English in helping children towards a critical understanding of the world and cultural environment in which they live. Children should know about processes by which meanings are conveyed, and about the ways in which print and other media carry values. (DES, 1989: paras 2.21–2.25)

When recently surveyed, three quarters of students following the Post-Graduate Certificate in Education (PGCE) English course at the University of Leeds stated that they believed the 'personal growth' model deserved most emphasis in the English classroom (Pike, 2002b) and such a finding is representative of the wider population of English teachers (Goodwyn and Findlay, 1999). Some of my PGCE students' comments illustrate why they thought 'personal growth' should be privileged:

> Personal growth is the most important aspect of English as I feel imagination is vital to all aspects of life and that English can enrich your life. (Kristina)

> I believe that the study of literature and language is enriching in terms of personal growth. Books give people access to many different experiences and viewpoints. In terms of education, the needs of the whole child should be considered. (Adam).

> I chose personal growth as the most important because through English children can broaden their range of experiences and learn to empathize with other people. Without personal growth, and a deepening of understanding of both literature and language, the other models become very difficult to achieve. (Alex)

The individual and aesthetic response

Those teachers of English who privilege the 'personal growth' model generally acknowledge that it has implications for their practice in two important areas. First, the individual and relationships are especially valued and, secondly, an important element of their role is to foster aesthetic response. These twin elements are also emphasized in a recent survey of subject teaching in secondary schools, which concluded that in the best English lessons teachers 'showed thorough knowledge of pupils as *individual* learners and commitment to their intellectual, cultural and *aesthetic* development' (HMI, 2001: 3, emphasis added).

Indeed, 'a recurring tenet of the philosophy of personal growth through English' is that English teaching must be based upon 'a special knowledge of the pupils as individuals' (Bousted, 2000: 24). There is an important place for the individual in English teaching and the comments below typify the views of many English teachers:

> Personal growth is the most important due to the emphasis on the *individual*. (Helena)

> *The individual* must be the central focus of the teaching of English. It is important to enable them to develop personal appreciation of literature. (Catherine)

> English needs to be taught with *the individual* in mind. (Pete)

> As an English teacher, I think *the pupil has to be at the centre* of everything I do. (Cathy)

In the best English lessons special attention is also given to 'aesthetic uses of language and form' (HMI, 2001: 3) and it is not, perhaps, surprising that individuality and aesthetic response go together as the following comments from student-teachers at the end of their PGCE course suggest:

> I chose personal growth because I think the ability to develop a child's *imaginative and aesthetic life* is crucial in discovering a full sense of self and nowhere else is there suitable room in the curriculum to do this. (Ruth)

> English should be about developing the *imagination*. If it is not, then why not just teach English within history or RE or across the curriculum? To have any value and importance as a subject, English needs to offer something that other subjects cannot. This is why English is important to develop the imagination. (Michael)

> 'Allowing' children to be *creative and imaginative* – through language and literature – is to liberate them. (Dawn)

> Personal growth is the main aim of life and *creativity* allows one to become the person one really is. (Helen)

■ The art of teaching English

The justification for considering English teaching to be an art (rather than a technology or simply a method) derives from the aims of English teaching, as exemplified by the comments of these student-teachers, which can only be achieved through the *art* of English. When asked to rank the models in order of importance one student explained that 'understanding both yourself and the world seems to me to be the aim of art – hence personal growth comes first'. The art of being an English teacher is to empower children to see through literature what they have missed in life as it is often 'art's ability to shock and inspire, to change vision, ideas and feelings' (Stibbs, 1998: 210) that is so potently educative for its purpose is 'to raise consciousness, not to evade or anaesthetise it' (Stibbs, 1996: 31).

Far from seeing teaching as an art, however, many consider only knowledge to be of central importance. Even some writers, such as Tolstoy, consider teaching to be a transmission of knowledge and distinguish between 'the handing on of what was known to former generations', which is seen as the business of 'teaching and learning', and 'the production of something new' which is creation or 'the real artistic activity' (Tolstoy, 1997: 169). Yet, many English teachers create something new every day they are in the classroom. Views of teaching like Tolstoy's are invidious because knowledge is seen as something to be 'delivered' and a harmful emphasis can then be given to explicitness, transmission teaching and inappropriate didactic methods. In contrast to Tolstoy, Dickens (like George Eliot) recognized that there is more to teaching than knowledge. We can learn a great deal from the second chapter of Dickens' *Hard Times*; what we need now in English teaching is not more 'fact' but more 'fancy', more imagination and less prescription:

Fact versus Fancy
So, Mr Choakumchild began in his best manner. He and some one hundred and forty schoolmasters, had been lately turned at the same time, in the same factory, on the same principles, like so many pianoforte legs. He had been put through an immense variety of paces, and had answered volumes of head-breaking questions. Orthography, etymology, syntax, and prosody, biography, astronomy, geography, and general cosmography, the sciences of compound proportion, algebra, land-surveying and levelling, vocal music and drawing from models, were all at the ends of his ten chilled fingers. He had worked his stony way into Her Majesty's most Honourable Privy Council's Schedule B, and had taken the bloom off the higher branches of mathematics and physical science, French, German, Latin and Greek. He knew all about all the Water Sheds of all the world (whatever they are), and all the histories of all the peoples, and all the names of all the rivers and mountains, and all the productions, manners, and customs of all the countries, and all their boundaries and bearings on the two-and-thirty points of the compass. Ah, rather overdone, Mr Choakumchild. If he had only learnt a little less, how infinitely better he might have taught much more!

Standardization, where either teachers or pupils are 'turned at the same time, in the same factory, on the same principles, like so many pianoforte legs' is no substitute for individuality.

English teaching at its finest, as an art, can flourish when 'responsive teaching' is practised for such teaching 'is founded upon a pupil's response' so that 'the starting point is where the pupil is and not where the teacher is' (Pike, 2000b: 20). If cues are taken from pupils, rather than exclusively from a prescribed curriculum or strategy, teachers are liberated to paint individual pictures for children instead of imposing a single diagram upon heterogeneous groups. Most importantly, children in our English lessons may become capable of painting pictures for themselves.

Responsive teaching recognizes that both the emotional and intellectual play a part in learning for 'the way it feels to the reader, what it does for him/her may yield a more lasting influence than any critical analysis aimed at advocating what is often regarded as an expert interpretation' (Britton, 1993: 88). The recognition that 'intelligence' and 'feeling' are 'mutually dependent aspects of human consciousness' is especially relevant in 'responsive teaching' (Wade and Reed, 1987: 56) as the 'broad range of affective components of appreciation, not just emotions properly so called, but also moods, desires, feelings, drives and attitudes or frames of mind' (Feagin, 1996: 9) are drawn upon. Such aesthetic response is likely to be enhanced and augmented through social interaction in the English classroom (Pike, 2003d) for while 'knowing how we see and read helps us to see and read things differently' (Stibbs, 2000: 43), we help others see as they help us and the sort of perception called for is often not only cognitive or even entirely rational.

Being and knowing: Heidegger and English teaching

Martin Heidegger, one of the twentieth century's greatest philosophers, provides us with a 'powerful philosophical basis for construing English teaching as a form of engagement and "being-with" students which acknowledges the aesthetic nature of literary study' (Pike, 2003a). Heidegger argues that there are important limitations on what we might call 'diagrammatic' ways of knowing and insists that we do not think in exclusively scientific, rational or objective ways because we are always *in* a situation in the sense that we are involved and engaged and are not passive or detached. Heidegger neatly reverses Descartes 'Cogito Ergo Sum' (I think therefore I am) and asserts that our primary way of being is not cognitive: we can only think because we exist. As a result of having experiences, we can think about them which is why the growth of experience (valorized in the 'personal growth' model) is central to English.

Heidegger's theory of knowledge is more significant than we might at first realize and has important implications for English teaching as he refutes the humanist view, underlying most educational thinking and especially the new managerialism, by claiming we can only ever know through involvement, engagement, interconnectedness, relationships and experience. For Heidegger, the aesthetic encounter (which English teaching should foster) is 'lived experience' (1993/1934: 204) as it opens up a fuller and truer knowledge than is possible in any other way. As such it brings about what the Greeks termed 'aleithia', the 'unconcealment and disclosure' of things or 'seeing in the widest sense of seeing' (ibid.: 184) and allows 'life in its highest complexity' (Eliot, 1866/1967) to be apprehended. The knowledge experienced in the English classroom is founded upon engagement and relationships for English teachers are not divorced from, but intimately involved with, human concerns. Heidegger's achievement is an important counter to 'the dominant rationalist view' which has 'screened out this engagement' and given us 'a model of ourselves as disengaged thinkers' (Taylor, 1993: 319).

Consequently, this book seeks to show how the formal curriculum can be implemented in a way that preserves what Heidegger would, no doubt, have termed the 'primordial' nature of English teaching. The English teacher's task is to bring about *significance* which is the sort of knowing that emerges from a way of *being*. Arguably, such an existence has a spiritual dimension and the quest for significance (Pike, 2003g) requires a spirituality of learning.

The spirituality of English teaching

According to Hegel, one of Heidegger's predecessors, 'art presents itself to sense, feeling, intuition, imagination' and therefore 'demands an organ other than scientific thinking' (1997: 142) and teaching that is genuinely aesthetic has a spiritual dimension. Indeed, according to Dewey, in *Art as Experience* (1934/1980), one of the last century's most influential works on education, we should not confine the 'spiritual' to places of worship any more than we restrict 'art' to what we see in 'theatres, galleries or museums' for both the aesthetic and the spiritual are 'present in the "significant life" of a community and within the story of our own human development' (ibid.: 7). The English classroom is a spiritual place and English lessons can foster spiritual development. The overwhelming importance of such learning in the lives of children is essential if one accepts that the 'spiritual' denotes 'something fundamental in the human condition which is not necessarily expressed through the physical sense and/or expressed through everyday language' (SCAA, 1995: 3). Indeed, the place of English as an arts subject can be justified by arguing that aesthetic education nurtures spiritual development (Pike, 2000e; 2002b; 2003f) for if pupils are 'not able to be moved by feelings of awe and wonder at the beauty of the world we live in, or the power of artists, musicians and writers to manipulate space, sound and language, they would live in an inner spiritual and cultural desert' (SCAA, 1995: 4).

The relation between aesthetic education and spirituality is well established and Hegel even considered that 'art and works of art, by springing from and being created by the spirit, are themselves of a spiritual kind' because art 'points through and beyond itself and itself hints at something spiritual' (1997: 145). When the dominant paradigm in teaching today is technical, rational and scientific an emphasis upon the spiritual and aesthetic is much needed and the theme running throughout this book is of English teaching as an artistic and spiritual endeavour. The challenge taken up here is to show how the *Framework for Teaching English: Years 7, 8 and 9* (DfEE, 2001) and the *National Curriculum for England: English* (DfEE/QCA, 1999) can be implemented in a way that is true to the ideals and values of most English teachers. We must counter attempts to reduce the aesthetic and inspired to the rational, methodological and explicitly diagrammatic and the following chapters demonstrate the importance of the 'picture' over the 'diagram' while recognizing that English is an applied art which has social obligations to fulfil.

Further reading

Dewey, J. (1980/1934) *Art as Experience*. New York, NY: Perigee.

Pike, M.A. (2003) 'On being in English teaching: a time for Heidegger?', *Changing English – Studies in Reading and Culture*, 10(1): 91–99.

Pike, M.A. (2003) 'From personal to social transaction: a model of aesthetic reading in the classroom', *Journal of Aesthetic Education*, 37(2): 61–72.

Pike, M.A. (2003) 'From the picture to the diagram? Literacy and the art of English teaching', *The Use of English*, 54(3): 211–16.

Pike, M.A. (2004) 'Aesthetic teaching', *Journal of Aesthetic Education*, 38(1).

Webb, E (1992) *Literature in Education: Encounter and Experience*. London: Falmer Press.

2

'Operational' lesson planning

Planning the English opera

When planning lessons, especially for the first time, there seems to be far too much to remember. So many essential elements cannot be left out of a lesson plan. Among others there are learning objectives, assessment opportunities, the plenary, resources, timing, transitions, pitch, timing, pace, the special needs of children, the curriculum, the examination requirements, setting homework, collecting books and liaising with other adults. The list just goes on. Remembering the simple mnemonic 'operational' can, therefore, be an easy way to ensure that all the essential elements are included. Each letter indicates a key aspect of English teaching that should be included in a lesson plan: O is for objectives, P for plenary, E is for En1, En2 and En3, R is for resources, A is for assessment and so on. After planning a lesson you can check that it is 'operational' and ready to teach.

Having an effective plan ensures you can put your creative ideas for a lesson into action. An 'operational' English lesson cannot, however, be created by teachers who are operatives and the mnemonic 'operational' is not intended here to signify scientific 'operations' or repetitive technical functions. Planning in English cannot be achieved by the 'operation' of exclusively rational methods and techniques and it will not be suggested here that planning in English should be 'operational' in any of these negative senses.

The stem of the word 'operational' is easily recognizable as the word 'opera' which, as an art form, is a dramatic composition and a multimedia event. Such a performance requires the careful co-ordination of speech and movement because parts are played by different people and the drama must sustain the interest of the audience. Analogously, the English class learns through response to both the art of the lesson and the art of the literary work that is experienced in the lesson. Planning an English lesson is planning for the opera to begin.

Opera-tional planning

Objectives – Have just a few clear learning objectives (LOs), plan how you will communicate them to learners and how you will know they are understood; display them and refer to them throughout the lesson; understand how they fit into your aims.

Plenary – In your *plenary* come back to your learning objectives, focus on what has been *learnt* and not just what has been *done* in the lesson; leave enough time for the plenary; 'clinch' the deal, *make* sense.

En1, En2 and En3 – Sometimes known in schools as 'chunking'; be clear about the different types of activities and tasks that will occur; divide your lesson into several different *events*; plan for some *speaking and listening, reading* and *writing*.

Resources –Your classroom, the examples you have prepared, worksheets, lesson plan, paper, pens, tissues, books, writing on the board, homework, the TV. You are the most valuable resource the school has so get some rest and relax too.

Assessment – Identify assessment opportunities so you can monitor the learning and assess *progress* as well as *attainment*. A is also for *aesthetic* so remember the most valuable things in life cannot be measured or precisely planned for.

Timing and transitions – Your tasks and learning activities will need to be carefully timed to ensure a sufficiently challenging pace is set. Smoothly manage the transitions between timed tasks and other events within the opera of your lesson.

Individuality – Do not take the 'one size fits all' approach as every child cannot do the same work at the same pace; think of children as individuals and you will address the need to differentiate and not discriminate on the basis of gender or ethnicity.

On the ball – Keep your eye on the ball, keep track of where the lesson is going in relation to your overall goal; make sure there is a close match between your learning objectives, the activities you set and the events you manage.

Needs (special) – Always take care to address the individual learning requirements of those children with special needs, understand their individual learning plan, have suitable alternative work ready, liaise properly, do some research on these special needs.

Adults – Liaise effectively with other adults in the room so they know how they can be most helpful; don't leave this to the last minute; see other adults prior to the lesson, prepare for them, make maximum use of support staff and respect them.

Literacy – Be aware of the literacy requirements of your lessons, have starter activities prepared that are relevant to your overall objective, have key words displayed and definitions ready, teach spelling and other literacy skills explicitly.

When you have, as part of your craft, all the elements of operational teaching, described in the mnemonic above, the art or opera of English can flourish and the performance of both teacher and learners can be a satisfying one. Including in a lesson plan attention to these key elements does not, on its own, ensure that the art of English is brought about but it does ensure that the craft upon which that art depends is in place.

English 'teaching is an art in that teachers, like painters, composers, actresses and dancers, make judgements based largely on qualities that unfold during the course of the action' (Eisner, 2002: 155) and as individuals have experiences in English that cannot be entirely planned for, teaching the subject continues to hold its fascination. Allowing for the 'creation of ends in process' necessitates 'a model of teaching akin to other arts' (ibid.: 156) for how 'humans learn in any rich sense is rather more messy and complex than the rational model implies' (Fleming and Stevens, 1998: 14–15). Planning for the unpredictability of English teaching is what makes it so challenging as it is, after all, not a science or a technology but an art.

O is for objectives

It is clear from *Qualifying to Teach: Professional Standards for Qualified Teacher Status and Requirements for Initial Teacher Training* (TTA, 2002), the document that specifies the competencies student-teachers in the UK must demonstrate, that you must 'set challenging teaching and learning objectives' that are 'relevant to all pupils' in the class (also see Chapter 9 on differentiation). When planning it is essential that your planning and teaching are informed by a detailed knowledge of the pupils in the class, evidence of their past and current achievement, expected standards and also the range and content of work relevant to those pupils (ibid.: 3.1.1)

Objectives should be taken from the *National Curriculum* or the *Framework*. The latter promotes teaching that is informed 'by clear, challenging and progressive objectives' and suggests that these objectives 'benefit from being explicitly taught and from being identified' (DfEE, 2001: 11). Some confusion may arise about which of these documents to quote on a lesson plan but while the *National Curriculum* is statutory and the *Framework* is not, it may be advisable to quote from the *National Curriculum* when selecting learning objectives.

Learning objectives should be challenging and must be designed to ensure progress is made. For instance, you can look carefully at the criteria for the award of Level 6 for writing (En 3) if you teach a boy who is regularly attaining a Level 5 for writing and can design teaching and learning so that it is possible for him to attain a Level 6. Educational objectives have to 'take adequate account of the range and type of pupils' abilities, their previous learning, and their progress towards future educational attainment' (Kyriacou, 1998: 16).

The currently accepted wisdom in the UK is that the learning objectives for a lesson should be clearly stated and communicated to learners. You need to explain to the class at the very start of the lesson what the purpose of the lesson is. It is important to emphasize that this is not the same as telling pupils everything that they will do. Certain activities will be introduced and signalled at given points during the lesson, but you do not have to disclose the content of the whole lesson in advance. All you need to say is something like 'Today, you're going to learn about the difference between tabloid and broadsheet newspapers, especially headlines'. Normally three lesson objectives (LOs) should be displayed where they are in clear view throughout the lesson so that the teacher can draw attention to them during the lesson. This ensures a focus on the purpose of the lesson's activities throughout and is helpful in the plenary at the end of the lesson where you assess the extent to which each LO has been achieved.

Communicating learning objectives

Communicating learning objectives needs to be done precisely and in language pupils understand for a good teacher is able to express and record learning objectives clearly. Writing the learning objective on the board is a good habit to get into, but it is even better to have these aims on the board before the lesson starts. At a school in West Yorkshire, I recently saw a fine example of how learning objectives can be handled effectively. Laura, the student-teacher, was not able to write her learning objectives on the board before the lesson because another teacher and class were in the room. As we waited in the corridor outside the classroom with a rowdy and boisterous Year 8 class, I wondered how Laura would settle the class, take the register and also write her learning objectives on the board.

Once the bell had sounded and the previous class left the room, Laura marched purposefully to the front of the class, took a large piece of colourful sugar paper (folded in four and ready to stick on each corner) from her bag, unfolded it and stuck it to the white board. Three learning objectives for that lesson were instantly displayed in large letters. Laura pointed to each of the three objectives in turn and explained them to the class. All this was accomplished in a businesslike and professional manner and took no more than a few minutes. Laura was certainly prepared for the visit of her university tutor. It appeared effortless but considerable time, thought and energy had been devoted to the planning and preparation of this lesson to make it effective. The effect of establishing and communicating learning objectives so quickly was noticeable as a calm, constructive and purposeful atmosphere was established.

It is also important to check with pupils that they have understood the learning objectives before progressing any further. After giving what you think is a perfectly clear statement about the learning objectives of a particular lesson it can be helpful to pause and check that the message you transmitted is the one that pupils have received. You can ask 'What have I said you're going to learn by the end of the lesson?' or 'Can anyone tell me what we're going to achieve in this lesson?' Such questions, after outlining your objectives, can keep a class on its toes and make sure pupils listen from the start. It is common for student-teachers to set too many objectives and having just three good learning objectives for most lessons is plenty.

Do tasks or learning objectives come first?

Do teachers start their planning by looking at objectives or do they think of a task and then think about the learning objectives that can be met by doing the tasks? I recently interviewed some of the students on the English PGCE course at the University of Leeds about their experience of planning lessons. One student, Luisa, explained that she started from the tasks and worked backwards so she could fill in the box at the top of her lesson plan labelled 'Learning Objectives'. In her words, 'You start by saying "I've got 6 weeks to read this book or these poems" and then you figure out what objectives you can fulfil'. Even if it is easier to think in terms of tasks you must 'work back' from the task and be clear about what it is that children should *learn* from completing the task. Only then can the decision be made about the appropriateness of the task and whether to go ahead with it or choose a different activity. What is not acceptable is to say that your objective is to 'get to the end of Act III scene 2' by the end of the lesson. You may well need to get to the end of Act III, scene 2 but need to be clear about what, specifically, will be learnt on the way. Simply occupying time with activity is not enough, you need to think about why you chose that activity, why the children should do it and what its benefits are.

Having a text or topic to build learning around is the way most teachers operate and this gives English not only continuity but also provides opportunities for aesthetic response and personal involvement. While you can plan for children to learn about metaphors and similes in a poem you cannot define the precise nature of their personal responses. What you can do is to plan for opportunities for such response. Clearly, the choice of topic or text will permit some objectives to be achieved more easily than others and the topic or text should be chosen with specific learning objectives in mind. A good question to ask when planning a lesson is 'Why have I chosen these tasks?' In other words, do the tasks ensure that the learning objectives will be accomplished? Ideally, you need to make it impossible for a child to fail. If the child does the task set, learning and success should be guaranteed.

P is for plenary

A plenary is where your learning objectives are revisited and pupils' learning is consolidated. Imagine that the Head of English is stopping random pupils after a lesson you have taught and is asking them one simple, straightforward question 'What have you just learnt in that lesson?' If your plenary is good the pupil should have a very clear understanding of what it is he or she has learnt and should be able to say precisely what he or she has learnt and not just what he or she has done. Many children might readily tell the Head of English that they played a game with cut-out newspaper headlines and put them into two groups (broadsheet and tabloid) or that they matched newspaper reports to headlines but doing and learning are two different things.

The plenary is important for many children as it can be in the final five to ten minutes of the lesson that what has been learnt becomes fully apparent and is crystallized. If we continue with our example, children should be able to say very simply and directly that they learnt about the main features of tabloid headlines and how they are different from those of broadsheets. The plenary is important in the final part of the lesson where everything 'comes together'. A plenary is more than a summary of the lesson and is not the same as rehearsing 'what we did' today. You might avoid asking 'What did we *do* today?' and could get into the habit of asking instead 'What did we *learn* today?' If a child describes what he or she *did* you could ask 'What did you *learn* by doing that?'.

One of the most common traps to fall into is not leaving enough time for the plenary and then to rush it. Generally, new teachers can underestimate how long activities will take. If a lesson is divided into four 'chunks' or parts (see 'E is for En1, En2 and En3 events' next) and each part runs over by a couple of minutes the plenary is likely to suffer and may even be missed out altogether. It is usually best to shorten an activity or phase of a lesson in order to protect the plenary time. On a plan you can mark the time (usually five or ten minutes before the end of the lesson) for the plenary to begin and it is best to be very firm with yourself and keep to this time. Children should not put coats on or give you anything less than their complete attention. The class should know the plenary is important and that it is to be taken seriously; you can even tell them that it is one of the most important parts of the lesson.

You must be absolutely clear in your own mind about what it was you wanted your class to learn; if you are not clear about this there is little hope of having a successful plenary. It is probably best to have a degree of formality for the plenary to ensure attentiveness. Make sure the transition from the last section of the lesson is clearly signalled so the children know it is over. When standing in front of a class the learning objectives should be displayed (to learn about the difference between tabloids and broadsheets, for instance). Recap on the start of the lesson and ask 'What did we say we were going to learn today?' Draw everyone's attention to the learning objectives displayed on the board. Then use your plenary wisely as an assessment opportunity (see 'A is for Assessment' below) as it is here that you can evaluate the success of the lesson. You may well want to choose pupils to answer and name them instead of asking for hands to be raised so you can differentiate the questions you ask according to ability. You might begin with less able children and ask 'What's a broadsheet?' or 'What's a tabloid?' and then move on to some more challenging questions directed at more able children.

The plenary is not normally the place for the teacher to give a summary and although the plenary has been promoted as a result of the National Literacy Strategy (see Chapter 5) the technique is just as good for sixth formers ending a double lesson, especially if they have been cultivating their social skills the night before. They too should be able to state clearly what they have learnt. We want students to know more than they did at the start, to be able to do what they could not do before or to have experienced something new and challenging. Teaching is about 'moving learners on' cognitively and the plenary is one place to see the extent to which that has happened. Learners often remember what is most recent so it is important to draw out the main learning points even if one of these was covered during the first ten minutes of the lesson which may have been forty minutes ago. The idea of the plenary is to concentrate on the important learning points and not merely the most recent ones.

A plenary should be highly interactive, have a fast pace and considerable momentum as a good plenary can create a real buzz and enhance motivation. It must engage everyone so try to involve as many children as possible. All children can be stimulated to think and can formulate answers even if they do not articulate them. Your plenary is crucial for continuity and is where you can achieve a sense of coherence by reminding pupils what they did before this lesson and what they will do in future lessons in pursuit of an overall learning objective. The plenary is important for you, as the teacher, because by assessing the learning that has occurred you can plan future lessons. The lesson you planned to teach next may need to be altered in the light of pupils' progress ascertained in the plenary.

▍ E is for En 1, En 2 and En 3 events

Variety is essential in teaching and it is usually a good idea to divide a lesson into three or four different events or sorts of activity. You might, for instance, begin with some whole-class speaking and listening, move on to small-group discussion and then switch to paired reading before fifteen minutes of individual writing. In schools this is sometimes known as 'chunking' as a lesson should be broken up into 'chunks' or sections. Recently, I was discussing a lesson plan with one of my PGCE students who was due to be observed teaching. Her plan was to read a short story to the class for about fifty minutes and then to ask them some questions about it in the remaining ten minutes. I told her that for a low-ability class to sit still and read for this long was optimistic and suggested that she 'chunk it' into manageable sections with some activities, such as paired prediction work, after the first ten or fifteen minutes of reading and again after the next part of the story. It seemed like good advice but a few days later, after the student was observed, the assessor described how the student had read a short story to the class for most of the lesson and suggested to me how the lesson might have been improved by dividing it into chunks or segments so that pupils could experience different activities!

Many teachers comment that teaching challenging children requires even more planning than teaching well behaved ones and this has certainly been my experience. After my first four years teaching English at a comprehensive school where about 60% of the pupils achieved five or more A–C grades at GCSE I moved to a city school where only 18% of pupils attained five or more A–C grades to gain experience of curriculum management. It was something of a culture shock and the immediate difference was that the children in my new school were far more 'in your face' than many of the polite middle-class pupils at my first school. No sooner had I set foot in the classroom with my Year 11 class than I was asked if I had a girlfriend, which football team I supported, where I lived, what sport I played and so on. These children were not passive or calm; they were rowdy, chatty and would misbehave if they were not 'on task'. I soon realized that my planning had to be far better and that I had to prepare more resources, think up different activities and swap from one activity to another more rapidly than before as their concentration spans were generally short. I had to have more activities ready than before and learning objectives had to be achieved by formulating short, manageable, time-specific tasks. Sometimes these tasks lasted no more than five minutes and had to be varied so that children stayed motivated and interested in what they were doing.

Our job as English teachers is not just to teach but also to motivate for we need to foster the *will* as well as the *skill* to learn. This is just as true when teaching very able children with a low boredom threshold who need to be constantly challenged or children of average ability who can produce work that is far above average if the lessons they experience propel them into mental activity. Choosing a topic or text that pupils are enthusiastic about can result in better work and greater motivation than would otherwise be the case. When planning your 'resources' and 'organization' you need to take account of 'pupils' interests' as well as their 'language and cultural backgrounds' (TTA, 2002: 3.1.2) (also see Chapter 9). Learning how 'to prepare resources based on topical material with which pupils will want to engage'

(TTA, 2000: 58) is part of the art of planning although we should not assume that what is topical is necessarily of greatest relevance to our pupils. When we divide lessons into pre-planned sections or segments we need to be careful that these do not restrict creativity by becoming predictable and routine as space needs to be left for individuality to flourish (see Chapter 5). We want to foster learners who are active rather than passive as many discipline problems can be averted through good planning which ensures children are challenged and have little time or inclination to misbehave. A possible structure is shown in Figure 2.1.

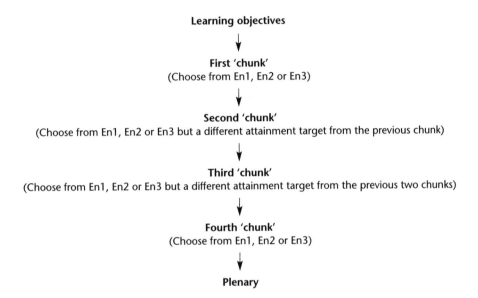

Learning objectives

↓

First 'chunk'
(Choose from En1, En2 or En3)

↓

Second 'chunk'
(Choose from En1, En2 or En3 but a different attainment target from the previous chunk)

↓

Third 'chunk'
(Choose from En1, En2 or En3 but a different attainment target from the previous two chunks)

↓

Fourth 'chunk'
(Choose from En1, En2 or En3)

↓

Plenary

Figure 2.1 *Planning structure*

R is for resources

Resources are more than stationery items; the teacher, the classroom and the whole environment are learning resources. The atmosphere and learning environment are important and a classroom should be neat, well cared for and have interesting displays of pupils' work which foster enthusiasm for learning. Litter should be in the bin (a teacher can ensure a class tidies up at the end of each lesson), the blackboard or whiteboard should be clean and the room should demonstrate a professional approach to teaching and learning in English. Children should want to be in your class just by looking at the displays of work. Your classroom should be tidy, well ventilated and must look inviting. You should be able to welcome pupils into your space rather than seeking to impose yourself on territory they have already occupied. Being early or at the very least punctual is a key element in the success of this strategy and needs to be carefully planned as it will not automatically happen. In most schools a teacher can be delayed on the way to a lesson for a multitude of reasons. Equally, you should not be setting homework after the lesson is scheduled to end or you can end up being late for the start of the next lesson.

It is worth itemizing on a lesson plan as a checklist all the resources that will be needed and then checking all are present before teaching. Having spares of items such as board markers (in case the one being used runs out) is recommended. So too is having the video at precisely the right place, set up ready to play on the television. Laying items out on the teacher's desk can help and checking you have everything is essential.

Recently, I was sitting at the back of a Year 9 lesson watching one of the best and most organized student-teachers on our PGCE English course. The room had displays of pupils' work and was a resource in its own right. The teacher welcomed the children into the class and was early. She communicated the learning objectives of the lesson well and recapped on what had been learnt in the previous lesson. Everything went well for the first quarter of an hour and then she realized that the pile of thirty textbooks she needed was not on the desk in front of her. Looking slightly bemused by this she walked to the far side of the room to get the books from the cupboard only to realize it was locked. She then had to leave the class (which had I not been there would have been unsupervised) to get the keys from a colleague. One thing led to another because a 'helpful' colleague had tidied the books away just prior to the start of the lesson. It is always worth checking you have everything you need before you begin.

▍A is for assessment

As the whole of the next chapter of this book is devoted to the subject of assessment it is sufficient to emphasize just three points about assessment in relation to planning here. First, an English teacher needs to plan for assessment opportunities and anyone seeking to gain Qualified Teacher Status (QTS) needs to show he or she can 'assess pupils' progress accurately' (TTA, 2002: 3.2.3). Secondly, an English teacher's markbook or planner should contain detailed assessment information about the children he or she teaches. If you are teaching a Year 7 class, for instance, it should be possible to see at a glance who attained a level 3, a level 4 or a level 5 in their Key Stage 2 test at the end of Year 6 and this assessment information should inform future planning. Thirdly, you should assess the extent to which planned learning objectives are met in a particular lesson or sequence of lessons as it is essential to 'evaluate pupils' progress towards planned learning objectives' (*ibid.*: 10, 3.2.1). Assessment is part of the teaching process where a teacher constantly evaluates pupils' understanding. Good teachers 'monitor and assess as they teach' and this makes it possible for them to give 'immediate and constructive feedback to support pupils as they learn' (ibid.: 10, 3.2.2). Assessment does not just happen; it needs to be planned for.

T is for timing and transitions

Dynamic English teachers often glance at their watches; they give time-specific tasks and set a pace in lessons that is deliberately challenging. Timing is certainly part of the art of English teaching as you need to sense when to give children more time and when to increase the momentum. It is important to tell learners how long they can devote to a particular task and to remind them of how long they have left on it. Transitions are normally signalled by the teacher exclaiming 'Two minutes left!' so that pupils know when the time for a task is coming to an end.

Timing when to give instructions can make a significant difference to the smooth running of the lesson. The rule is to give all your instructions before movement so that you are not trying to shout over the sound of scraping chairs and desks. If the class is assembled around you at the front of the class and are to move back into groups, you can tell them what they will do in their groups before they move so they are not wasting time waiting for your instructions after moving and you do not have to establish silence again. It is important that transitions between tasks are signalled, smooth and efficient.

I is for individuality

The TTA document *Qualifying to Teach: Professional Standards for Qualified Teacher Status and Requirements for Initial Teacher Training* states that student-teachers should ensure that 'girls and boys, from all ethnic groups, can make good progress' (TTA, 2002: 3.1.2). Clearly, gender and ethnicity are important features of a learner's identity and you need to be aware of the way these aspects of identity influence learning (see Chapter 9). Yet, seeing children as individuals ensures you will not discriminate unfairly or unwittingly on the basis of gender or ethnicity. Individuals have different learning styles and differ in character, personality, likes, dislikes, interests and so on. What interests one learner may not be of the slightest interest to another and it is essential to get to know the children you teach as individuals. By fulfilling the requirement to 'plan opportunities for pupils to learn in out-of-school contexts' (ibid.: 9, 3.1.5) you can begin to get to know the children you teach as individuals.

■ O is for 'on the ball'

When planning lessons it is essential to 'keep your eye on the ball' and be aware of the direction events are taking. The activities you plan must closely match your stated learning objective. Just as essay writing requires that you identify the key words in the title and ensure that everything you write is relevant to this title, the activities of a lesson must be relevant to your stated title, the declared learning objectives. If a task or explanation is not going to help to achieve your objective, there may be little point wasting valuable time on it.

If your learning objective is to get pupils to understand the words and actions of Macbeth and Banquo in a particular scene of *Macbeth* there is no point spending the time analysing a Shakespearean sonnet. While such a mistake is so obvious, it is rare; an easier error to make with this learning objective is to spend the lesson focusing predominantly upon Banquo. One of my student-teachers did just that when I observed her teach. After the lesson she was quite pragmatic and told me she should have either changed the learning objective so that Banquo was the main focus or, if she taught the same lesson again with the same learning objective, she would need to devote more attention to the character of Macbeth.

If you have been working hard setting tasks, maintaining order, giving instructions, managing transitions, setting homework and doing what seems like a thousand and one other tasks it may seem that anyone observing you is being unnecessarily pedantic if they persist in drawing subtle distinctions between *tasks* and *learning*. Yet, learning is the reason for the tasks and 'keeping your eye on the ball' means that there must always be a 'tight fit' or close match between the tasks set and the intended learning. This is most helpfully demonstrated as a diagram. A handy way of making sure you get the most important features of planning lessons right is to think of it as a 'three-way match'. The first part of the three-way match in planning is to match the tasks and the teaching to the learning objective *within* the structure of the lesson. The other 'matches' are *between* the child and the curriculum and *between* the learner and the lesson. The aspect of the three-way match focused on here is the internal one. At the planning stage it is important to have this internal 'fit' right (see Figure 2.2).

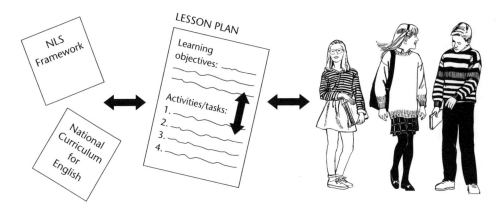

Figure 2.2 *Planning as a three-way match*

When planning it is necessary to consider *tasks* and *objectives* together. A common misconception among some student-teachers and those in the early stages of their career in English teaching is to confuse *learning* and *doing*. Conflating *activity* with what will be *learnt* is common. Hayley, a talented student-teacher who reflects below on my visit to see her teach a Year 8 class during her first teaching practice at a school in Harrogate, notes the difference between the two:

A cold mid-December morning; a chill wind whistled eerily down the corridors of my first placement school: Mark was coming. University observation time had come. The feeling of nausea that normally accompanies a visit from the in-laws, or a trip to the dentist, is the only way to describe this kind of fear.

'So', says Mark casually, as I frantically photocopy my lesson plan for him, 'tell me about the lesson I'll be seeing.' What my tutor meant by this is 'What will the kids be *learning* in your lesson?' He certainly did not mean 'What are you going to *do* for the hour that I'll be watching?' 'Well, Mark, what we're going to *do* is . . . .' Too late, the words were out.

While the learning objective was clear in my mind, it was not communicated to my tutor, and had he not pointed this out, it wouldn't have been communicated to the kids which would have been an example of how *not* to begin a lesson. . . .

▌N is for needs (special)

Every English teacher needs to read and refer to the inclusion statement in the *The National Curriculum for England: English* (DfEE/QCA, 1999) as it is necessary to plan with 'barriers to learning' in mind and to provide an 'appropriate challenge'. Teachers of English will find *Introducing Special Needs – A Companion Guide for Student Teachers* (2001) by Philip Garner and John Dwyfor Davies especially helpful. While you will plan to differentiate routinely, some children have needs that are 'additional to' and 'different from' those an English teacher might ordinarily differentiate for. These children will either be the focus of 'school action', 'school action plus' or will have a 'statement of special educational need' (see Chapter 9 for a further explanation).

In schools, the English department often has a special relationship with the special needs department and English lessons can be especially beneficial for children with special needs. An inspirational book that English teachers will find immensely valuable is *Literature for All* by Nicola Grove (1998). The principle underlying this book is that literature is an art that can and should be experienced by everyone. Many examples of activities that help children with special needs to experience literature are given. There are also a number of excellent books that provide positive images of children or young people with special needs. Recent books such as *Running on Empty* by Anna Patterson (Lucky Duck Publishing) and *Falling for Joshua* by Brian Keaney (The Watts Group) are well worth reading. *Running on Empty* tells the story of a girl with an eating disorder whom boys in your class may care greatly for.

■ A is for adults

English teachers need to 'plan for the deployment of additional adults who support pupils' learning' (TTA, 2002: 9, 3.1.4) and *Introducing Special Needs – a Companion Guide for Student Teachers* by Garner and Davies (2001) is especially helpful in this respect. Guidance on liaising with support staff can be found in Appendix 11.ii where an 'example of an adult helper briefing sheet' provides a clear structure for working with special needs assistants.

It is all too easy to rush into a classroom and begin to teach without informing other adults in the room, such as the special needs assistant, what is going on. Clearly, they need to be informed of the aim of the lesson and how the child, or children, they work with can be helped to achieve the objectives you have in mind. Many of these adults only receive a copy of a worksheet when the pupils do but they would willingly study it beforehand to see how they can make it accessible for the child they work with if it was given to them in advance. Out of respect for the professionalism of your adult assistant you should communicate with them before the lesson. When you are observed (be it by an inspector, county adviser, external examiner or university tutor) he or she is likely to ask the adult helper in the room about liaison and whether you discussed the lesson with him or her beforehand.

Student-teachers need to take part in 'teaching teams' (TTA, 2002: 3.1.4): one such team is made up of you and the special needs assistant. Adults in the classroom should be briefed so that they are aware of the particular purposes and requirements of the lesson and can be most effective.

L is for literacy

Last but not least is literacy although it is only dealt with briefly here as it is explored at greater length in Chapter 5. Essentially, English teachers should be especially aware of the literacy requirements of the work they are doing and their planning should not simply focus on English but specifically on literacy. It is, perhaps, sufficient here to point out that English teachers need to be aware of the literacy demands of the texts pupils read, the literacy needs of learners and how to teach writing and reading explicitly. Careful preparation and planning are especially necessary for literacy teaching where resources such as exemplars of text-types, writing frames, starter activities, 'shared' and 'guided' reading and writing tasks are needed and where an overhead projector, appropriate transparencies and working marker pens are indispensable.

Further reading

Eisner, E.W. (2002) *The Educational Imagination: On the Design and Evaluation of School Programs* (3rd edn). Upper Saddle River, NJ: Merrill/Prentice Hall.
Fleming, M. and Stevens, D. (1998) 'Planning', Chapter 2 in *English Teaching in the Secondary School – a Handbook for Students and Teachers*. London: David Fulton.
Kyriacou, C. (1998) 'Planning and preparation', Chapter 2 in *Essential Teaching Skills*. Cheltenham: Nelson-Thornes.

3

'Metre' reading: assessment in English

Metre reading?

In a world where great faith is put in numbers, there is a temptation to think of assessment in English as something as straightforward as metre reading. When the gas or electricity metre is read some numbers are scribbled down to record the measurement. When it comes to assessment in English, measurement is involved and is recorded but there the similarity with metre reading ends. In English teaching assessment is not primarily about numbers, it is about people and about supporting teaching and learning.

This chapter, however, employs the mnemonic 'Metre' as a framework (M is for Motivation and monitoring, E is for Educational feedback, T is for Teaching, R is for Recording and reporting, E is for Evidence of effectiveness) for although the most well-known definition of a 'metre' is the unit of measurement in the metric system the other meaning of the word 'metre', familiar to students of English literature, that refers to poetic rhythm, is equally important. There should be an almost poetic rhythm to assessment because it should be part of the flow and pattern of English teaching. Assessment is an integral element of 'responsive teaching' (Pike, 2000b) because the teacher is concerned to understand the responses of learners. Just as the rhythm of a poem is not the point of it, assessment is not the point of, or reason for, English teaching.

The rhythm of a poem may help us to understand its meaning but is not the reason for the existence of the poem. Analogously, the purpose of assessment is to help facilitate teaching and learning and must not become an end in itself. There should be a close relation between assessment and teaching in English where the former always supports the latter. When the art of English is practised there should not be a disjunction between teaching and assessment but a skilful and almost seamless relation between the two where one informs the other. Dissonance is the result when assessment is divorced from teaching and becomes an end in itself.

The most important questions to ask when it comes to assessment in English are: What is the point of doing it? Why am I assessing? What purpose does it serve? What will it achieve? Assessment can be a morally justified and ethical activity for the English teacher if it is an element of the art of English teaching. Using the mnemonic 'metre' is a helpful way of remembering the most frequently given reasons for, and purposes of, assessment but each reason for assessment requires careful consideration. This chapter will seek to 'read' the 'metre', the system of measurement, in English.

Metre reading

M – Motivation and monitoring. Assessment can provide the extrinsic (as opposed to intrinsic) motivation some pupils require to achieve what they are capable of. If a learner is praised and achieves success this can boost self-esteem, readiness to work and enthusiasm for the subject. Assessing how pupils work enables the teacher to monitor the teaching and learning situation as well as progress and attainment.

E – Educational feedback. Assessment in English can give valuable feedback to the pupils about their learning and the progress they are making. In formative assessment there is a close relation between the teaching situation and the learning experience and learners can receive advice about how their work can be improved.

T – Teaching. One of the most convincing reasons for assessment is that it enables a teacher to learn about his or her teaching by assessing learners' responses to topics, texts and teaching methods. The kind of feedback this sort of assessment gives the teacher is invaluable as it can help to improve teaching and learning.

R – Recording and reporting. Arguably, there is a need for teachers to be accountable and it is therefore necessary to record pupils' progress as well as their attainment in relation to their ability. Reporting assessment information to the child, parents, carers, managers in school and the local education authority can support the child's learning in a variety of ways. Keeping useful records over time can enable trends to be identified which can inform future planning. Evidence in the form of clear records is needed to justify extra help and resources for particular children.

E – Evidence of effectiveness. Assessment can enable judgements to be made about the performance of teachers and schools and how effective they are. If children of similar ability and from similar socioeconomic backgrounds attain much better results in one class or school than in another judgements can be made about teachers' and managers' abilities, skills and effectiveness. How valuable these schools or teachers are to society, how cost-effective they are and the value for money they provide for tax-payers can be evaluated.

■ M is for monitoring and motivation

Monitoring

Assessment in broad terms has been defined as 'any activity used to appraise pupils' performance' and comprises the 'techniques you can use to monitor pupils' progress in terms of specific learning outcomes' (Kyriacou, 1998b: 102). This is generally a helpful definition although not everything in English can be measured and it is notoriously difficult to measure significance or aesthetic response in relation to a 'specific learning outcome'. Measuring how a child's store of experience has been augmented or the extent to which empathy has developed as a result of an English lesson is hard to quantify.

Monitoring can certainly take the form of informal assessment and should be part of a teacher's normal daily activity. What is important to recognize, especially as a new teacher, is that you cannot wait for aspects of the performance of those you teach to be unavoidably obvious; you have to go looking. Some children give the impression of understanding and know when to smile and nod to keep the teacher happy when, in fact, they do not understand and do not want to let you or the class know they do not understand. Clearly, 'monitoring should be investigative and active, in the sense that you actively probe pupils' current understanding and difficulties rather than simply rely on this being drawn to your attention in some way' (ibid.: 108). Our attention is often drawn to the 'best' and 'worst' students and it is easy to neglect a mass of children between these two extremes. You must not fall into the trap of monitoring the progress of those who immediately catch your attention and must frequently monitor all your pupils. The art lies in the ability to do so unobtrusively and to interweave such monitoring with your teaching. One of the most immediate and effective ways of monitoring pupils is by marking their work, that done in class and for homework too, as most schools generally schedule two homeworks per week for English.

Marking to monitor progress

Marking is part of everyday life for an English teacher and it is not always an easy part of it. You cannot just mark something as right or wrong and give a numerical score for it as very little marking in English lends itself to such a simple and clear-cut approach as qualitative judgements come into play. Marking itself is a subject whole books have been written about but in this short introduction it is important to recognize that you cannot mark and correct every error in every child's work. Doing so demoralizes both you and the child and serves little purpose. Our guiding principle regarding assessment is that it should facilitate learning and it is far more helpful to target certain errors that you want a child's attention to be drawn to. You can tell the child you have only focused on punctuation or certain spelling patterns this time, for instance, but you should always make the criteria clear and ensure children understand how they are being assessed. When marking a piece of work it is essential that you refer to National Curriculum levels for Key Stage 3 (see Chapter 5) and grade descriptions and assessment objectives for GCSE (see Chapter 6), AS and A2 (see Chapter 7). You can use phrases from the criteria or convert them into child-friendly language but you must show that you have referred to the criteria when marking because the audience for your marking is not just the child. It should be evident to the child, parents, your curriculum manager, advisers, inspectors and examiners why you have awarded a particular mark. Communicating assessment information to parents or guardians should enable them to help and support the child's learning. Your marking and especially your written and verbal comments should justify the grade or level you have awarded. When writing your comments you should note achievements and also give advice. Generally be positive in your opening comment and specific when you subsequently explain how the work could be improved. Ideally, you should explain how the next level or grade could be achieved, so that a clear and achievable target is evident from your marking.

Marking and motivation

You cannot survive as an English teacher and maintain your sanity if you engage in very detailed marking of every piece of work you receive as there are not enough hours in the day to do this. One strategy is to target particular errors that it is important to avoid or which are frequent in a piece of work. Shorter pieces of work at Key Stage 3 will be impossible to allocate a level to. Even allowing for this you will end up with a heavy marking load as an English teacher which is time consuming if you do the job well; during your first year or two as an English teacher you might be shocked by the sheer volume of marking you have to undertake. It is, therefore, important to balance your marking load and to design teaching so that you avoid collecting Year 13 A level coursework, GCSE coursework, mock KS3 test papers and a short story from Year 7 all in the same week. It is advisable to try to balance and regulate when you have major pieces of marking to do. The art is to plan your teaching so you do not have piles of marking from lots of different classes coming in at the same time. As you may teach over two hundred different pupils in as many as seven different classes each week, this requires careful planning.

Little and often is the best approach to take. If you finish teaching at three or half past three in the afternoon, you can get through a considerable amount of marking by staying a couple of hours after school for a few nights in a row and, although this takes discipline, it can be a good habit to get into. Most English departments have policies which specify how often you should mark work and the turn-around time needs to be planned into your schedule. At the end of his teaching practice one student-teacher, Tom, spoke from experience when he commented, 'stick to the homework timetable as this will avoid unnecessary build-up; it's as important to know when each piece is due as it is to know when it is set'. Clearly, you cannot have children writing in their exercise books if they are in a pile on your desk at home waiting to be marked, so working out when the best time is to take work in is important. You also need to be familiar with the marking policy of your English department if you are going to fit into the English team in your school.

Marking in English can take place as continuous or terminal assessment. Coursework in English is continuous as the final assessment of coursework tends to be based on what has been done over several terms. While this can appear to be less stressful than sitting examinations, if work has improved over several terms early efforts can weigh down overall attainment. If a child has Cs to start with but scores Bs for the final couple of pieces, on a 'best-fit' basis and averaging out the pieces of work, the candidate may only attain a C grade overall. In English at GCSE and A level a combination of coursework and examinations makes up the final result. The class teacher normally marks the coursework and a sample is moderated by a moderator employed by the exam board. Terminal assessment is nearly always carried out in an examination. There is no reason why this has to be the case, as it is simply an assessment of the pupil's attainment at the very end or termination of a course. At Key Stage 3 an examiner marks the three test papers although you will have marked past examinations yourself in preparing children in Year 9 for the Key Stage 3 test. At GCSE, AS and A2 level exam scripts are marked by external examiners although coursework is marked by teachers and then moderated internally and externally.

Motivation

One of the most serious dangers of assessment is that 'pupils who find that the feedback on their progress indicates that they are doing less well than their peers or some standard of attainment of value to them, may become disheartened and upset by this' (Kyriacou, 1998b: 103). If a C grade in English is valued to the exclusion of all else in Year 10 and Year 11 then children not capable of this grade may indeed become disheartened. In some schools, where a D or E grade is not valued, the difficulties of teaching the lower sets are exacerbated because of the poor motivation that failure can cause.

For one child a grade E is a very satisfactory achievement and can be more of an achievement than the B grade gained by another child who could have done much better. English teachers who teach lower sets in the secondary school often teach children who have been labelled as failures at the ages of

7, 11 and 14 and motivating such children for yet more assessment at 16 is a challenge. Reinforcing failure and underachievement can lead to the creation of an underclass in school who are disenfranchised and excluded from a success culture.

A 'personal best' should be aimed for and our motives and those of managers should derive from what is best for the learner and not just what looks good in a league table. On the other hand, many children find pleasing results highly motivating and assessment can reinforce success and challenge children to do better as competitiveness spurs many on. In English we should always strive to foster intrinsic as well as extrinsic motivation where the work itself is valued and not simply the grade attached to it, where pleasure is taken in the crafting of writing and not just in the assessment of it, as attitudes need to be fostered that leave children feeling good about who they are and what they are doing.

E is for educational

Communicating assessment information to learners

The professional standards document *Qualifying to Teach* (TTA, 2002) makes it clear in Section 3.2 ('Monitoring and assessment') that to be awarded Qualified Teacher Status (QTS) student-teachers must have evidence that they 'involve pupils in reflecting on, evaluating and improving their own performance' (ibid.:10, 3.2.2) and should also use their records of pupils' progress and attainment to 'help pupils review their own progress' (ibid.: 10, 3.2.6). Assessment is ultimately most worthwhile when it helps the pupil to learn more effectively. If pupils are to have co-ownership of the learning process with their teachers they need to be able to evaluate their progress.

A central issue is how we communicate assessment information as this can lead to some children becoming more motivated and others less motivated. Some English teachers express concerns that communicating assessment information to certain pupils, who are doing well, can lead to them lessening their efforts and underachieving and that communicating poor results can have similar effects if other children give up when they realize they are too far away from their desired target. Other English teachers claim that we should be open and honest and provide learners with accurate feedback and that how an individual interprets and reacts to this information is a matter of individual responsibility. Consequently, even the communication of assessment information is the subject of controversy.

I have a vivid memory of my very first curriculum managers' meeting as a young and newly appointed Head of English, Communications and Drama at a large comprehensive school because the subject of the meeting was assessment. After school, more than a dozen of us assembled in the conference room around the polished oak table with the headteacher presiding at the top. My strategy, carefully worked out in advance, was to say as little as possible until I saw the way the view of the meeting was going. It appeared to be a rather formal occasion as staff sat in near silence waiting for the meeting to begin and there were only occasional hushed whispers between colleagues sitting next to each other. Once the meeting began it soon became apparent that there was a difference of opinion on the subject of assessment. Some heads of department believed assessment information, such as predicted GCSE grades, should be communicated to pupils and others felt it should be 'for teachers' eyes only'. Before I could find out who was on each side a senior colleague looked directly at me across the table and asked me what my view was. With that all heads turned to see what the newcomer had to say. After what seemed to me like a very long pause, I took a deep breath, decided to have the courage of my convictions and explained that I could not see the point of wasting time assessing students unless we communicated that information to them; if learners were to have ownership of the learning process it was important that they should be aware of their current level of attainment.

How assessment information is communicated to pupils and how grades are valued in the school is especially important. For a student to know only the result achieved in a test or given for a piece of work can be decidedly unhelpful. As a pupil I can remember going into the Chapel block at Bishop Wordsworth's School in Salisbury and looking on the noticeboard at a list of boys' names and scores as we were ranked in the end-of-year internal examinations. I walked away with a percentage in my head and knew how I had done relative to everyone else but had not the faintest idea how to improve, except maybe by working harder next time. It was only later when the English master sat down with me and talked me through my examination script that I learnt how to improve. Assessment should be an integral part of the learning process so that a child's individual learning needs are the central focus. Rather than a child simply knowing he or she gained a D grade in English, children need to know what they have to do to move up a grade so they can build on their strengths while addressing areas of relative weakness. In English this is especially important because strikingly different levels can be awarded in each attainment target. Explaining in simple and practical terms what is needed to ensure progress and improvement should be part of the process of communicating assessment information.

Assessment should be about learning and should have a justifiable educational purpose. Assessment should help learners learn. Consequently, formative as distinct from summative assessment is especially valuable. Assessment is not simply for the teacher's or the school's benefit as the purpose is to identify how the child can be helped to make progress. Formative assessment can show the teacher what the child has not understood and needs more help with. In this sense the assessment is diagnostic for the precise nature of the problem the child is having can be identified. Is it spelling, punctuation, paragraphing, reading between the lines, comprehension beyond the literal or sentence cohesion that need to improve? If it is spelling, what aspects of spelling is there a difficulty with? Is it pluralization, modifying words ending in e or confusion about antonym prefixes? Diagnostic assessment is a form of formative assessment and is different from summative assessment which is explained shortly in 'R is for recording and reporting'.

T is for teaching

The analogy with which this chapter opened was of assessment being like the metre of a poem, supporting the content, the really important element of it, but not being the sole purpose of it. The rhythm or metre exists for the poem and not the poem for the metre. Put in a more down-to-earth way, if the dog is teaching and the tail is assessment, the tail should not wag the dog. Assessment should help us teach and we can tell if the tail is wagging the dog when assessment takes up too much time and draws teachers away from teaching and planning teaching.

Assessment is invaluable even before you teach. When you start a new job and are given a timetable or are on teaching practice you should be given a list of names and some statistical data about the children as well as their marks for previous pieces of work. You need to understand this information and having the teacher you are taking over from talk you through this data is very helpful indeed. Arguably, you cannot plan a lesson effectively without an assessment of those you want to teach as appropriate tasks cannot be designed or pitched at the right level without a sufficient assessment of learners.

Some of the most commonly used quantitative data on pupils in most schools in the UK are CAT scores. Often the whole year group is taken to the school hall during Year 7 and again in Year 9 to be tested. The CAT test is a cross between the 11+ and an IQ test and gives teachers information about a child's NVQ (non-verbal reasoning), VQ (verbal reasoning) and quantitative skills. These data give you an idea of a child's *ability* which is quite distinct from his or her *attainment*. For English the verbal reasoning is the most useful data to have and you should beware if this figure disappears and you are given a mean or average CAT score instead. The relation of CAT scores to GCSE grades is presented in 'E is for evidence of effectiveness' at the end of the present chapter.

Assessing speaking and listening, reading and writing

As an English teacher when it comes to assessment you need to ask yourself if you are using the right tools (or combination of tools) for the job. You do not use a screwdriver if you need a hammer but it is easy to set an inappropriate task to assess a particular skill. You need to consider what the best way is of getting access to the knowledge or skills you are assessing. The nature of the assessed task, whether it is En 1, En 2 or En 3, needs to be considered and all three attainment targets should be assessed regularly.

Arguably, the most natural way of assessing speaking and listening is when it is integrated with the topic or text being studied. Children can even be informally assessed so that they are not put off by knowing an assessment is taking place. If a particularly good argument breaks out over whether Macbeth, the witches or Lady Macbeth are to blame for Scotland's descent into anarchy and a child argues a view effectively, this mark can be recorded as an example of negotiation, argument and persuasion. In assessing speaking and listening, feedback can be given to students that directly addresses features of their performance and facilitates improvement. Specifically commenting on the way a group works and the roles adopted can be especially valuable and allocating specific roles as a learning game can enable group members to see and understand the processes at work.

We should bear in mind that pupil-talk generally decreases as teacher-talk increases. Teachers in general, and English teachers in particular, can be prone to talk too much. Further, much classroom discourse is artificial and contrived. We often ask questions we know the answers to which is the opposite of most real-life situations. If I am at a bus stop and ask the man next to me in the queue what time it is he assumes I do not have a watch. He does not assume I have a watch and know the answer and am just testing him. Yet, that is precisely what we do in school. In English lessons we often ask questions we know the answers to. Creating realistic conditions in an English classroom is the challenge English teachers need to rise to on a regular basis.

Assessing reading presents the problem of getting inside someone else's head. We never have direct, unmediated access to reading (comprehension and understanding). All we know of a child's reading ablility is derived from what the child says or writes about what he or she has read. Put another way, we only find out about reading via what comes out of their mouths or their pens and, as such, assessing reading is problematic as it depends upon a child's powers of written or oral expression. Assessing someone's reading through speaking and listening can produce very different results from assessing reading through his or her writing, especially if the individual experiences difficulties with the mechanics of writing.

Equally, it is quite possible for a piece of writing to be awarded two completely different grades, one for reading and one for writing; you have to look at the piece of work through one lens to assess writing and through a different lens to assess reading. Some of the most relevant work on assessing writing has emerged from Myhill's (1999b) research which analyses the linguistic features of the different grades at GCSE (see Chapter 6). This is an invaluable resource for teachers wanting to know about the assessment of writing.

R is for recording and reporting

To gain QTS you need to show that you 'record pupils' progress and achievements systematically to provide evidence of the range of their work, progress and attainment over time' (TTA, 2002: 10, 3.2.6). In my experience the key word here is 'systematically' for while most English teachers are innovative and enthusiastic communicators they are not always systematic when it comes to recording numbers in boxes in a markbook. The challenging aspects of English teaching, for which a real gift is required, are often dismissed with aplomb and the routine and mundane task of entering numbers in a column is sometimes a challenge. It may be for this reason, and because numbers often conceal as much as they reveal, that many English teachers write notes and comments as well as numbers next to pupils' names. The best record-keeping is both quantitative and qualitative and there are many advantages to combining numerical scores with prose comments. Keeping accurate, systematic and detailed records is essential and you need to have the date on which the assessment was administered as well as the title of the task and whether En1 (speaking and listening), En2 (reading) or En3 (writing) was being assessed because you need to have clear evidence of the range of pupil's work and also information about 'progress and attainment over time' (ibid.).

With such information you can provide colleagues, other professionals or parents with information about progress and can form hypotheses to account for particular peaks and troughs. You can show that you 'are able to use records as a basis for reporting on pupil's attainment and progress orally and in writing, concisely, informatively and accurately for parents, carers, other professionals and pupils' (ibid.: 10, 3.2.7). You should be able to show your Head of English your markbook at any time and not be filled with dread. You should not be embarrassed if anyone asks to see your records for a particular class. If you are training to teach, you need to able to show your tutor your systematic records and refer to these when planning lessons so you can 'identify and support' both pupils who are 'more able' as well as those 'who are working below age-related expectations' and those 'who are failing to achieve their potential in learning' (ibid.: 10, 3.2.4). Recording detailed observations concerning pupils 'who experience behavioural, emotional and social difficulties' (ibid.) is also necessary if patterns are to be identified and strategies devised.

Your teacher's planner or markbook should contain assessment information about each child you teach and having the most essential assessment information to hand each time you plan a lesson can inform your teaching. You must, however, beware of self-fulfilling prophecies for your expectations of a child and faith in his or her abilities can influence performance as children often conform to their teachers' views about them. It is good to have a healthy scepticism of numerical scores and to have high expectations of pupils regardless of their ability as this gives them the benefit of the doubt and imposes no artificial ceiling on them.

Recording and reporting pupils' progress can be summative where attainment is measured at the very end of a course or key stage or it can be formative which enables development to occur. Assessment is also either norm-referenced where grading is determined by how well everyone else does in the test or criterion-referenced where grades or levels are awarded in relation to a given criterion such as a grade descriptor. With norm-referenced assessment a judgement is made about a student's attainment in relation to the rest of the population for comparative purposes. With criterion-referenced assessment anyone matching, for instance, the B grade criteria gets that grade regardless of whether he or she is the highest or lowest-achieving student in the country. Under a norm-referenced system the 'best' candidate would automatically get an A.

Summative assessment is normally external as opposed to internal assessment and is undertaken by examiners outside the school. Sometimes summative assessments (such as GCSE coursework) are marked by the class teacher and then finally moderated by external examiners. Summative assessment is normally formal, known about well in advance and very different from informal formative assessment. Summative statements about pupils' attainment are required by employers as they are often not only an exit qualification but also an entry qualification to other courses or careers.

E is for evidence of effectiveness

Curriculum managers will often compare CAT scores with examination results to assess your abilities and performance as a teacher. For instance, the NFER (1996) found from a sample of nearly 24,000 children that those with CAT scores of 125–130 attained a GCSE grade A in English, those scoring 115–124 were awarded B grades and children with CAT scores between 95 and 114 achieved C grades. If the class you taught for two years at GCSE had an average CAT score of 100 and all got A grades you would be deemed to be an exceptional teacher indeed. On the other hand, teaching children with CAT scores of 120 and ending up with a clutch of C grades would not be so good for your career. The problem with such analysis is that the motivation and educational aspirations of the child are ignored.

Your effectiveness as a teacher will also be judged by comparing results at the end of each key stage to assess the extent to which value-added progress (that which is in excess of normal development and improvement over time) has been achieved. Generally, anything in excess of 1.7 levels per key stage (roughly 2 grades at GCSE) is termed value-added. Children are expected to improve by a grade per year in the normal course of events and value-added denotes progress in excess of this. For instance, a level 5 at Key Stage 3 is roughly equivalent to a grade E at GCSE, so if a child is at this level at the end of Year 9 he or she stands a reasonable change of getting a C grade two years later at the end of Year 11. If you taught this child during Year 10 and Year 11, and he or she attained a B grade you would have demonstrated value-added progress.

Many curriculum managers have kept their own local records of the correlation between CAT scores and GCSE grades for some years now and have a good idea of the CAT scores of children who have gained certain grades in their particular school. This is more useful, in some ways, than the national survey as it reflects the quality of teaching and the educational aspirations or motivation of children in a particular area. Similar analysis of value-added progress can be undertaken by comparing, for example, end of Key Stage 3 results with end of Key Stage 4 results. While some teachers argue that relating ability to attainment in this way is problematic as they do not have control over how hard children work, others see it as their job to motivate children through their teaching. While CAT scores are widely used now a note of caution is advisable. In one school where I was responsible for managing GCSE the Year 11 pupil with the highest CAT score in the year achieved the lowest grades as he truanted in order to earn money working with his dad fitting carpets in nightclubs. While assessment can identify learning needs and measure end results it does not on its own provide strategies for improvement. That is left to the English teacher's professional judgement and artistry and such teaching and learning can be planned in the light of such information.

■ Further reading

Kyriacou, C. (1998) 'Assessing pupils' progress', Chapter 7 in *Essential Teaching Skills*. Cheltenham: Nelson Thornes.

Myhill, D. (1999b) 'Writing matters: linguistic characteristics of writing in GCSE English examinations', *English in Education*, 33(3): 70–81.

Stibbs, A (1979) *Assessing Children's Language – Guidelines for Teachers*. London: Ward Lock/NATE.

4

English teachers' professional development

The art and spirituality of professional development

The notion of English teaching as an art rather than a technology, that runs throughout this book, is developed in this chapter as any improvement in teaching must necessarily be a development of the art of teaching. The professional development of an English teacher must be seen in its aesthetic, ethical and even spiritual aspects. Here, the improvement of the practical 'craft of the classroom' skills that make the art of English teaching possible is explored and classical spiritual disciplines are drawn upon in exploring the professional development achieved through action or practitioner research and reflection.

Recently, moves have been made to introduce aesthetic approaches into teacher development such as the art of reflective writing where teachers learn through narratives (Winter et al., 1999), and many teachers are also 'ready to look beyond technique for whatever guidance may come from spiritual traditions' (Palmer, 1993: x) as there is a growing recognition that learning and spiritual development go hand in hand. Yet, as we saw in Chapter 1, teachers are increasingly viewed as technicians (Muijs and Reynolds, 2001) whose task is to be more efficient and effective rather than professionals who deliberate the aims of education; consequently, the inadequacies of technical-rational models of teacher education are rooted in their failure to acknowledge the need for professionals' development to be holistic, especially at a time when there is an 'increasing appreciation of the importance in professional practice of non-cognitive aspects of being' (Knight, 2002: 231).

Many English teachers now recognize that 'empirically-grounded knowledge is not the only true or valid kind of knowing' for, while reason 'is excellent for scientific enquiry and proof', we know that 'there are other ways of knowing and other kinds of knowledge which are just as valid even though

they cannot be proved by scientific means' (May, 1981: 24). Ev¹
is a need to draw upon a 'new knowledge' as one 'does not d
pedagogy simply by choosing from a grab bag of teaching t¹
1993: 30). The realization that 'knowing is a profoundly cₒₗ.
(ibid.: xv) moves us in the right direction for 'real and genuine knowleᵤᵍₑ
also comes via commitment' as one 'can never truly know another human
being . . . unless one is prepared to commit oneself in trust, whole-heartedly,
to the other person' (May, 1981: 24). Arguably, the pain of disconnection
that pervades education arises from the attempt to find rational solutions to
relational problems.

A professional's development begins by seeing differently and having a
renewed vision of the possibilities within a particular context, and spiritual
disciplines provide 'exercises that can help us see and be whole' (Palmer,
1993: xxvi) for these are 'disciplines that empower us to do the sort of teaching that can help re-form our students, our schools, and our world as well'
(ibid.). Classical spiritual disciplines such as 'the study of sacred texts, the
practice of prayer and contemplation, and the gathered life of the community itself' (ibid.: 17) are reflected in our schools where reading, reflection
and responsiveness to others are still practised. As teachers, we are formed by
the reading we do, the reflection we engage in and our responsiveness to our
community. All these disciplines are incorporated into action research which
seeks to improve professional practice by acknowledging the communal
nature of understanding.

■ Action research for improving English teaching

The 'long term aspiration' of action research is 'always a collaborative one'
(Altrichter et al., 1993: 6) as it is 'the study of a social situation with a view
to improving the quality of action within it' (Elliot, 1991: 69). Consequently,
the English teacher's role is 'not to be an objective, dispassionate and impar-
tial spectator, but to be an integral part of the action that improves a
situation' (Pike, 2002a: 34–5) for 'development and innovation are an essential part of professional practice' (Altrichter et al., 1993: 201). Although at
the 'heart of teaching lies the complexity of social interactions (usually
involving large groups) in which there is always opportunity for improvement' (ibid.), action research is 'about your action, not the action of others'
(McNiff et al., 1996: 17) because 'there is an emphasis on your deliberate
intention to intervene in your own practice to bring about improvement'
(ibid.). Rather than aiming 'to fit personal practice to another person's
theory, it concerns itself with enabling individuals to develop their own personal theories' (McNiff, 1993: 17) which is a hallmark of the professional as

the sort of questions addressed are of the type: 'How can I improve . . . .?' (McNiff et al., 1996: 17).

Such an approach is helpful in both initial teacher training and staff development. English teachers can work on the following research questions: How can I improve my teaching of Shakespeare in Year 9? How can I improve my starter activities? How can I improve the pace of A level lessons? How can I differentiate more effectively? How can I incorporate the effective use of ICT into Year 10 lessons on the anthology? How can I improve children's literacy? How can I teach spelling patterns more clearly? How can I manage whole-class discussion better? How can I improve my teaching of poetry so that boys in Year 10 enjoy it more? How can I ensure children in Year 8 are challenged by reading activities? The same approach can, of course, be taken by whole English departments and experienced teachers responding to new challenges.

Reflective practice is now 'taken to be a key ingredient of professional development in a variety of practitioner domains, including education' (Bryant, 1996: 106) and learning to teach or how to improve one's teaching is a process where an improvement in a 'person's conscious understanding of his/her praxis' (McNiff, 1993: 6) is brought about as 'the individual is encouraged to be critical of personal practice, and use her deepened insights to move forward' (ibid.: 20). Consequently, 'action research is a way of defining and implementing *relevant* professional development' (Lomax, 1990: 6–10). The aim of English teachers engaged in action research is, therefore, 'the development of a sensitive and self-critical subjective perspective' (Stenhouse, 1975: 35). Narratives and reflective writing are so valuable in this respect because an 'important benefit of reproducing one's perceptions, as a writer, is that the act of representation tells the observer, not just about what was seen, but about the lens through which it was seen' (Pike, 2002b: 29).

An approach to such reflective practice that will be of particular interest to English teachers can be found in *Professional Experience and the Investigative Imagination: The Art of Reflective Writing* (1999) by Richard Winter, Alyson Buck and Paula Sobiechowska, which shows how professionals can 'explore and represent their professional practice through "artistic", and "imaginative" forms of writing, in particular, "fiction"' (ibid.: 1). This text takes its cue from Donald Schön's notion that reflective practice is 'artistry' as it requires that we deal sensitively with 'situations of uncertainty, instability, uniqueness, and value-conflict' (1983: 50) where there is no single correct way of acting. Evidently, deciding how to act and respond in a particular situation 'is the literature teacher's art' because it involves a consideration of 'where, when and whom to flood or focus; when to pester, when to nudge, and when to leave alone' (Stibbs, 1996: 37).

Teachers employing action research can also, of course, describe the action with 'factual accounts based on transcripts of conversations and meetings, or summaries of data from questionnaires and interviews' (McNiff et al., 1996: 19).

Certainly video or audio-taping is a way of recording data although diaries and personal reflections can also be used. As explanation and evaluation follow the description of the action, it is essential, however, to 'involve other people to check out your interpretations' (Lomax, 1991: 102–3) and this 'means sharing the findings with other people, particularly colleagues in the work context, and checking with them whether your perceptions are reasonably fair and accurate' (McNiff et al., 1996: 27). What is important is that reflection is made critical, which entails 'exploring its significance from a range of different perspectives' (ibid.: 20).

Action research which fosters reflective practice is of such value in English teachers' professional development because it can generate pedagogic knowledge which is a knowledge of processes. For this to be the case, the teacher's action must be *informed* in the sense that 'you need to be proactive in exploring your own motives and values' (ibid.: 17); it should be *committed* because 'the action researcher needs to be a stakeholder in the action' (ibid.: 18); and it needs to be *intentional* because the intention is 'to improve practice, to be systematic, to invite criticism' (ibid.). In this way, the professional teacher is able to show how transformation has occurred. Practical strategies are needed in such investigations for if 'one is not forced into working out the practical implications of one's aims . . . then there is every chance that the feel-good satisfaction of boasting about the humanising effect of one's work are not likely to lead to much actual good in the classroom' (Davies, 1996: 29). One benefit of action research is that it provides English teachers with 'the methodological tools needed to transform practice and to set their own agenda for change' (Pike, 2002b: 34) because a cycle of planning, acting, observing, reflecting, planning is followed. Reading the journals *Changing English*, *The Use of English* and *English in Education* can help teachers to reflect upon their own practice in the light of that of others, and the UK government offers Best Practice scholarships for teachers who have taught for four or five years to enable them to investigate aspects of their work.

Lesson study: action research from the USA and Japan

One application of action research for teaching currently gaining ground and winning converts in the USA is known as 'lesson study' (Fernandez et al., 2001). This system originally came from Japan where it forms part of the professional development of teachers in schools where the aim is to bring about steady incremental improvement rather than a 'quick fix'. In fact, teachers meet for up to a year to 'design, implement, test and improve' a lesson which is related to a theme for professional development at school level. It illustrates one way of working collaboratively to improve practice and there are many variations that can be equally successful.

Eight stages are part of the lesson study process. At 'Stage 1: defining the problem', the particular area for professional development becomes the focus for a particular lesson. At 'Stage 2: planning the lesson' the objective is to plan (see Chapter 2) an effective lesson and to understand why and how it might work. Research is carried out and then the plan is presented at a departmental meeting for discussion. 'Stage 3: teaching the lesson', comprises both teaching and observation for when the lesson is being taught all the other teachers come to watch, walk around and take careful notes about what students are learning. The lesson may even be video-taped. 'Stage 4: evaluating the lesson' entails teachers staying after school to express their views about it, with the teacher who taught the lesson going first. The focus is the lesson (rather than the teacher who taught it) as it is group property and was planned by the whole group so teachers engaging in criticism of the lesson are actually critiquing themselves. During 'Stage 5: Revising the lesson' teachers redesign the lesson based on the evidence they have. At 'Stage 6: Teaching the revised lesson' the redesigned lesson is taught by a different teacher to a different class. At this point all the school's teaching staff attend and watch! In 'Stage 7: Evaluating and reflecting again' the department and perhaps an outside expert are involved in comprehensive evaluation. During 'Stage 8: Sharing the results' written reports are shared and the teachers collaboratively adopt an action research strategy to bring about further improvements.

Self-knowledge through others: mentoring and paired observation

The 'lesson study' sequence just described is only one way of carrying out action research and engaging in reflective practice. It is also common, for instance, for a student-teacher to plan a lesson for his or her mentor to teach so he or she can observe its progress. Such school and university-based tutors are 'essential for the development of more effective teaching behaviours' as teachers are often 'so busy in the moment-by-moment events that they could not recollect with any clarity the specifics of their behaviour' (Huebner, 1979/1999: 305) or, indeed, that of their pupils. The observer can 'help see the totality and bring before the teacher those events and behaviours that were not part of his or her conscious memory' (ibid.). Video-taping is similarly valuable as this enables teachers to view a lesson, rewind and view parts of it again so they can be 'independent of their own fallible memories' and 'can become students and researchers of their own teaching, and gain control over future behaviours' (ibid.).

Many student-teachers who watch the successful lessons of experienced members of staff come out feeling intuitively that what they have seen was aesthetically pleasing without being able to identify rationally why it was so successful and are then unable to replicate such success. Clearly, both intuition and reason are required for 'the "skills" of art (or rather the understandings of and capacities for art) are responsive and developing and benefit from continual self-examination' (Stibbs, 1996: 32). Yet, if teaching is approached as a technology, development can only be achieved through limited propositional knowledge (if I do x then y will happen) and English teaching is not that simple. Knowledge about English teaching cannot exist independently of the practitioner.

Artists tend to engage with the work of other artists in order to be inspired and challenged, and proficiency in 'a craft develops slowly and requires the concentration, patience and practice which goes with any discipline' (Huebner, 1962/1999: 33) because the properties of the medium can only be understood by experimenting. When learning to teach it is worth knowing that the fastest learners do not always make the best teachers and your learning will continue after you are fully qualified. Even the experienced artist can become aware of new characteristics of the medium as new ideas and techniques are tried. Above all English teachers generally have a love of teaching and it is this love for our art that prompts us to innovate. The experienced artist knows the possibilities of the medium and understands how its properties work. The spirituality of such activity lies in the way the teacher must have a vision of what is desired and may intuitively bring that vision to fruition without being able to explicate beforehand exactly how it was to be achieved. Arguably, a kind of faith is needed to conceive the image of the situation one wants, and to believe not only that it is possible but that it will be realized. The teacher initially experiences something aesthetically dissatisfying, if you like, and has a vision, a picture, of what would be satisfying and this sense, feeling, intuition and belief often preceed analysis and rational attention to details of the craft. Having a vision of your expectations being fulfilled is necessary as is believing in yourself and in the power of your words and abilities to create.

Such an approach to teacher development may be more likely to work with English teachers than managers' grids, targets and data projections. This way of going about professional development is more likely to foster spiritual well-being than issuing teachers with targets that must be achieved by a specified date. Paired observation can be especially helpful for experienced teachers. When I led an English faculty in a comprehensive school, we addressed the issue of staff development by dividing into six pairs for observation of lessons. The teacher being observed nominated the focus for observation. Some areas for focused observation could be communicating learning objectives, starting the lesson, explanations, setting tasks, maintaining a good working environment, interacting with pupils, assessing pupils, differentiation, pace, pitch, use of the plenary, how well the task or teaching matched the learning objective, classroom management, managing transitions between activities, managing hands up and so on. Focusing on just three or four of these aspects of teaching and using methods of action research to collect evidence in order to examine closely what is going on can be invaluable as teachers benefit from more than their own viewpoint and enable critical insight to develop.

Regrettably, in many schools the capacity of English teachers to help colleagues in their department to develop by undertaking paired observation is neglected, and for an English team to discuss teaching (as in the lesson study example) is all too rare. Clearly, an atmosphere of trust and openness is necessary if such honesty and development is to be possible. We need to make time to benefit from the skills of existing staff which could have a significant impact on the development of teaching. We also need to ensure that departmental administration does not detract from our central focus, which is teaching and learning in English. Meetings should regularly concentrate on how to improve teaching and learning where teachers share their best lessons and discuss ways of teaching an innovative media assignment or a new way of teaching a Shakespeare scene. People are an organization's most precious asset and, as a resource, their creativity, ideas, experience and reflection need to be released so that they are empowered to develop. A teacher needs to give other teachers the benefit of his or her perspective and also to listen to the perspectives of colleagues so that teaching can be evaluated from different viewpoints. Teachers have to work openly and collaboratively if improvement is to be possible for 'the improvement of teaching requires a democratization of the work place and a redistribution of those resources that give teachers control over their own destiny as teachers' (Huebner, 1979/1999: 311).

Professional development and personal experience

Life-history affects professional practice and reflecting on the teaching one experienced as a child can be a valuable way to begin. In the case of teaching, reflective practice entails reflection, to some degree, upon the past, and although Gadamer suggests we can only see the past through the limited perspective of the present it would also appear to be true that we can only understand what we do in the present by recourse to past experience. At Edith Cowan University in Perth, Western Australia, the unit on 'Life History' (for their one-year Graduate Diploma in Education) is especially valuable as the influence of early life on professional identity cannot be ignored when fostering reflective practitioners (Trotman and Kerr, 2001). A student-teacher has, after all, experienced at least twelve years of schooling and has observed teachers at work. Teachers are influenced by how they were taught at school but may not realize what a powerful influence their own education exerts upon their practice. Arguably, the way we were taught influences how we teach. One task of professional development is to enable an individual to reflect on his or her tacit understanding in order to improve practice and we need to recognize that personal experience acts as a critical filter. The recent work of a highly perceptive PGCE student shows that the personal and the professional should not be separated:

> When I was in Year Nine, and under tuition of an English teacher by the name of Mr Horsforth [a pseudonym], our class spent an entire term reading a novel *Collision Course*. I'm sure it was a great book; it was, after all, written by the marvellous Nigel Hinton who produced the children's classic *Buddy*. However, the only memory I have of this book is that I loathed it. I found it boring. It made me, for the first time in my life, dread my English lessons. This was no mean feat, because even at the young age of thirteen, sitting in that dull Year 9 lesson, I knew I wanted to be an English teacher. I knew I wanted to make people love the subject as much as I did.
>
> So what was so terrible about *Collision Course*? Nothing, really. The problem was in the way Mr Horsforth chose to teach it. He took what I now know to be the easy option; he let the class read the novel aloud, one page each, going clockwise around the room. And then starting again when we reached the end of the chain. This didn't represent much of a challenge for those of us who were able readers, but for those who struggled (and my class seemed to have quite a few of these) it was a nightmare. One girl in particular took at least ten minutes to read her page, in a lifeless and barely audible monotone.
>
> While this girl was bravely ploughing through her page of text the rest of the class were getting bored and fidgety. The boys at the back of the room were starting to create their own amusement in the form of bits of rubber that they could flick at the backs of those in front. The children sitting by the window were gazing outside distractedly. Even those, like myself, who were not known for our deviant behaviour, had started to talk in low whispers and scribble notes to each other in our jotters. And what did the teacher do about all this? Nothing. Because he wasn't really teaching anymore. He had shut down. Sometimes he even used this time to mark books at his desk, completely oblivious to what was going on around him. The point of this anecdote is to illustrate that the best form of teaching has to involve interaction. The teacher, at all times, has to be aware of what is going on in his or her classroom. They simply cannot, as Mr Horsforth did, let the lesson run itself and hope for the best.

Clearly, Joanne learnt a lot about how to teach (and how not to teach) from engaging in this reflection about teaching and learning from her own school-days. A number of judgements are made about what is good and bad teaching. Combining approaches from biographical studies (Erben, 1998) to enhance reflective practice with action research is valuable for it is 'located at the social justice end of the political continuum' (Day, 1998: 273) and is not only concerned with achieving change that enables the English specialist to be more efficient or effective but, more fundamentally, with 'how to act rightly' (Bryant, 1996: 116).

Practitioner-research can perform a 'transformative social role, not simply because it facilitates the development and implementation of appropriate pedagogy, but because it has the potential to transform the professional culture' (Pike, 2002a: 36). This is especially important now because since the 1980s the notion of teachers' professionalism has been redefined in the UK and there is a growing tendency to see professional reflection as the activity of paying attention to means not ends. The Hay McBer research (2000) specifies the characteristics teachers are to have and develop so that even the definition of what it is to be an effective teacher is centrally controlled and enshrined in national standards. Truly professional development for the English teacher cannot separate means from ends, the past from the present or effectiveness from ethics, for English teachers engaged in action research 'tend to be working intentionally towards the implementation of ideas that come from deep-seated values that motivate them to intervene'. (McNiff et al., 1996: 9–10). For professional development to be of value it must value teachers and address their needs in a way that acknowledges the ethics, aesthetics and spirituality of English teaching.

Further reading

McNiff, J. (1993) *Teaching as Learning: An Action Research Approach*. London: Routledge.

Palmer, P. (1993) *To Know as We are Known – Education as a Spiritual Journey*. San Francisco, CA: Harper.

Pike, M.A. (2002) 'Action research for English teaching: ideology, pedagogy and personal growth', *Educational Action Research: An International Journal*, 10(1): 27–44.

Winter, R., Buck, A. and Sobiechowska, P. (1999) *Professional Experience and the Investigative Imagination – the Art of Reflective Writing*. London and New York, NY: Routledge.

PART II

Teaching the English curriculum

5

Literature and literacy at Key Stage 3

Literature or literacy?

There is a tension at the very heart of English teaching and nowhere is it more evident than at Key Stage 3. As English teachers, we have a responsibility to foster children's love of literature and also their capacity to function as literate members of society. We seek to empower young readers to be imaginative while recognizing the need for them to be accurate. We attend to appropriateness but also seek to foster insight. This chapter explores the tension between literature and literacy and the changing nature of English in the early years of the secondary school. I argue here that imagination and aesthetic response to literature are more central to the development of literacy skills than is often acknowledged and that literate citizens are not fostered simply by learning literacy skills but by acquiring a love of literature.

We need to remember that literacy is not always acquired in the most obvious of ways. If Albert Einstein had only focused on the symbols on the paper in front of him, he would never have achieved his breakthrough. What was needed more than anything else was an imaginative leap, an act of creativity, for Einstein's Theory of Relativity 'was formulated as a result of his imagining what it would be like to ride a shaft of light into outer space' (Ousbey, 1991: 18–19). Imagination is sometimes more important than knowledge.

The time-honoured practice of English teachers, before the start of the present century, was to teach the skills of literacy through imaginative literature. Now all that is changing and with the advent of the National Literacy Strategy (NLS) a far greater emphasis has been placed upon literacy, in its own right, in the early years of the secondary school. The rules and conventions of a range of texts (many of them non-literary) are to be explicitly taught and there is a greater emphasis than before on grammar, syntax and grapho-phonological knowledge. Key Stage 3 English is being transformed and this chapter seeks to provide a clear and succinct description of the most important changes while emphasizing the centrality of literature in English teaching. To begin, though, we need to look at our motivation for reading and writing: at both its *purpose* and the *pleasure* derived from it.

Reading and writing for *purpose*

Eighty per cent of the data stored on the world's computers is in English and 75% of the world's surface mail is in English (McCrum, et al., 1987: 20). One quarter of the world's entire population can speak English reasonably fluently and a billion people (that is one thousand million of them) are currently learning English. It has been argued that the 'greatest legacy the English have bequeathed the rest of humanity is their language' (Paxman, 1998: 234) and it is easy to forget the value that the rest of the world attaches to English if you are a native speaker. When a German meets his or her Japanese counterpart to discuss business they will speak English; when the Dutch captain of the aeroplane taking them from Cologne to Tokyo talks to air traffic controllers of different nationalities on the way, they converse in English; if the plane were ever to be hijacked by terrorists they would bark their commands in English. English is the language of international politics as well as of travel, science, commerce and technology. Language is power and to be literate in the world's most powerful language is to be empowered indeed. Being able to communicate in the global language empowers the individual to function in the global village.

Being literate in English is especially necessary if one happens to be living in England. It is sobering to consider how disempowered a person is who cannot read the letters that come through the letter box, the signs in the doctor's surgery, the newspaper, the voting card, a tax return or the stories his or her children love. Various statistics indicate that between one sixth and one eighth of adults in the UK have problems with literacy and while everyone seems to use different measures to assess literacy it is generally agreed that literacy levels are too low in the UK. Around 30% of pupils fail to achieve a level 4 in English at the age of 11 and are, consequently, ill-equipped to benefit from the broader secondary curriculum. The literacy demands of books in geography or religious studies render them out of reach and children are excluded from both learning and lessons as a result. To participate and be included in a society, where one can exercise rights and responsibilities, demands a level of literacy that enables the individual to function.

Reading and writing for *pleasure*

Yet, enjoyment is important too and is often left out of the debate about literacy. When adults who have made the journey from illiteracy to literacy are asked about their new life they often talk about being able to read the stories their children want to hear. A much neglected point in the debate about literacy is that if you are attempting to teach someone to read or write, he or she needs to *want* to do so. Policy-makers would do well to consider what makes 11–14-year-olds *want* to read and write. Many teachers of English have long understood this and those with experience of adolescents are acutely aware that motivation is central to the achievement of our goals however egalitarian they may be. Any approach to secondary English teaching that focuses too exclusively on the acquisition of skills and does not take sufficient account of the human will and the motivation of the adolescent learner is destined to fail.

There 'needs to be more emphasis on motivation, on helping children to enjoy reading' (Cox, 1998: x), and Roy Hattersley rightly asserts that while literacy is a necessity, it should be 'the most universal and easily accessible of pleasures' and not merely 'like good manners and clean shoes, essential to the prospect of employment' (1998: 50). We must ensure that there is not such a focus on form and function or accuracy and appropriateness that children get out of the habit of reading for enjoyment.

Literature in English at Key Stage 3

Two of the most effective ways of motivating children in the 11–14 age range to read and engage with texts is for the English teacher to employ DARTs (Directed Activity Related to Texts) and active approaches. These pedagogic strategies are closely related and have enlivened countless classrooms. DARTs are designed to enable readers to reflect upon their reading by adopting active approaches to texts. Examples of DARTs are segmenting the text, prediction exercises, drawing diagrams, highlighting, underlining, annotating, sequencing, cloze procedure and so on. Lunzer and Gardner pioneered the use of DARTs and their book, *The Effective Use of Reading* (1979), provides a more detailed description of their use. Small-group and paired work is normally suitable for DARTs although some activities can be done individually. Usually, DARTs are relatively short, time-specific, 'hands-on' tasks. The DART is alive and well in the English classroom and student-teachers who view the video *Supporting Assessment for the Award of Qualified Teacher Status: Secondary English* (TTA, 2000) of student-teacher Juliet teaching *Romeo and Juliet* will see that when her pupils sequence quotations from the play in order to focus on Shakespeare's use of the nurse for humorous effect, they are using a DART. Such approaches are also actively encouraged by the NLS.

Active approaches, with a performance element and often involving social and physical activity, have been successfully developed for the teaching of

Shakespeare whereby pupils can respond in a variety of ways because multiple interpretations are legitimated (Gibson, 1998). Each play is treated as a script and incorporates the principle that 'Shakespeare is to be enjoyed!' (Gibson, 1994: 147). The *Cambridge School Shakespeare* series of books gives many examples of active approaches and focuses on the imaginative experience so central to English teaching. A few of the active approaches to Shakespeare listed by Rex Gibson (1994: 144) are:

> acting out of scenes; tableaux; all varieties of choral speaking; improvizations; companies; parodies; trials; missing scenes; short versions; confessions; hot seating; intercutting; dreams; sequencing; insults; greetings; partings; commands, and oaths; games of all types; directing; designing; mimes; casting; role playing; inquests; interior monologues; alter egos; voices off; blocking; director's notes; brainstorming; echoes and whispers.

Active approaches can be modified and used with a wide range of texts as dialogue in the class reader can be turned into a script. At an appropriate level texts such as *Holes* by Louis Sacher, *Boy* by Roald Dahl or even *Mrs Frisby and the Rats of NIMH* by R.C. O'Brien allow children the opportunity to enter other worlds and to experience life from a different point of view as they engage in an active approach to a text.

When so much that is written about the teaching of English at Key Stage 3 is currently dominated by a concern with literacy it is important to reassert the central importance of literature within the English lessons of 11–14-year-olds. As well as considering *how* children can be encouraged to read literature we also need to think about *why* they should read literature and why English teachers consider literature to be of primary importance. What is the point of reading fiction? What is the point of reading poems or plays? A student-teacher could derive the impression from the National Literacy Strategy that the point of children studying certain text-types as models and examples is so that they can produce their own and we have to admit that most children are not likely to need to write a novel or a poem in the workplace after they leave school.

Having a rationale for the reading of literature is vital. One of the 'great functions of literature for the young is to give them models of life which both deepen the *experience* they have and suggest, explore, ranges of *experience* they don't have' (Byatt, 1998: 45, emphasis added). Indeed, it has been suggested that the literary work is quite unique and entirely different from any other type of writing because, unlike other forms, it 'diverges from the real experiences of the reader in that it opens up perspectives in which the empirically known world of one's own personal *experience* appears changed (Iser, 1971: 8, emphasis added). The literary work 'allows the reader to place himself within the world of fiction' and one of the chief values of literature is that it is able to give everyone 'the chance to enter other worlds' (ibid.: 44).

The transformation of English at Key Stage 3

The implementation of the National Literacy Strategy at Key Stage 3 has provoked diverse reactions. Clearly, there are benefits of the new emphasis upon teaching language skills but also disadvantages due to increased prescription and the pervasive and growing emphasis derived from functional grammar. It is important to explain some of these changes simply and to consider what they mean for the English teacher of children in the early years of the secondary school.

A knowledge of the conventions of the most common non-fiction text-types is now essential, and English teachers' syntactical and grapho-phonological knowledge has become increasingly important. Syntactical knowledge relates to sentence-level work as it is concerned with grammar and how words function in a sentence; grapho-phonological knowledge focuses on the relation of sounds to letter symbols, patterns of spelling and morphology. Phonics is no longer the preserve of the primary school teacher as English teachers now need phonic knowledge in order to improve children's spelling and there is a more coherent, planned and systematic focus on spelling than was common previously. English teachers are now required to focus on sentence-level knowledge and to know the metalanguage of English. Words and phrases such as 'subordinate clause', 'noun phrase', 'auxiliary verb' and 'determiner' did not often roll off the tongues of English teachers before the implementation of the NLS, and English teachers with literature degrees now have to augment their own linguistic knowledge and know the parts of speech, more accurately known as word classes, in order to teach literacy.

The shift towards non-fiction such as transactional writing and the growing importance being attached to the ability of pupils to report, explain, instruct and so on may be evidence of the 'bleak spectre of utilitarianism' which 'hangs over our schools like a pall' if the focus on literacy is only 'to enhance our economic performance' (Marshall, 1998: 109). On the other hand, advocates of the NLS are keen for us to see the new emphasis on literacy in terms of human growth and often like to focus on the power of literacy to transform society. The change in the types of text studied will, undoubtedly, have major consequences for English as a subject as the 'textual materials mostly read and written in English have customarily been to do with what might broadly be described as "the literary arts": a focused, rather small portion of literacy; possibly best characterised as "literary literacy"' (Dean, 2002: 10).

The Literacy Strategy, in the form of the *Framework for Teaching of English: Years 7, 8 and 9* (DfEE, 2001) directly addresses pedagogy and ways of teaching as one of the reasons for the introduction of the NLS was a concern that insufficient attention was being paid to the explicit teaching of literacy in English. Just a few examples from the *Framework* document will suffice. The NLS promotes teaching that is 'Direct and *explicit*' (ibid.: 16) and the simplicity of this ideology is apparent in the admission that the 'implications . . . for lesson organization are few, but very significant: more *explicit* teaching' (ibid.: 17). We are told that '*explicit* attention to language learning' (ibid.: 66) will be of great benefit and that teachers must 'clarify *explicitly* the similarities and differences' (ibid.: 65) between spoken and written English. Further, the 'transfer of skills from one lesson to another' should be 'part of the *explicit* teaching agenda in all lessons' (ibid.: 15) as objectives 'benefit from being *explicitly* taught and from being identified' (ibid.: 11). (my italic)

Explicitness is increasingly seen as a panacea for all perceived pedagogic ills, and the government's prescribed treatment may have side-effects upon children's motivation and engagement. English teachers need to ensure that heavy doses of explicitness, regularly administered, are not all there is to English teaching at Key Stage 3. Children must experience the art of reading and writing so that they are sufficiently motivated to learn more. The whole emphasis on the explicit is, of course, problematic in English teaching for, while English teachers do not normally advocate deliberate obfuscation and have always recognized the importance of clarity, the emphasis on the explicit in English can be taken too far and we need to work hard to ensure that its converse, the implicit, is not marginalized.

A distinctive feature of any literary text is that it has gaps in it which 'are a basic element for the aesthetic response' (Iser, 1971: 12) as they are filled at a peculiarly individual level and, analogously, lessons are also texts that children read. By increasing the degree of explicitness in the lesson and focusing on knowing and applying the conventions of different text-types the nature of the intellectual space inhabited by learners is radically altered in English. With the introduction of the National Literacy Strategy there is an attempt to bring about a radical shift in the boundaries within which the learner thinks and responds in English at Key Stage 3; we need to be aware that the fewer the gaps the lesson supplies, or the more routinized they become, the less personally involved the learner may be.

Having the right sort of gaps in the text of an English lesson is a precondition for high levels of motivation and also aesthetic response. Gaps need to exist that stimulate the learner to bring vision, creativity, imagination and personal experience to the lesson and we must be wary of initiatives that seek to prescribe and routinize the nature of the text (the lesson) that students participate in. Gaps in English lessons are opportunities to respond individually as a result of something being left unsaid. Like the literary text, the English lesson provides a degree of implicitness that allows the reader to make the text his or her own. English teaching must not be reduced to a method with an undue emphasis on the explicit and, consequently, the literacy strategy needs to be implemented with considerable skill and discrimination.

While explication, when it comes to knowledge about language, is entirely appropriate we should not forget how learners are motivated as it may only be as a result of the reader being interested in a text and perceiving its relevance that the motivation to explicate comes about. When English teaching becomes more focused on acquiring skills and knowledge than on providing literary experiences that motivate, there are likely to be very grave consequences. English teaching misses the point if it concentrates on the style and form of texts and their linguistic features and devotes insufficient time and space to personal and aesthetic response.

The model of language in the NLS

Put simply, the model of language implicit in the NLS can be summed up in two questions a reader or writer can ask about any text: (1) *Who* is it for? and (2) *What* is it for? The assumption enshrined in the NLS is that if I need to produce a piece of writing and I know the answers to these two questions I can select an appropriate form and style for the writing. If I possess a sufficient knowledge of *audience* and also of *purpose* then I can select from my repertoire of text-types and choose the most appropriate one. If I know the conventions of this text-type (at text, sentence and word level) I can produce an appropriate text in the most appropriate form given its purpose and audience. If I need to write an explanation it helps to know that explanations answer how and why questions and to know the common features of explanations. If I need to write instructions I can write in an appropriate way if I know whom I am instructing and have internalized the common conventions for writing instructions. A prediction in terms of register is being carried out: if I know the situation I can get the language 'right'.

Such a theory or model may seem pleasingly neat and simple as an explanation of how language works and it is certainly very useful when it comes to finding a socially justifiable way of teaching standard English and encouraging children to use this dialect rather than a regional one. While the method of ascertaining the *purpose* of and *audience* for a given text is helpful when teaching certain aspects of English in school, it would appear to be insufficiently discriminating to apply such a model to the whole of English during an entire key stage. Yet, the NLS is founded upon the 'functional grammar', expounded by linguists such as Halliday (1978), Kress (1989), Littlefair (1991; 1992) and Derewianka (1990) which claims that the purpose of a text determines how it works. Halliday argues that in order to know how to behave linguistically we need to know about the social context because 'the language we speak or write varies according to the type of situation' we are in (Halliday, 1978: 32). Certain claims from *Language as Social Semiotic*, in the light of the NLS, sound strangely familiar as Halliday observes that the 'ability to control the varieties of one's language that are *appropriate to different uses* is one of the cornerstones of linguistic success, not least for the school pupil' (ibid.: 28) for 'language is as it is because of what it has to do' (ibid.: 18–19). It is important to realize, though, that this is only one way of thinking about texts and how we read and write them. There are alternatives and the model of language underpinning the NLS, with its emphasis upon social convention and appropriateness, does not privilege the writer's voice as something unique and original that is to be encouraged and developed. Nor does the model of language implicit in the NLS appear to draw on critical literacy to any great extent so that communication might be understood as ideologically determined.

Literature and literacy at the start of Key Stage 3

Many teachers of English have long believed that language and literacy are best taught through literature. If the reader can enter another world, the world of fiction, and be captivated by a story, a description or a memory then that child is likely to want to find out what made the piece of writing so extraordinarily powerful and effective in the first place. Pupils can then be inspired to write their own stories, descriptions and memories after being absorbed in reading fiction they enjoy.

One of the Key Stage 3 National Strategy booklets to hit just the right note, in this respect, is *Transition from Year 6 to Year 7 English – Units of Work* (DfEE, 2002). The work for Year 7 is based around the rather wonderful story *My Father is a Polar Bear* by Michael Morpurgo. As a class reader the story is only fifteen pages long and appears in *Hereabout Hill* although it is reproduced in full in the *Transition* booklet. The narrator tells the story of growing up with his mother and step-father, always haunted by thoughts of his real father, an actor, whom he first saw as a 5-year-old one Christmas Eve on stage as a polar bear in *The Snow Queen*. Throughout life he spots his father in different roles in theatres and on television, eventually meeting him face to face as an adult at the end of the story. This is a tremendously engaging story that undoubtedly enables young readers to escape the confines of their classroom and place themselves in the world of the fiction, longing to meet an absentee father, the famous actor rejected by their mother, only glimpsed through theatre make-up in a series of costumes on different stages. The story is about growing up, the reasons adults do things, their relationships, secrets, families and one's own personal and intimate hopes and dreams.

In just a few pages Morpurgo's *My Father is a Polar Bear* is guaranteed to capture the attention of Year 7 pupils in their first fortnight at secondary school. The *Transition* booklet shows how literacy skills can be acquired by pupils reading this story in a way that fosters their 'critical reflection and personal response' (DfEE, 2002c: 12). While focusing their attention on such a well crafted story on a theme they can relate to, children also 'study how an author structures a text to prepare for the ending' and learn about 'the differences between an oral recount and a narrative' while they are 'consolidating their understanding of the use of complex sentences' and 'securing the correct spellings of vowels in words' (ibid.). Whoever it was at the Standards and Effectiveness Unit who wrote these lesson plans understood the importance of achieving clarity in literacy teaching while fostering the personal growth of 11-year-olds.

Writing in journals is employed to develop thinking (and not simply to record it after the event), and pupils' own wider reading is used to 'celebrate the class's range of reading and validate personal preferences' (ibid.: 14). Children work in pairs, in groups and individually; they read, write, speak and listen in one short period of time and learn about the structure of a narrative, such as how the final paragraph relates to the rest of the story; they also recall events from their own personal lives and reflect on the way they were when younger. All the ingredients of successful English teaching are here. The resources are superb; the annotation of the short story is helpful for teachers and the detailed lesson plans are clear and informative. Teachers could benefit greatly by undertaking a careful analysis of the way the two weeks of lessons have been planned as this demonstrates how literacy and literature should be mutually interdependent.

Literacy without literature at Key Stage 3?

Some of the literacy taught at Key Stage 3, however, does not appear to be intended to be taught through literature. Significant sections of the progress units, while explicitly targeting children's literacy skills, do not do so by looking at the use of language in children's literature and there has been considerable debate about the value of teaching language out of context. In Year 7 pupils at level 3 should have additional support and focused teaching to enable them to catch up with their peers. To this end there are six 'progress units': *Writing Organization, Information Retrieval, Spelling, Reading Between the Lines, Phonics* and *Sentences.*

The emphasis in these progress units is on intensive and explicit teaching directly focused on an area that is a persistent difficulty for the Year 7 pupil. Teachers can quickly check whether a child should follow a given progress unit by performing a simple and straightforward diagnostic assessment provided at the start of each unit. For instance, the teacher can test the child's spelling with the list of words provided and if a score below a certain level is recorded the spelling progress unit would be deemed appropriate for that child. By following the unit the child would be explicitly taught how to spell correctly the sort of words he or she was spelling incorrectly. Teaching notes are provided and a plan for each session is given so that an accomplished teaching assistant could work with a small group of half a dozen pupils following the plan. Schools implement the teaching of the progress units in different ways although they are not supposed to take time away from normal English lessons as they are seen as additional support.

The *Year 7 Spelling Bank* (DfES, 2001) is a superb resource for starter activities and is excellent material for word-level work which imaginative teachers can relate to other work children are doing. Vowel choices, unstressed vowels, doubling consonants, pluralization, vowel and consonant suffixes, classical prefixes, homophones, common roots and word families are all covered. Other helpful resources are the *Key Objectives Bank: Year 8* (DfES, 2002a) and *Key Objectives Bank: Year 9* (DfES, 2002b), which suggests an imaginative range of activities and assessment opportunities.

The *National Curriculum* and the *Framework*

Two essential documents ensure that attention is devoted to both literature and literacy at Key Stage 3 and it is necessary to have a good understanding of both of them. They are *The National Curriculum for England: English* (DfEE/QCA, 1999) and the *Key Stage 3 National Strategy: Framework for Teaching English: Years 7, 8 and 9* (DfEE, 2001), normally termed the *National Curriculum* and the *Framework* or *Literacy Strategy*. There can be confusion about the relation between these two documents and it is helpful to note that '*The Framework for Teaching English* is based closely on the programmes of study for English in the revised National Curriculum of 2000' and that '*Framework* objectives for Years 7, 8 and 9 provide a framework for progression and full coverage of the English Order' (DfEE, 2001: 9). At the risk of oversimplification it might be worth thinking of the *National Curriculum* as telling us *what* we have to teach and the *Framework* telling us *how* to teach it.

The *National Curriculum for English*

It is worth rendering the whole notion of a single 'national' curriculum anthropologically strange in order to consider what the point of having one is and to evaluate its contents critically. It is also worth remembering that, for many years, until 1989, English teachers in England did not have a national curriculum to tell them what to do although they had to prepare pupils for examinations set externally by examination boards. It is certainly worth pondering what you would have in a curriculum for English if you could write your own and whether you would choose to have a single curriculum that all teachers and children should follow. This sort of exercise can be quite revealing as it tells you about your own beliefs and values with regard to the subject of English. What sort of emphasis would you put on language and what on literature? Would you include the teaching of formal grammar? What about slang, soap operas, adverts, literature in translation or Shakespeare?

Unlike the *Framework*, the *National Curriculum* is statutory. It prescribes which subjects should be taught in school and which are assessed formally in a Key Stage 3 test towards the end of Year 9. *The National Curriculum for England: English* (DfEE/QCA, 1999) covers all four key stages but the last two of these (Key Stage 3 and Key Stage 4) are the most directly relevant to life in the secondary English classroom. Key Stage 3 covers Year 7 (11 and 12-year-olds) to Year 9 (13 and 14-year-olds) and Key Stage 4 covers Year 10 (14 and 15-year-olds) and Year 11 (15 and 16-year-olds). The 'programmes of study' for English prescribe what should be taught and divide into three distinct attainment targets known as En1 (Speaking and listening), En2 (Reading) and En3 (Writing). Each attainment target is further divided into 'Knowledge, skills and understanding' (KSUs) and 'Breadth of study'.

If we take the second attainment target in English (En2: Reading), we read under 'Knowledge, skills and understanding', for instance, that children need to be able to 'extract meaning beyond the literal' (1a) and should also be able to 'distinguish between the attitudes and assumptions of characters and those of the author' (1i). They also need to be taught 'how and why texts have been influential and significant' (2a) and to learn about the qualities of literature from 'different traditions and cultures' (3c). Children also need to learn about ICT-based information texts as well as moving image and media texts and about language structure and variation. Such knowledge, skills and understanding, however, are to be cultivated while ensuring children experience a specific range of texts that appear under the heading 'Breadth of study'. This lists the range of literature as well as non-fiction texts to be studied so that knowledge, skills and understanding are to be taught through the range of texts (DfEE/QCA, 1999: 35) written by selected authors (ibid.: 36). Similarly, with the attainment target 'Writing' (En3), 'Knowledge, skills and understanding' comprises composition where children need to be taught how to write to 'imagine, explore and entertain'; to 'inform, explain and describe'; and to 'persuade, argue and advise' as well as to 'analyse, review and comment'. They need to plan and draft as well as punctuate and spell but all this is to be achieved through the production of texts for a range of purposes and readers and in a variety of forms. Under the heading 'Breadth of study' we are given a list of these forms and children must, for example, write poems, autobiographies and diaries, memos and minutes, advertisements, articles and letters as well as essays.

The *National Curriculum* is linked to a programme of assessment and examinations are taken at the end of Key Stage 3 (the Key Stage 3 test) and at the end of Key Stage 4 (the General Certificate in Secondary Education or GCSE). For each attainment target, En1 (Speaking and listening), En2 (Reading) and En3 (Writing), there are levels of attainment which you will find on fold-out A3-sized sheets at the back of *The National Curriculum for England: English* Although levels 1–8 are given on these sheets, pupils at the end of Key Stage 3 normally sit a paper for which the levels 4–7 can be awarded. Even though there are descriptions of each level it is advisable to see some examples. Studying a portfolio containing some level 4 writing and some level 5 writing helps you to recognize the difference between the two with confidence.

Much has been written about the political manoeuvring and reasons for the introduction of a national curriculum, and two books worth reading are *Cox on Cox: An English Curriculum for the 1990s* (Cox, 1991) and *The Battle for the National Curriculum* (Cox, 1995). Far less, however, has been written about the *Framework* document as most general guides to English teaching (Brindley, 1994; Davison and Dowson, 1998; Fleming and Stevens, 1998) were published before it began to transform Key Stage 3. Consequently, more space will be devoted here to the *Framework* as much is available elsewhere on the *National Curriculum* and the developments that led to its current form.

The *Framework*

The *National Curriculum* is supported by a *Framework* for English teaching as part of the extension into secondary schools of the National Literacy Strategy. Although it is not statutory, English teachers were expected to teach according to the objectives outlined in the *Framework for Teaching English: Years 7, 8 and 9* (DfEE, 2001) from the start of the academic year in 2001. Teachers are advised to implement the four-part lesson, to teach to the objectives contained in the *Framework* and to focus on language at text, sentence and word level far more explicitly than previously. Although it is not statutory, rigorous target setting underpins the strategy and considerable resources, training and staffing have been invested to promote literacy.

The *Framework* attempts to promote a view of literacy as more than basic skills and defines literacy as 'the ability to recognize, understand and manipulate the conventions of language' so that pupils can learn 'to use language imaginatively and flexibly' (ibid.: 9). The *Framework* has brought about the need for a significant reorientation in what English teachers do at Key Stage 3. Knowing the conventions of certain text-types is the starting point for further progress so that children do not only understand the relationship between instructional and explanatory text, for instance, but can 'rewrite the contents of one text type in the manner of the other' (Dean, 2002: 16).

Reading and writing according to the Literacy Strategy

A glance at the Year 7 objectives listed under 'Sentence level' illustrates the change taking place within English at Key Stage 3. In Year 7 children need to know 'the stylistic conventions of the main types of non-fiction' which are listed as 'Information . . . Recount . . . Explanation . . . Instructions . . . Persuasion . . . Discursive writing' (DfEE, 2001: 23). It has been suggested that before the Literacy Strategy there was 'an assumption in considerable numbers of English classrooms that pupils naturally know how to read texts placed in front of them'(Dean, 2002: 44). Considering what is meant by 'reading' in the strategy is worthwhile and the reading objectives (DfEE, 2001: 11) indicate that reading is about research and study skills, comprehension (reading for meaning), understanding style (the author's craft) and the study of literary texts.

When assessed, children often have a higher reading than writing level as defined by the *National Curriculum* and, consequently, writing is a major focus of attention in the NLS. By the end of Year 6, their last year at primary school, children should have attempted reading and writing the following non-fiction text-types: recount, non-chronological report, explanation, instruction, persuasion and discussion. These need to be revised and revisited in Year 7 and during Key Stage 3 children should augment their repertoire with two further text-types: analysis and evaluation. During Key Stage 3 the *Framework* states that children should be able to write for specified purposes, grouped as 'triplets', and should be able to 'Imagine, explore and entertain', 'Inform, explain and describe', 'Persuade, argue and advise' and also to 'Analyse, review and comment'.

Although teachers in primary school teach a daily Literacy Hour, divided into four parts, in secondary schools where children often have only three hours of English a week, a Literacy Hour has been impossible to implement. While we are told 'there is no single structure for lessons using the framework' (DfEE, 2001: 17), the 'four-part lesson' increasingly exerts an influence upon the structure of English lessons. The *Framework* is quite specific about what should happen in each part. A short starter activity is followed by teacher exposition or questioning where the main teaching points are introduced, after which these points are developed through group activity and finally a plenary that should 'draw out the learning' (ibid.). While English departments do not have to adopt the four-part structure and not every lesson has to have a starter, it is recommended and many senior managers and OFSTED inspectors may expect to see English lessons that conform to this model.

The starter

A lesson starter, lasting about ten minutes, is where spelling rules as well as aspects of punctuation and vocabulary can be introduced. The rationale for the starter is to begin the lesson in a focused, interactive and purposeful fashion. The starter is intended to set the pace and is seen as the ideal place for word-level work. The *Year 7 Spelling Bank* (DfES, 2001) is a helpful resource that can easily be turned into starter activities by English teachers as it presents patterns of letters and word families (morphology) very clearly. Starter activities should be fast and interactive with little explanation and the rapid completion of short tasks should stretch pupils and also foster motivation by reinforcing success. The aim is for the first part of the lesson to be intense, interactive and short. The approach to word-level work is 'little and often' and although it is not essential to relate the starter activity to the rest of the lesson some of the best lessons do have imaginative connections. Starter activities need to be mapped in a departmental scheme of work over the course of a half term, a year or even the whole key stage.

Shared reading and writing

What is termed *shared* work in the second part of the lesson is where the main teaching points are introduced through the teacher's questioning and direct instruction. Shared literacy work is described as the part of the lesson where 'the teacher demonstrates and models the process of comprehension or composition with the whole class' (DfEE, 2001: 17). In the four-part lesson structure the second part of the lesson is 'shared' literacy work and the third part is 'guided' work. What is termed 'shared' work is whole-class activity that is teacher led. The teacher explains, demonstrates and questions and an OHP is commonly used with a transparency designed to focus attention on a certain text-type or genre as the starting point. The whole class looks at the words already written or being written on the screen and listens to the teacher's direct, explicit and well rehearsed instruction and exposition. Pupils engage in a rapid, highly interactive and focused question-and-answer session and teachers often consider about a quarter of an hour to be the optimum time for such intensive, whole-class activity.

If the *shared* literacy activity is focused on reading a particular text-type or genre (such as an explanation) an example is projected onto the screen. The teacher, armed with felt-tip pen, draws the attention of the whole class to the key features and conventions of the particular text-type or genre by underlining, boxing and annotating particular parts of the text. The key conventions of that text-type and the rules that govern it are clearly identified and explained. Direct and explicit whole-class teaching in this second stage of the lesson is not simply instruction, for the marking-up of the text before the children's eyes often takes place as an integral part of the question-and-answer session so that a word is marked when a child gives an answer.

An integral part of the new teaching at Key Stage 3 is that 'nothing is taken for granted' so that in shared reading all the 'hidden, usually silent, mental processes that are normally intrinsic and unremarked by experienced readers should be brought to the surface and made obvious' (Dean, 2002: 44). In shared reading the teacher 'takes the pupils through all the very evident stages, speaking out loud and sharing those moments at all points, as if from the view of the learner' (ibid.). The form the discourse might take during shared reading could look like this:

> Teacher: 'Now I have been asked to look out for . . . I have been informed that this text is a good example of . . . My teacher has suggested that I look at pages . . . because there are some instances of . . . I have found the pages, and immediately I should be looking for . . . I could ask myself at this point, "how long are the sentences? Which word, or sort of word keeps reoccurring? What do I notice about the way this group of words has been put together?" So, from this evidence I am beginning to think that . . .', etc. (ibid.: 45).

If the *shared* literacy activity is focused on writing rather than reading, similar sorts of interactions occur but with one important difference. Instead of appearing ready-made the text is created on the screen during this part of the lesson. As the text is a joint construction there may be even more whole-class participation. Just as the attention of pupils was drawn to key textual conventions in shared reading, in shared writing attention is drawn to the decisions a writer makes as the text is drafted by the teacher in response to children's suggestions or answers. Shared writing is concerned with modelling the creation of a certain text-type. The process is interactive and a central objective is to teach children explicitly about the processes a writer goes through, the questions that are asked in order for the text to take an appropriate shape and conform to the conventions of that text-type at text, sentence and word level. The teacher slows down and makes explicit the sort of processes that are rarely seen explicitly in an experienced and accomplished writer. Writing and reading are, of course, intimately related and it is important for children to have read (often during shared reading) the sorts of texts they are expected to write.

Guided reading and writing

What is termed *guided* literacy work is the small-group work part of the lesson where the main teaching experienced by the whole class in the previous *shared* part of the lesson is developed through small-group activity. *Guided* literacy work is defined in the *Framework* document as the part 'in which the teacher dedicates substantial time in the lesson to support and stretch a particular group' (DfEE, 2001: 17). During guided reading, which takes place between a teacher and a group of no more than eight children, the focus is upon specific aspects of the text being considered and the small-group context is to allow the teacher to focus on individual learning needs and to differentiate (see Chapter 9) more easily and effectively than is sometimes possible with a whole class.

After children have experienced a highly interactive whole-class *shared* reading or writing session it is time to move on to what the strategy terms *guided* literacy work. Children work in small groups rather than as a whole class. The teacher does not simply walk around the different groups pausing to stand behind one group here and another group there to answer the odd question while the children are working. *Guided* implies that the teacher will sit down and work intensively with one small group for an extended period of time so that a group of half a dozen pupils benefits from direct and sustained teacher involvement for around a quarter of an hour. The children are grouped according to ability and, as in the shared work they have just experienced, the teacher engages the children in discussion and question-and-answer interaction appropriate for the needs of that group. In the next lesson it will be the turn of a different group during the *guided* part of the lesson. The Key Stage 3 National Strategy in conjunction with NATE (the National Association for the Teaching of English) have recently published material on guided reading on their website to broaden the scope of pupils' independent reading which English teachers will find helpful as active reading strategies that address specific objectives from the *Framework* are explained.

If the teacher is not circulating and is spending up to twenty minutes giving undivided attention to one small group, the rest of the class have to be willing to work unsupervised. It has been suggested that with a less able class the teacher 'might elect to spend no more than ten minutes or so with any group' (Dean, 2002: 47). Teachers have to ensure they spend time with each group and need to devise a rota so that no group is left out. A range of reading abilities may be evident in the same class and therefore during guided reading one group may be working with the teacher on simply decoding of the text while another is working at quite a sophisticated level considering not only meaning but how it is conveyed. During guided reading the teacher may want to pay attention to what the child was doing for homework and to engage with the ongoing reading of individuals. A range of options are on offer for this part of the lesson and we are told that 'pupils appreciate the access that guided sessions give them to the teacher' (DfEE, 2001: 18).

The principle behind guided writing is that pupils should have to 'justify and explain choices they have made in more demanding one-to-one situations' and for the teacher 'to intervene more potently into pupils' work while it is being composed, or even while it is being planned' (Dean, 2002: 48). Having helped to compose a text on the OHT as a whole class and having considered the sorts of choices a writer of a text makes, and its conventions and form, children compose their own text during the guided session based upon this model. The advantage of the one-to-one interaction that takes place during guided writing is that the teacher can respond immediately to the cognitive and linguistic processes observed in the child.

The sequence of moving from *shared* to *guided* writing can ensure pupils understand what it is they have to write and how to write it as they can copy the style and conventions of the text they have just read. In *guided* writing the teacher may work with a group about to embark upon writing who are at the planning stage; they may be making choices about the type of text to write and how to structure it while a group that is further ahead might be reviewing what they have written to see if they have achieved the form they intended to write. The *guided* writing session is an opportunity for the teacher to work with a group selected according to ability where a whole text or a shorter segment of text can be the focus of attention.

The plenary

The plenary is an essential and invaluable part of any English lesson (see Chapter 2). It is in the plenary that learning is crystallized. A plenary requires skilful handling and reinforces the point of the lesson by making what has been learnt explicitly clear to the learner. It is easy, however, for the plenary to be 'squeezed out' of the lesson. The children may still be finishing an activity and homework may need to be set. Yet, the plenary is neglected at our peril. If an inexperienced teacher plans to spend five minutes on a plenary it can disappear from the lesson entirely or be so rushed it is pointless. If such a teacher planned to spend ten minutes at the end of the lesson on the plenary he or she might get five minutes if everything else is going according to plan. If too much has been planned for a lesson it is generally better to leave out an activity or cut it short rather than miss the opportunity for a plenary. The plenary has for many primary teachers been the most difficult part of the lesson to accomplish successfully. Secondary English teachers generally recognize how important the plenary is and they are also aware that it does not always have to be at the end of the lesson.

The plenary has been described as the part of the lesson 'where pupils share some reflection on what they have done, how well they have done it, and the extent of the learning they have taken from those activities' (Dean, 2002: 50). While 'reflection' is important it does not communicate the vigour, energy, dynamism and motivational impact that a good plenary should have. Children should be challenged and should know what, of real significance, has happened during the lesson. They should be aware of their learning experience and derive a real sense of purpose from it. Children should know that something worthwhile has been achieved and be able to say exactly what it is. They should be zealous to share their new-found knowledge, even to show off with it and to revel in their new vocabulary, that moment from a story or the line from the poem. The key to a good plenary is the start of the lesson where learning objectives are communicated. These are revisited in the plenary so that children know why they have done what they have done and what they have learnt from it. They must know the rationale for and purpose of their time in the classroom.

Assessing English at the Key Stage 3

A detailed overview of issues relating to assessment was given in Chapter 3 but with regard to the assessment at the end of Key Stage 3 it is important to note here that children's attainment in reading (En2) and writing (En3) is assessed. They are awarded a reading level and a writing level. From 2003 new tests have been introduced to assess reading and writing at the end of Key Stage 3 because the old tests were formulated before the *Framework* and the advent of the NLS. The new tests are designed to assess the level of attainment of children who have followed the *Framework* during the first three years of secondary school. Three examination papers ('Reading', 'Writing' and 'Shakespeare') are taken by pupils. A brief summary of the tests is provided below as further details, including sample examination papers and mark schemes, are available from the QCA.

The 'Reading' paper

This test lasts for 75 minutes although 15 minutes is reading time. Three texts, different in genre and style, are provided to reflect the breadth of the reading diet of children in English. Texts are chosen, according to QCA, that work well together. There are fifteen questions and each question assesses one 'assessment focus'. Questions are set that assess children's ability at text, sentence and word level. Emphasis appears to be placed upon children's knowledge of style and form in writing and they need to be able to write about writers' uses of language, such as grammatical and literary features.

The 'Writing' paper

This paper lasts for 45 minutes although 10 minutes of that time is to be spent planning. Writing at the end of Key Stage 3 is assessed in two papers. The longer writing task is part of the 'Writing' paper and a shorter writing task is completed when candidates take the 'Shakespeare' paper. The writing candidates produce in this paper is to take the form of one of the 'triplets' specified in the *Framework*. If, for instance, pupils' ability to engage in writing specified by the triplet ('Analyse, review, comment') was tested in this paper a teacher could be sure that in the two shorter written tasks on the 'Shakespeare' paper candidates would have to show their ability in the other triplets ('Imagine, explore and entertain' or 'Inform, explain and describe' or 'Persuade, argue and advise').

The 'Shakespeare' paper

This paper lasts 75 minutes and comes in two sections. Some 30 minutes is to be spent on Section A (shorter writing tasks) and 45 minutes is to spent on Section B (Shakespeare reading tasks). In the first section candidates have to produce writing related to a theme in the play they have studied. Normally one play from a choice of three is made. Currently the three plays are *Macbeth*, *Twelfth Night* and *Henry V*. As explained above, the written tasks in the first section of this paper address the framework triplets ('Imagine, explore and entertain' or 'Inform, explain and describe' or 'Persuade, argue and advise' or 'Analyse, review, comment') although whichever triplet has been assessed in the 'Writing' paper will not be assessed again here. The emphasis in Section A is on the ability of candidates to be concise and to write with precision. In this first section only En3 (Writing) is assessed and not understanding of the play. In the second part of this paper, Section B, lasting 45 minutes, the Shakespeare reading task, one task is set on each play and pupils have to refer to two extracts from the play. The task focuses on character, theme, language and performance and is assessed for reading only; candidates' understanding and response to the play and not their written expression is assessed.

The statutory assessment of children in these tests ensures that the skills and knowledge set out in the *National Curriculum* and issued as an explicit teaching agenda in the *Framework* are taught. There are seven different reading assessment focuses and eight different writing assessment focuses for teachers to teach towards. Questions in the tests assess a child's attainment in relation to each focus. Of the seven reading assessment focuses the last four are particularly relevant for most Key Stage 3 pupils. Thirteen and fourteen-year-olds should be taught to:

- identify and comment on the structure and organization of texts, including grammatical and presentational features at text level;
- explain and comment on writers' uses of language, including grammatical and literary features at word and sentence level;
- identify and comment on writers' purposes and viewpoints and the overall effect of the text on the reader; and

■ relate texts to their social, cultural and historical contexts and literary traditions.

Of the eight writing assessment focuses two are singled out as being especially appropriate for children at Key Stages 3. We are informed by the QCA that 'When children become older what is more valued in writing is their ability to make independent choices at whole text, sentence and word level in ways that are appropriate for task, reader and purpose. Thus assessment focuses 2 and 5 are likely to carry greater significance' (QCA, 2002: 6). Focuses 2 and 5 describe children's ability to:

■ produce texts which are appropriate to task, reader and purpose;
■ vary sentences for clarity, purpose and effect. (QCA, 2002: 6)

Clearly, a particular model of language underpins the literacy strategy and these tests are designed to assess children's attainment in relation to that model. It is evident that writing for 'purpose' (readers will recall that this chapter opened with a distinction between literacy for 'purpose' and for 'pleasure') is of central importance and it is clear that pupils will need to be able to comment on language and a writer's style and technique. Although the notions of appropriateness, audience and social context are central to the strategy English teachers know that reading and writing for purpose is rarely effective if young readers and writers do not read for pleasure.

Further reading

Cox, B. (ed.) (1998) *Literacy is not Enough*. Manchester: Manchester University Press.
Dean, G. (2002) *Teaching English in the Key Stage 3 Literacy Strategy – a Practical Guide*. London: David Fulton.
Goodman, S., Lillis, T., Maybin, J. and Mercer, N. (2003) *Language, Literacy and Education: A Reader*. Stoke-on-Trent: Trentham Books/Open University.
Hannon, P. (2000) *Reflecting on Literacy in Education*. London: Routledge/Falmer.

6

Teaching GCSE English and English literature

The challenge of GCSE English and English literature

Teaching GCSE can be one of the most rewarding experiences for an English teacher as the age of the students, the variety of the courses and the choice of texts are a challenging combination. Often, there is also a greater sense of 'ownership' of a class at GCSE than lower down the school where the teacher is likely to have a Year 7 class for one year but may not teach those children again when they move up to Year 8. At GCSE, by contrast, English teachers take their classes from the first day in Year 10 until the end of their compulsory education at the end of Year 11. During this time students change a great deal; many look very different at the end of Year 11 from the way they appeared at the start of Year 10 and they certainly think very differently. As a developmental stage this period of time is fascinating for adolescents are asking important questions, coming to terms with their own identities and personalities, and maturing rapidly. Being their teacher of English, with all that entails, through this period can be enjoyable but also demanding.

The demands come from a number of sources. The students themselves need to be motivated and inspired and it is also expected that the teacher will bring about a significant improvement in attainment and gain the highest grades possible for students. Another challenge is that the curriculum has to be covered in a very short time indeed. Realistically, there are only five terms of teaching time to get students through two GCSEs (English and English literature) with about three hours a week allocated to English. Transition from Key Stage 3 to Key Stage 4 presents new challenges as a considerable amount of coursework needs to be completed (none is required at Key Stage 3) and 'Speaking and listening' (En1) is assessed and accounts for 20% of the marks for GCSE English. How good a preparation for GCSE the new approach at Key Stage 3 will be remains to be seen. There is certainly a shift in emphasis between the two key stages as a considerable proportion of work at GCSE consists of reading and writing about poetry which appears to feature very little in the literacy strategy.

An integrated approach to teaching GCSE English and English literature

In this chapter an integrated approach to GCSE is advocated and described whereby a certain amount of synergy can be experienced throughout the course. Arguably, children across the ability range should study both GCSE English and GCSE English literature as elements of one course can prepare students for elements of the other. Indeed, within just one GCSE, coursework in one area prepares and helps children to succeed in another. It is especially important that reading and writing are integrated so that children's reading informs their writing and vice versa; likewise speaking and listening should pervade the learning experience at GCSE for thinking and talking go hand in hand. Integration requires that teaching should be carefully planned for over the whole course so that learning at GCSE is coherent and progress in one part of the course informs learning in others. My recommendation that most children should follow both GCSE English and GCSE English literature is informed by both principle and practice.

The two subjects are not equals and GCSE English is more valuable in our market economy than GCSE English literature. In one sense, the two most valuable qualifications a person can have today in the UK are GCSE English and GCSE mathematics. There is, consequently, a risk that with limited time allocated to the study of English at GCSE, the study of literature may be marginalized. Further, the emphasis of the Literacy Strategy prior to GCSE upon functional and transactional forms of English may lead to a questioning of the value of literature. If English departments opt to enter most candidates for only GCSE English the place of literature within the curriculum and in children's lives will be reduced and we shall all be the poorer. The temptation to follow just GCSE English and not to bother with GCSE English literature is especially acute when deciding which course 'borderline' candidates (those who could get a C or a D) should follow. The argument is sometimes put that if more time is spent on GCSE English without the distractions of GCSE English literature, the all-important C grade might be attained. It is important to explain why such thinking is generally misguided and a retrograde step.

Pressure is being put on literature and it needs to be vigorously defended. A scenario not uncommon in secondary schools will illustrate. When I arrived at a new school as Head of English, Communications and Drama

I was dismayed that only the very top sets followed GCSE English literature as well as GCSE English. In my view, this was not only elitist but also counterproductive because, as English teachers frequently assert, children learn about language through the literature they study. It was my belief that all children, across the ability range, should enter both GCSEs and this provoked some heated debate in the English department. Some experienced colleagues expressed the view that the all-important GCSE English results would suffer if they devoted the little time they had to the study of English literature. After listening to the views for and against joint entry I took the decision that all pupils, regardless of ability, would study both GCSE English and GCSE English literature. Very little extra work was required to gain two GCSEs rather than one because of 'cross-over' work that could be assessed for both qualifications and the skills assessed for GCSE English could be developed while working on assignments for English literature.

In the belief that an integrated approach could work, that language skills can be developed while studying literature and also that it was indefensible for only the most able to be given the opportunity to study the texts set for English literature, we embarked upon the new approach of dual entry. It was something of a relief, therefore, when after two years of the new system, the 9% (A*–C) improvement of the previous year had not only been maintained but had improved by another 13% for GCSE English language (a rise of 22% over three years) even when precious time was spent on English literature and no extra time was allocated to English. While this rise in GCSE results cannot be attributed entirely to entering more students for English literature it does show that an integrated approach can work well and that studying both subjects can be a positive and complementary experience for pupils. In addition many pupils who did not gain a C grade for GCSE English were delighted at achieving a C grade for English literature.

For such a policy to work, planning the teaching of English and English literature at GCSE over five terms, almost two years, requires some skill as it is important to ensure the best sequence is followed that facilitates cumulative improvement and creates synergy. An integrated approach can enable students to derive maximum benefits from the way their course is followed. What follows is not a detailed description of a syllabus but an overview which is necessary to illustrate how an integrated course works.

Integrated teaching for GCSE English

Integration is encouraged by the AQA as they have 'cross-over' pieces of coursework but it is helpful to identify other ways in which preparing for one element of the course is helpful for other elements. For instance, key themes and background material read in conjunction with *To Kill a Mockingbird* for GCSE English literature can prepare students for reading non-fiction/media texts for GCSE English. One could study newspaper reports and magazine articles about the death penalty and Death Row as well as the civil rights movement for racial equality in the USA as such work can help pupils understand Tom Robinson's plight. Part of the skill of teaching GCSE is to plan for such connections so the course is thematically coherent and a particular activity can serve more than one purpose.

The texts upon which reading is assessed in Paper 2 of GCSE English are provided in the AQA *Anthology* (2002a). The teaching of 'Limbo' by Edward Kamau Brathwaite and 'Night of the Scorpion' by Nissim Ezekiel will be discussed here to give an overview of the sort of reading students need to be prepared for when studying GCSE English. The poems are not reproduced here as 'Limbo' and 'Night of the Scorpion' both appear in the anthology which each pupil has a copy of. In 2004 some annotation of poems is permitted although from 2005 this will be phased out completely. As well as some explanation of the poems for teachers, ways of approaching them and a possible teaching strategy will be considered. These poems have been chosen as they deal with important issues and there are many ways of enabling pupils to engage with them.

'Limbo' is a challenging poem to teach because it contains far more than is at first apparent. Even the title of the poem has a double meaning. The word 'limbo' can refer to a dance where dancers move with their backs thrown backwards under a stick which is lowered to make it more difficult each time the dancer passes under it. Eventually the stick is practically touching the ground and it is a fascinating performing act to watch in the Caribbean even today. The dance is, however, also associated with slave galleys and is thought to have been developed as a therapy for cramped conditions. The other meaning of the word 'limbo' is more closely related to the common expression of being 'in limbo' to indicate being between things or the feeling of not having anything particular to do. Limbo comes from the Latin word *limbus* which in early Catholic teaching described the region just outside Hell where it was believed that unbaptized infants awaited the Last Judgement. It is a prison, a place of confinement and a condition of neglect. 'Limbo', therefore, is the region between two worlds and signifies a state of suspension.

Clearly, 'Limbo' is a metaphor for the history of Caribbean people because they have been uprooted from Africa and transplanted to the Americas. The prisoners on the slave ship are between two continents and also between the two states of freedom and slavery. There are two passages in the poem, the passage under the stick in the dance and the middle passage of the Triangular Trade, the sea voyage of captives to the Americas. A rite of passage is depicted in the poem ('down, down, down . . . up, up, up'). The line 'hot slow step on the burning ground' refers to the Africans' first step on new soil in the Americas and the description of it as 'burning ground' is ominous, has connotations of the act of branding, and also conjures up infernal images associated with Hell. An understanding of imagery is important when studying this poem because two sets of imagery are apparent. Superimposed on the imagery of the limbo dance ('And limbo stick is the silence in front of me' line 1) is the imagery of the slave ship ('long dark deck and the water surrounding me'). The poem begins with the dance and moves on to the idea of slavery while the refrain and rhythm recreate the music of dance and drum. Together with the use of the present tense this presents us with a dramatic re-enactment of past experience.

One aspect of the art of teaching English is how you lead children to such knowledge without giving them a lecture and telling them to write down what you say, which is not the sort of teaching advocated here. As there are really only five terms in which to teach GCSE English, it may be best practice to prepare children for Paper 1 of GCSE English (where they have to read non-literary and media material) in conjunction with the poems chosen. For instance, various forms of writing on slavery can be read in conjunction with the poem 'Limbo' and the same pattern can be followed elsewhere so that study for one element of the course prepares students for another part of it. This poem is a good choice as many children study the slave trade as a topic in history in Year 9 and will be familiar with the diagrams you can show them of the cramped conditions aboard the slave ships. For those less familiar with the slave trade Colin Palmer's article 'African slave trade: the cruellest commerce' with photographs by Maggie Steber and paintings by Jerry Pinkney in *National Geographic* magazine (1992) can be helpful. Reading such an article is a good preparation for the other reading students have to do for GCSE English Paper 1.

The film *Amistad* (1997) directed by Steven Spielberg and starring Nigel Hawthorne, Anthony Hopkins, Djimon Hounsou and Morgan Freeman or the novel of the same name by Alexs Pate (1997) is a superb way to prepare children for 'Limbo'. The film is based on the 1839 mutiny on a Spanish slave ship, *Amistad*, where 53 young people won their freedom and returned home to Africa. It tells the story of Cinque, the son of a Mende chief, who is enslaved and courageously leads the revolt. The book follows Cinque's trial in the Supreme Court, where the argument that he was illegally enslaved changes a nation's history. *Mutiny on the Amistad* is a good book for teachers as it depicts the events that inspired the film. It is written by Howard Jones, Research Professor of History at the University of Alabama, and is fascinating as it tells the true story of how the mutiny resulted in a trial before the US Supreme Court where former President John Quincy Adams came out of retirement to defend the Africans against the federal government. The court's landmark decision was to free the slaves and permit them to return to Africa. Speaking and listening tasks such as the replication of the court scene further integrate the GCSE course.

Learning about the poet can help to supplement students' engagement with a poem. Edward Kamau Brathwaite was born in Barbados, won a scholarship to university in England and then went to work in Ghana as an education officer. When he went home to Barbados he reports that he felt as though he had not left as he was experiencing Africa in the Caribbean and was completing his own triangular voyage following his ancestors. A similar approach can be taken with Nissim Ezekiel, writer of 'Night of the Scorpion' in the students' anthology. In *Naipaul's India and Mine* (1965) Ezekiel explains he is not a Hindu and that his background makes him an obvious outsider. Ezekiel is Jewish and attended a Catholic school in Bombay which is a predominantly Hindu city.

Any writing on the theme of outsiders and of cultures clashing can inform study of 'Night of the Scorpion'. Writing on the theme of 'outsiders' can prepare pupils for the culture clash they witness in the poem which tells the story of the night the narrator's mother nearly died, and begins 'I remember the night my mother/was stung by a scorpion'. In the poem, everyone tries to ensure the mother survives the night and various interpretations are offered to account for her pain and suffering. As she writhes in agony in the dark room where there has been the 'flash of diabolic tail', possibly indicating suffering inflicted by Satan, the mother is surrounded by people who try to cure her. As the family are Bombay Jewish and the neighbours who come to help are from the local Hindu community we are presented with different interpretations of the event. Throughout the night there are 'more candles, more lanterns, more neighbours/ more insects, and the endless rain' as the mother twists and turns on the mat. One Hindu attempts to 'tame the poison with an incantation' and the child, the narrator, distances himself from the neighbours with the repetition of 'they said'. The neighbours' interpretation of the event is quite different from the child's and this can be seen in the way the neighbours are described: they 'came like swarms of flies' and 'buzzed the name of god a hundred times/ to paralyse the Evil one'. Any work on the theme of 'outsiders' from non-literary sources or of the differences between belief systems is a 'tie-in' to the poem and ensures both examination papers are prepared for with a degree of thematic coherence.

The structure of GCSE English and English literature

The examples above are only one way of beginning to integrate different elements of a GCSE course, and the first stage in planning such thematic coherence, where what is learnt from one element of the course supports learning elsewhere, is to have an overview of the requirements for both GCSE English and GCSE English literature. All examination groups in England must ensure that the range of reading assessed includes prose, poetry and drama. The range must, however, specifically include a play by Shakespeare, a work from the English literary heritage by at least one major writer with a well established critical reputation, texts from different cultures and traditions, non-fiction texts and also media texts. Here, an overview is given of the AQA specification A for GCSE English and English literature as it appears likely to be the most popular from 2004.

Reading and writing for GCSE English

For 'Reading' (En2) at GCSE English candidates are currently required to read non-fiction and media texts for Section A of Paper 1 and their response in this question is worth 15% of the total marks. They also read poetry from different cultures and traditions in the AQA *Anthology* for Section A of Paper 2 in English which is also worth 15% of the total marks. Other reading is required for coursework and candidates read a Shakespeare play and some prose texts; the assessment of their reading of each is worth 5% of the total marks. Teachers will note that in the examination the only fiction candidates write about is poetry and their response to this question is worth 15% of the marks whereas a whole piece of coursework, where they read prose which is assessed for En2 (Reading) is worth only 5% of the marks, as is Shakespeare. Certain areas of the course, such as poetry, carry most of the marks and response to this genre is likely to change a student's overall grade, for better or worse, far more than others.

For 'Writing' (En3) at GCSE candidates write to argue, persuade or advise in Paper 1 Section B which is worth 15% of the total marks and write to inform, explain or describe in Paper 2 Section B, also worth 15% of the total marks. The writing candidates do for media and original writing coursework is each worth 5% of the total marks. There is no reason why writing cannot emerge from reading that has been engaged in for English or English literature. All genres, both pre- and post-1914, are studied as are media and non-literary texts as these provide a rich source of inspiration for children's writing and offer them models and forms to experiment with.

Speaking and listening for GCSE English

'Speaking and listening' (En1) is assessed for GCSE English and three oral activities (each in different contexts) must be assessed as this accounts for 20% of the total marks available. An integrated approach can be adopted with speaking and listening as students are assessed in relation to 'triplets' of skills: 'explaining, describing, narrating', 'exploring, analysing, imagining' and 'discussing, arguing, persuading' (AQA, 2002b: 31), and teachers have the freedom to match activities to contexts however they wish so long as three contexts and three units of work are included. The contexts are described by the AQA (ibid.) as an 'individual extended contribution', a 'group interaction' and 'drama-focused activity'. Texts or themes explored in English literature or as part of candidates' reading for English can provide the basis for a speaking and listening task and assessment. If we take the example of *To Kill a Mockingbird* and 'Limbo', candidates could perform their group task where they 'discuss, argue and persuade' in relation to the death penalty or the trial scene in *Amistad*. Planning ahead clearly saves valuable time and brings greater coherence to the students' experience.

Reading for GCSE English literature

Seventy per cent of the total marks for GCSE English literature are awarded on the basis of two questions answered in 105 minutes in the exam room. One question must be answered on a post-1914 prose text (such as *To Kill a Mockingbird*, *Of Mice and Men*, *Lord of the Flies*, *A Kestrel for a Knave* or short stories in the *Anthology*) and one question on pre- and post-1914 poetry from the AQA *Anthology* (featured post-1914 poets are currently Seamus Heaney, Gillian Clarke, Carol Ann Duffy and Simon Armitage; some of the featured pre-1914 poets are Robert Browning, Shakespeare, Tennyson, Wordsworth, Blake, Whitman, Hopkins and Clare). Coursework makes up the remaining 30% of marks with three pieces of coursework worth 10% each (pre-1914 drama such as Shakespeare, pre-1914 prose and post-1914 drama). As the piece of coursework on Shakespeare and that on the pre-1914 prose text can be 'cross-over' pieces that count towards GCSE English coursework it means that the difference between doing just GCSE English and two GCSEs (in English and English literature) is just one extra piece of coursework and one short examination.

Improving writing at GCSE

It has already been suggested that reading and writing should be taught in an integrated fashion but that does not mean that writing will automatically improve so long as children read enough. Children's insights regarding what they read often develop as they mature but improving writing is something that needs to be explicitly and skilfully taught for writing can be improved through direct instruction. The booklet *Improving Writing at Key Stages 3 and 4* (QCA, 1999b) and Myhill's 'Writing matters: linguistic characteristics of writing in GCSE English examinations' (1999b) are valuable to teachers of GCSE because they provide analysis of the features of children's writing at different grades. Characteristics of different grades of script (helpfully divided according to spelling, punctuation, sentence/clause structure, word class usage, paragraphing and textual organization) identify the specific aspects of writing which children attaining different grades need to be taught (QCA, 1999b: 5).

For instance, if we focus on punctuation, most children gaining C grades use commas to demarcate some clauses and in lists, but rarely use commas parenthetically (ibid.). If you were teaching a child who was performing at the grade C level for writing it would be important to check his or her work for the parenthetic use of the comma. If this was, as it is in most cases, an area for development, the way subclauses in sentences work should be explicitly taught to enable candidates to improve on the C grade, in terms of punctuation at least. What is so helpful about this booklet is that it clearly shows which aspects of writing English teachers can target to bring about improvement:

> The analysis suggested specific areas in which teacher intervention was likely to make a significant difference to the quality of pupils' writing and the standard of work in examinations. For example, the characteristics of writing identified explicitly at grade C provide a focus for teaching pupils working below that level (ibid.: 28).

An important point is that the explicit teaching of writing can be missed out at GCSE for while some 'features, such as spelling, punctuation and paragraphing, are often addressed in marking' we know that 'this is in response to errors made or omissions, rather than teaching a constructive understanding of the way the feature works' (ibid.) and that 'clause structure or patterns of word class usage, are rarely referred to, either in teaching or marking' (ibid.). The report recommends that English departments plan 'to identify how and where teaching of each of these features best fits current schemes of work' (ibid.). One example will be sufficient to illustrate the point. The least-used type of comma at GCSE is the parenthetic comma and it is important because:

> [In] narratives, parenthetic commas allow the writer to expand upon the immediate action (Mr Brooks, the older farmer, was leaning anxiously against the barn wall). In non-narratives, the parenthetic comma can act as an aside directly addressed to the reader (as you may have observed) or can emphasise an argument (Britain, on the other hand, is opposed to joining a common European currency) (ibid.).

Clearly, the comma is a tool for crafting and shaping writing but this is only one example to illustrate the pattern of assessing writing diagnostically (see Chapter 3) and teaching to target areas of weakness and to build on relative strengths. Such focused, clearly identified, targeted teaching can achieve dramatic improvement in results and in the quality of pupils' writing. The art is to integrate such teaching at the right point into the sequence of work as children are preparing to write. Integrating the teaching of reading, writing and speaking and listening is a key to success at GCSE; showing children examples of such features in the texts being read at GCSE and explaining their value enables children to see why they should use them too. It is most helpful to show pupils preparing to write about *To Kill a Mockingbird* examples of parenthetic commas from the text to help them become more discerning readers and to see how Harper Lee involves her audience and writes with such style while improving their own writing skills as a result. The value of such an approach is that integrating the teaching of reading and writing has benefits for both. There is nothing wrong with marking that responds to what a child has written so long as different ways of writing and new techniques or constructions are taught and advice is not limited to the correcting of existing writing.

As candidates have to write to argue, persuade or advise (Paper 1, Section B, GCSE English) and also to inform, explain or describe (Paper 2, Section B, GCSE English) certain sections of *Improving Writing at Key Stages 3 and 4* (QCA, 1999b) are invaluable. Pages 40–3 focus on writing to inform, explain and describe and pages 44–7 focus on writing to argue, persuade, advise. What is helpful is that teaching strategies and pupil activities are described which foster these skills. If the topic for such writing was linked to the text being read or topic being discussed, effective and coherent integration of the modes of language use assessed at GCSE would be complete.

The importance of speaking and listening at GCSE

It is especially important that speaking and listening is not perceived as an activity in English that has little relation to reading and writing. We learn through talking with and listening to others and use language to think; consequently, reading and writing can be developed through speaking and listening. One of the most influential theorists of the relation between learning and talking is Vygotsky, and teachers who wish to pursue the subject further will find *Thought and Language* (1986) helpful. The value of Vygotsky's model of cognitive development for English teaching lies in the emphasis it places upon learners and teachers as language users and the acknowledgement that 'children solve practical tasks with the help of their speech, as well as with their eyes and hands' (ibid.: 26). In other words, language is not simply a way of communicating socially, it is also the method by which learners are enabled to reason for it is through spoken language that they can collaboratively create and modify meaning.

The value of interaction and discussion between peers has been emphasized in a number of reports (Bullock, 1975; Cockcroft, 1982; Dearing – DES, 1995) and in the latest National Curriculum for English 'group discussion and interaction' (DFEE/QCA, 1999: 31.33) forms a distinct area of the knowledge, skills and understanding to be acquired by pupils. Various researchers have concluded that speaking and listening can enable learners to make more progress than they would achieve without it. It appears, however, that certain sorts of dialogue are especially productive and can bring about extraordinarily rapid development. Judy Dunn's detailed ethnographic study of learning in very young children concluded that 'the important developmental changes are . . . those in which they attempt to argue, persuade and negotiate' (1988: 186) and such findings have significant implications for the cognitive development of older children when they negotiate with a teacher or peer in English where speaking and listening is formally assessed.

The social nature of knowledge and learning is central to Vygotsky's model of cognitive development. According to Vygotsky, cognitive development progresses from social to individual, from intermental to intramental (and not vice versa as Piaget believed). In a subject where originality of interpretation and creativity are highly prized it is important to recognize that these can be fostered by social interaction and verbal exchange (Pike, 2003d). Indeed, reflection and metacognition, the ability to think about one's thoughts, is part of the mental maturity which, for Vygotsky, is brought about through the learner interacting with more competent members of the society he or she is being ushered into. Development is seen as an apprenticeship where certain cultural tools eventually become part of the child's own resources.

Reading and writing through talking in GCSE English

For Vygotsky, the notion of 'potential' was central to the Zone of Proximal Development (ZPD) which is the area of especially productive development defined as the 'distance between the actual developmental level as determined by independent problem solving and the level of potential development as determined through problem solving under adult guidance or in collaboration with more capable peers' (Vygotsky, 1978: 86). The teacher or other learners can 'scaffold' learning or can provide support (rather like stabilizers on a bicycle) until they are ready to be taken away. According to Vygotsky it is what the child turns out to be able to do with another person through assisted or guided learning that points us to what the child will eventually be able to do alone. Clearly, paired and group discourse work can facilitate the development of understanding in reading.

Vygotsky's view was that children grow into the intellectual life of those around them but there has been little exploration of the practical application of such theorizing in relation to literature teaching. This is despite the fact that literature is an essential part of a child's culture and that 'most learning in most settings is a communal sharing of the culture' (Bruner, 1986: 127), and Margaret Meek (1985: 56) has noted that literature texts can be ZPDs for children. Bruner offers good advice for getting a child to cross the threshold of a ZPD and suggests that we should make entry appear to be 'play' where teachers are actively 'minimising the cost, indeed the possibility of error' (Bruner, 1986: 94). Arguably, paired talk is so valuable because the 'cost' of losing credibility is not as great in this context as it is when an adolescent engages in dialogue with a teacher watched by thirty peers.

There are certain problems when it comes to talk in the classroom. Whereas interactions at home are often spontaneous and child-initiated, the discourse between pupils and teachers in school is often contrived, has special rules and is adult controlled. The artificial nature of much classroom discourse has been described as 'ritual' knowledge where a pupil is able to 'go through the motions' or to perform a mechanical set of procedures without fully understanding why, for instance, a particular inference is more valid than another. A lack of such understanding characterizes 'ritual' knowledge which is 'a particular sort of procedural knowledge, knowing how to do something' (Edwards and Mercer, 1987: 97) rather than 'principled' knowledge which is 'explanatory' and shows an understanding of how and why certain conclusions are logical or valid.

In English, a child may move from 'ritual' to 'principle' and develop as a reader when verbal exchange with a more able partner, be it teacher or classmate, ensures that assisted learning occurs. The value of pupils' speaking and listening, when working collaboratively, is that it is real discourse whereas much pupil–teacher discourse is based on rituals rather than real understanding. This is because teachers' 'questions are often not real questions; that is they are not questions to which the answers are not already known, questions that arise from genuine curiosity and promote enquiring' (Edwards and Mercer, 1987: 7). Integrating speaking and listening with reading and writing (as in the example of the court scene based on 'Limbo', *Amistad* or *To Kill a Mockingbird* above) can provide opportunities for adolescents to argue, negotiate and persuade and can lead to dramatic gains in understanding.

Another way of integrating the three attainment targets in English is through the study of the media. When I organized a Media Day for a Gloucestershire school, with the help of the local Newspapers in Education (NiE) journalist, I was struck by the way activities such as writing newspaper articles or scripts for radio or television news can integrate many of the assessed elements of English at GCSE in a purposeful and enjoyable way. The headlines in the local newspaper were revealing and one in particular read 'Pens poised for an incident packed day' as it shows a group of pupils standing with clipboards and pens at the ready, watching a staged incident of a firecrew cutting the roof off a car in which a victim was trapped. Writing and reading was involved and these children listened and asked questions. GCSE students had to read, write, speak and listen in order to problem solve and produce the news.

Cub-reporters were separated into editorial teams of ten working on either television, radio or newspaper reports. During the day they received 'tip-offs' about incidents happening across the city and had to meet a deadline for the early evening news. As the local newspaper put it:

> Fire brigade officers staged a road accident and chemical spill actually cutting trapped victims from a car; a police sniffer dog tracked down stolen computer tapes; police officers mocked up the scene of a stabbing; a 'patient' collapsed in the waiting room at St James Surgery; Tesco reported dangerous structural problems that could put shoppers' safety at risk and Taylors Estate Agents told of a pop star who wanted to move to the area (Senior, 1995).

The day was great fun and even won £500 from the Local Education Initiative Award Scheme, Gloucestershire Training and Enterprise Council and Nuclear Electric, which paid for the next year's Media Day! While not every school will wish to stage these incidents a simulation can be just as effective where a team has to read and write headlines and articles, negotiate, deal with other people and meet a deadline.

Such media activity can be conducted through a role play based on a robbery where half a dozen students are allocated a role (police spokesperson, victim, community worker, young offender, shop owner, witness and so on) and give a press conference. The teacher can provide details (such as address of shop, background of victim, views of community worker) on cards for each pupil to help them get into role. At the press conference the rest of the class can ask questions, take notes and then hurry back to teams to write their reports on the incident; they have to read the report for the news and fit their story into a sequence of other stories you have provided. An integrated approach where all the modes of language use are employed and combined can be most fruitful with both literary and non-literary texts at GCSE.

Further reading

Myhill, D. (1999) 'Writing matters: linguistic characteristics of writing in GCSE English examinations', *English in Education*, 33(3): 70–81.

Pike, M.A. (1999) 'Reading the writer, reading the reader: pre-twentieth century poetry in the English literature examination', *The Use of English*, 51(1): 41–52.

QCA (1999) *Improving Writing at Key Stages 3 and 4*. London: QCA.

7

Teaching English 16–18: Advanced level

For most English teachers, teaching A level is the 'icing on the cake' as it is one of the most satisfying and intellectually stimulating aspects of their work. Working with a smaller group of students than at GCSE who have chosen to study English alters classroom dynamics in important ways. From the teacher's perspective, having a timetable with some periods of sixth-form teaching provides a welcome contrast to working with children lower down the school. Yet, while there are important differences from teaching younger children, many of the innovative and imaginative teaching strategies developed with other classes can be put to good use in the A level lesson.

Recently, post-16 education in the UK has been revised. The changes to English at A level have not only been structural, in that the curriculum is designed differently, they have also brought about a significant reorientation in the subject. The nature of English at this level has changed. This chapter describes and analyses these changes and sets out the most important features of the new A levels in English. The main focus in this chapter is on A level English literature because this is the most popular version of 'English' at this level although the course structure of English language as well as the joint English language and literature is also presented here. The chapter sets out the new assessment objectives for English literature, common to all examination groups. One specification (previously known as a syllabus) from the Assessment and Qualifications Alliance (AQA) is dealt with in the most detail. Ways of teaching some texts from the second AS module, in particular, are considered.

Changes at A level

The old A level awarded at the end of two years' of sixth-form study has been replaced by two qualifications in English, the AS and A2. The changes have come about as a result of Dearing's *Review of Qualifications for 16–18 Year Olds* which identified two priorities. First, it recommended that after the age of 16 students should follow a broader curriculum as restricting the range of subjects to just three at A level was considered to be too narrow. Secondly, according to Dearing, students should develop to a higher level their abilities in new key skills. These key skills were drawn up by Dearing and include, among others, ICT, working together, problem-solving and improving one's own learning. All the courses are modular, each unit or module can be retaken and the same pass grades (A–E) as before are awarded.

The new AS level is designed to improve progression from GCSE and one of the reasons for its introduction is to make the transition from GCSE to sixth-form level English less difficult. The new AS level is different from the old AS level because it is not assessed at A level standard. Before the changes some students took AS level as a sort of consolation prize if they found the number of texts studied for A level too demanding. From 2000, everyone begins by studying AS level in the first year of their A level course. The new AS is not assessed at the same standard as the final A2 qualification; it is intended to be easier than the old A level and can be a 'stand-alone' qualification or the first year of English courses leading to the award of A2.

Through the three AS modules taken in the first year of sixth-form study, students can begin to develop the skills they need for A2 level study. At AS, for English literature, the three main literary genres, including a pre-twentieth-century work, are studied. At least one module requires a 'closed-book' examination to be taken. Three more modules are taken in the second year of the sixth form so that a total of six are required for completion of the A2 course, three in the first year for AS and three in the second year for A2.

A 'suite' of courses, as the AQA calls them, is available at AS and A2. They are: (1) English language, (2) English language and literature or (3) English literature. Students usually follow just one of these in addition to three or four other AS subjects. At A2, just three subjects are usually taken. Each of these three options is outlined below. Alternative specifications for these subjects are available from the AQA as well as from other examination groups.

A typical course in English language (AS and A2) (AQA Specification B 2000)

AS modules:

■ Module 1: Introduction to the Study of Language.
■ Module 2: Language and Social Contexts.
■ Module 3: Original Writing.

A2 modules:

■ Module 4: Investigating Language.
■ Module 5: Editorial Writing.
■ Module 6: Language Development.

A typical course in English language and literature (AQA Specification B 2003)

AS modules:

■ Module 1: Introduction to Language and Literature Study.
■ Module 2: The Changing Language of Literature.
■ Module 3: Coursework – Production of Texts.

A2 modules:

■ Module 4: Coursework – Text Transformation.
■ Module 5: Talk in Life and Literature.
■ Module 6: Critical Approaches.

A typical course in English literature (AS and A2) (AQA Specification B 2003/4)

AS modules

■ Module 1: Introduction to the Study of Literature.
■ Module 2: Genre Study: Poetry and Drama.
■ Module 3: Shakespeare.

A2 modules

■ Module 4: Comparing Texts.
■ Module 5: Set Texts: Drama before 1770; Poetry before 1900.
■ Module 6: Exploring Texts.

Below is a more detailed description of each module in these three different examination subjects but you should consult the AQA's specification for the full and current descriptions.

English Language Module 1: Introduction to the Study of Language

This module aims to enable candidates to investigate the range of uses and contexts for written and spoken English. The importance of audience and the choices available to writers and speakers in terms of structure and style are covered. Students learn and apply lexical, grammatical (word, sentence and text level), phonological, semantic and pragmatic frameworks to texts. They should know about idiolects (an individual's language style based on ideology, experience and personality), dialects (language derived from geographical situation) and sociolects (language caused by education, occupation and social class). Students will also need to identify, apply and discuss the language system and should be familiar with lexis (choice of vocabulary), grammar (the language structure), phonology and phonetics (the way the voice communicates meaning), semantics (the way meaning is understood) and pragmatics (the way social conventions are encoded in language). One 90-minute written paper is taken, all questions have to be answered and the texts in the exam are 'unseen' before the paper is opened.

English Language Module 2: Language and Social Contexts

This deals with the relation between language and social context. Each year different areas are prescribed such as 'Language and Gender', 'Language and Power' or 'Language and Occupational Groups'. Candidates are assessed in one examination lasting two hours. Two questions are to be answered, each one from a different topic area. Like Module 1, this is based on 'unseen' texts.

English Language Module 3: Original Writing

Candidates can write to entertain, persuade, inform or to advise and instruct as in the third module of the AS English language and literature. Students can write anything from advice about how to use computer software to a short story but have to submit a commentary as well as the original writing itself. Two pieces of original writing are completed for coursework. In total both pieces should come to between 1,500 and 3,000 words. Two different pieces (in terms of form, audience and/or purpose) are required. The commentary should be about 1,000 words in length.

English Language Module 4: Investigating Language

This is also a coursework module and students conduct a small research investigation into an aspect of written or spoken English. A range of investigations can be undertaken. Students could transcribe everyday discourse, analyse linguistic features of the media, study the spelling system of English, transcribe a regional variety of English and so on. Between 2,000 and 4,000 words are to be written although this excludes appendices of data such as transcripts.

English Language Module 5: Editorial Writing

The compositional and editorial process is studied. Two sets of pre-released source material are given to students three days before the examination. In the exam candidates complete one task and write a new text in an appropriate style and register based on the source material.

English Language Module 6: Language Development

This module on language acquisition and change is synoptic and draws on what has been learnt in the previous five modules. Literacy development in children from 0 to 7 years of age is studied as are diachronic changes to the English language. One written paper lasting two hours is taken and two question are answered, one on language acquisition and one on historical changes to our language.

Teaching language at A level

Teaching language at A level, as can be seen from the module outlines above, is not restricted to the study of linguistics but, with this board, is more concerned with sociolinguistics which, to my mind, is far more interesting. One of the reasons this area of study is so fascinating is that it is relevant to our lives. Language is a pervasive aspect of our interaction with each other and is the most sophisticated symbolic system we have. Studying linguistic diversity is especially relevant in the UK as we now live in a multilingual society and important minorities speak languages rarely heard on this island before the 1960s. Even before that Britain was, of course, linguistically diverse and the history of Gaelic, Cornish and Welsh makes fascinating reading. The future development of language is especially relevant and David Crystal's *Language and the Internet* (2001) shows how the range and variety of language is expanding as a result of the impact of the Internet.

The topics that can be studied for English language at A level are an important opportunity for the teacher. What self-respecting 17-year-old could not be interested in topics such as 'language and power' or 'gender and language'? Those interested in business studies and economics can examine language in institutions or the language of marketing and the media. Sixth formers studying psychology may like to explore psycholinguistics and budding sociologists can look at language and class. There really is something for everyone here, not least in the form of an opportunity to engage in original writing. An area relevant to every member of the class is certainly that of language and education. The variety of topics here is an opportunity to consider issues that effect your students directly. Language and educational attainment, the relation of thought and language, language development in the early years of life, literacy and cognitive development, communication in the classroom, whether grammar should be taught, how people learn to read – all these topics can be studied as part of A level English language.

Some superb resources are available for teachers of English language at A level. The Open University MA (Ed) course *Language and Literacy in a Changing World* (E844) and accompanying *Language, Literacy and Education: A Reader* (Goodman et al., 2003) are excellent resources if teachers need to augment their own knowledge in this area. I studied a predecessor of this course when I was in my second year of teaching and found that I understood much more about classroom interaction and communication and derived greater satisfaction from teaching as a result. I can readily recommend such courses to all English teachers and getting hold of the *Open University Study Guide* for this course is the next best thing to becoming an OU student as it provides helpful insights into various aspects of language. One of the best books on the market specifically for teachers and students of A level is *Living Language – Exploring Advanced Level English* by George Keith and John Shuttleworth (2000).

Neil Mercer's *Words and Minds* (2000) and David Crystal's *Discover Grammar* (1996) should also grace the shelves of an A level English language teacher and Melvyn Bragg's recent four-part BBC television series *The Adventure of English*, screened for the first time late in 2002, is an excellent resource for teaching about the major turning points in the English language, as is *The Story of English* by McCrum et al. (1986), which is still one of the best and most accessible overviews available. Two absorbing and very high-quality texts to recommend are *Using English: From Conversation to Canon* (Maybin and Mercer, 1996) and *Learning English: Development and Diversity* (Mercer and Swann, 1996). All these books can, of course, be used for the combined language and literature A level which is described briefly below.

AS and A2 English Language and Literature

Module 1: Introduction to Language and Literature Study

This module requires a critical assessment of literary and non-literary sources around a central poetry text. A small anthology on a given theme accompanies this module. For 2003, 2004 and 2005 the theme is 'Education, education, education'. Students have to look at the creation of values and attitudes as well as context and must be able to describe and interpret both meaning and form (structure and style). There is one written paper of two hours consisting of one question on the central text and one on a text of students' own choice from the anthology. Any annotation of the anthology taken into the exam room must be restricted to cross-references and glossing odd words as no essay plans or detailed notes are allowed.

Module 2: The Changing Language of Literature

This module focuses on the way language changes diachronically and also how it changes according to social and cultural context. It examines how attitudes and values are presented and the ways in which texts vary according to context. Students study concepts of purpose and audience. How texts are structured (lexis, grammar and semantics) as well as the contrasts between texts is the focus of attention. In the examination, students answer on one pair of texts, written about a hundred years apart. For instance, from January 2003 Edgar Allan Poe is paired with Raymond Chandler. Poe's texts are *The Murders in Rue Morgue*, *The Purloined Letter* and *The Gold Bag* and are to be contrasted with Chandler's *The Big Sleep*. Teachers should check the specification for other pairings. One written paper of 90 minutes is taken and one question on the chosen pair of texts is answered. Candidates are allowed to take their texts into the examination room.

Module 3: Production of Texts

This module develops students' own expertise as writers for different audiences and purposes. Students can write to entertain, persuade, inform, advise or instruct. To persuade, students could write a report, a moral fable or an advertisement. To entertain, they might write a short story or a radio script. To advise or instruct, they might focus on some aspects of personal computing such as how to make use of specific software. An accompanying commentary to the original writing is required. Students have to write two pieces one for a reading audience and one for a listening audience. In total the two pieces should come to between 1,500 and 3,000 words. The total for the commentary should come to no more than 1,500 words. Students must write for a different purpose, audience or form for each of the two pieces of the coursework module. The aim is to develop the students' skills as writers and to take up where GCSE left off.

Module 4: Text Transformation

Students take a literary work in one genre and change it into another. They may alter the purpose and audience too (this builds on Module 3). The imaginative teacher can come up with a wide range of possibilities for students. Some examples given by the AQA board are Frost's poems such as 'Out, Out' and 'Mending a Wall' changed into newspaper stories, *Twelfth Night* transformed into a script for a cartoon version, *An Inspector Calls* made into a detective short story and so on. This is a coursework module.

Module 5: Talk in Life and Literature

This module focuses on spoken language in everyday situations and also in literature such as plays. The texts are transcripts of conversations from real life and literature. In the examination students respond to unseen texts. One play by Shakespeare is studied from a list of four, currently *Othello*, *Richard II*, *The Winter's Tale* and *Much Ado About Nothing*. In the examination two questions are answered, one on the Shakespeare play and one on the unseen texts. The focus is on the way everyday conversation and meaning are constructed in plays and poems. Students study how conversation can be understood and interpreted and concentrate on context and discourse conventions as well as phonological characteristics like intonation and pace. Interactional features such as pauses and modes of address as well as lexico-grammatical features such as rhetoric and uses of imagery are also studied.

Module 6: Critical Approaches

This module is 'synoptic' and is intended to draw on all the modules studied so far. The emphasis is on developing a synthesis of all previous learning in response to a range of spoken and written texts. These texts, seen and unseen, familiar and unfamiliar, from the present and also the past need to be critically analysed and students' judgements should be informed by a range of linguistic and literary approaches. Students must show evidence of critical reading and be aware of how context can influence interpretation. Students need to know and apply both literary and linguistic frameworks and perceive the connections between literary and linguistic studies. Students need to show they can read and be critical of any text in this module. The examination is two and a half hours long but this includes half an hour of reading time. Material is pre-released three days before the examination and can be taken into the examination room although only very brief marginal annotation is permitted.

AS and A2 English Literature

Module 1: Introduction to the Study of Literature

Here *one* text is chosen and studied from a list of seven. These range from pre-twentieth-century classics like Mary Shelley's *Frankenstein* and Emily Bronte's *Wuthering Heights* to modern works such as Achebe's *Things Fall Apart* or Ian McEwan's *Enduring Love*. Texts to be examined for the first time in January 2004 are *The Color Purple* by Alice Walker and *Waterland* by Graham Swift. As the texts change every few years teachers need to be absolutely sure that a question on the text they have chosen will appear on the examination paper at the end of the year. One examination paper lasting one and a quarter hours is taken and only one question on one of the seven texts is to be answered. Students can take their copy of the text into the examination room and can highlight it, gloss words and cross-reference but are not allowed any more detailed notes. The assessment objectives for this module are AO1, AO2i, AO3, AO4 and AO5i, although the largest single share of the marks is awarded for AO1 and AO3 (see pages 92–93).

Module 2: Genre Study: Poetry and Drama

For this module there is a choice of poems and plays from each genre. Poets include Chaucer, Donne, Milton, Blake, Elizabeth Barrett Browning and Emily Bronte. Dramatists include Arthur Miller, Tenessee Williams, Samuel Beckett, Robert Bolt, Caryl Churchill and Willy Russell. Students take one written paper lasting two hours and answer two questions, one on a twentieth-century drama text and one on a pre-twentieth-century poetry text. The assessment objectives for this module are AO1, AO2i, AO3 and AO5i, although more marks are available for the last three of these than the first one.

Module 3: Shakespeare

This is a coursework module where students write either one or two pieces of work not to exceed 2,000 words in total. The module is designed to enable them to increase their understanding of different critical interpretations and the importance of cultural context. The largest share of the marks in this module is given for AO4 although AO1, AO2i and AO5i are also assessed. Students study one Shakespeare play but it cannot be one they have studied before at Key Stage 3 or for GCSE.

Module 4: Comparing Texts

For this module students compare one prose text with one other text and there is considerable flexibility. The second text can be prose, poetry or drama but if it is a prose text it must be of a different type or from a different period. Although teachers are given the opportunity to exercise their professional judgement in the choice of texts, these must be of 'sufficient substance and quality to merit serious consideration' (AQA, 2001: 26). The assessment objectives for this module are AO1, AO2ii, AO3, AO4 and AO5ii.

Module 5: Set Texts: Drama before 1770; Poetry before 1900

This focuses on pre-Romantic and pre-1900 texts (poetry and drama). Students study for a two-hour written examination and answer two questions, one on poetry and one on drama. Texts cannot be taken into the exam room; it is a 'closed book' examination. Different assessment objectives are tested with each genre. For the poetry, AO3 and AO4 are assessed and, for the drama, AO1 and AO5ii are assessed. Currently, candidates can choose from set poems by Chaucer, Shakespeare, Herbert, Coleridge, Tennyson and Dickinson for the poetry before 1900 section. For the drama before 1770 section one text is to be chosen from a list of six texts by such authors as Marlowe, Shakespeare, Webster, Middleton, Behn and Congreve.

Module 6: Exploring Texts

This is the 'synoptic' module as it addresses all the A2 assessment objectives. Students should synthesize the knowledge and skills they have acquired throughout their course of study and have to apply this knowledge and understanding to both the pre-release material and the unseen texts on the examination paper. The texts are literary (prose, poetry and drama) or literature related (such as reviews, articles, biography). Students are 'required to show evidence of the ways in which contextual factors and different interpretations of texts will illuminate their own reading' (AQA, 2001: 31). This module has to be the last module covered because it draws on all the skills they have developed so far. The aim is 'to focus on the candidate's awareness of the approaches to and methods of study of literary texts' (ibid.). Both pre-release material and unseen texts are written about. The written paper lasts for three hours although this includes 30 minutes' reading time. The pre-release material is usually distributed three days before the examination. Usually students can read the texts over the weekend before the exam, which is usually on a Monday. In this exam all the questions have to be answered. Over the three days students can discuss the material with each other and do research but they are not allowed to discuss the pre-release texts with their teachers. The advice the AQA gives is that students 'will be best prepared for this Unit if they are very conversant with the Assessment Objectives' and if they have 'read widely a range of literary material' (ibid.: 32) over the two years of the course. The other advice the board offers is that they should have read critically and considered 'different interpretations of texts' (ibid.). The focus is on analysing particular features of texts and comparing texts.

▮ Key skills

Whichever of the three 'subjects' above is chosen key skills have to be taught and evidence of students' attainment in these skills needs to be recorded (full details regarding key skills are available from the QCA). In order to gain the National Qualification in Key Skills attainment must be demonstrated in three 'main' key skills – Application of Number, Communication and Information Technology. Wider key skills are desirable but are not assessed in the Key Skills Qualification. 'Wider' key skills are Improving one's own Learning and Performance, Working with Others and Problem Solving.

The exam boards show in more detail how key skills can be integrated into A and AS courses in English. This does depend on how the course is organized and the English teacher has to be quite skilful about this. For instance, discussion is the main mode of learning in most English classrooms where students speak to the rest of the class and often give full presentations. All these activities are key skills. To count as key skills, evidence of these activities need to be kept to show that they are being addressed and covered. Little by little, just like assessing speaking and listening at Key Stage 3 or GCSE, the development of key skills can form part of most lessons. One requirement of the system is that an image needs to be included in writing (for instance, from a production of a play, the cover of novel or an advertisement). Research on the Internet and assignments word processed on a personal computer can provide the necessary evidence for ICT.

Teaching AS and A2 English literature

There is not the space here to discuss all three versions of English (English language, English language and literature, English literature) in detail but English literature will be analysed in more detail to show a model that can be followed elsewhere. The model could be described as: Aims of Course + Assessment Objectives = Relevant Teaching.

When you are preparing to teach at this level, you must take the time to read the relevant specification to find out what the overall aim of the course is and understand its underlying principles. For English literature, the AQA say that their specification 'encourages students to develop interest in and enjoyment of English literature, through reading widely, critically and independently' (AQA, 2001: 9). In 'Underlying principles' they state that 'this specification seeks to highlight the way meanings are made and how they are received in relation to personal and public ideologies, social contexts and individual experience' (ibid.). This board values coursework and declares that the 'AQA believes this form of assessment to be the most effective in ensuring that certain Assessment Objectives (AOs) are met' (ibid.). It could be added that certain key skills can best be assessed through coursework too.

When teaching or planning to teach a new AS and A level course you should have at the forefront of your mind the assessment objectives. You need to know which assessment objectives are being assessed in each module, and also the relative weighting given to each assessment objective in each module. This information is contained within the specification. The assessment objectives (AOs) for English literature are as follows:

For AS level English literature
AO1   communicate clearly the knowledge, understanding and insight
       appropriate to literary study, using appropriate terminology and
       accurate and coherent expression
AO2   respond with knowledge and understanding to literary texts of
       different types and periods

AO3   show detailed understanding of the ways in which writers' choices of form, structure and language shape meanings

AO4   articulate independent opinions and judgements, informed by different interpretations of literary texts by other readers

AO5i   show understanding of the contexts in which literary texts are written and understood

For A level English literature

AO1   communicate clearly the knowledge, understanding and insight appropriate to literary study, using appropriate terminology and accurate and coherent written expression

AO2ii respond with knowledge and understanding to literary texts of different types and periods, exploring and commenting on relationships and comparisons between literary texts

AO3   show detailed understanding of the ways in which writers' choices of form, structure and language shape meanings

AO4   articulate independent opinions and judgements, informed by different interpretations of literary texts by other readers

AO5ii evaluate the significance of cultural, historical and other contextual influences on literary texts and study

▌ Grade descriptors

In addition to having an understanding of the overall course aims and a secure knowledge of which assessment objective is being assessed in each module, it is also helpful to look at grade descriptors, particularly the bottom and top of the range to get an idea of what is being expected of students in the subject being taught. Detailed grade descriptors are available from the board as the following descriptions of A and E grade students are only intended to give a feel for what students can achieve and of the sort of criteria employed at this level. In addition, collecting examples of work at each level in a portfolio is advisable.

What is a grade A student of A2 English literature capable of?

The A grade student has a 'comprehensive, detailed knowledge and understanding of a wide range of literary texts from the past to the present, and of the critical concepts associated with literary study' (AQA, 2001: 47). The student gives detailed responses to 'the ways authors use form, structure and language to create meaning, as well as showing some awareness of contextual influences' (ibid.). When interpreting texts this student is able to 'relate their own judgements to those of others' and skills of intertextuality are apparent. The student can also construct and sustain a line of argument.

What is a grade E student of A2 English literature capable of?

An E grade student can 'demonstrate some knowledge and understanding of a range of texts' and is capable of 'sometimes supporting their views by reference to the links between meanings and author's uses of form, structure and language' (AQA, 2001: 47) This student can note the 'possible effects of context' and might show some awareness and understanding of 'how other readers interpret texts' as he or she tends to point to the broad similarities and differences between texts but he or she does not necessarily do this 'within a wider critical framework' (ibid.). This student sometimes supports what he or she says by reference to the text and sometimes uses the appropriate terminology.

▌ Teaching Texts for A level English literature

The texts dealt with in the following section have been selected from the second AS English literature module to provide further insight into A level teaching. More students will take this AS module than any of the A2 modules and I have chosen an early module because many student-teachers begin with a lower-sixth group during their PGCE year, as do newly qualified teachers when they take up their first teaching post.

Teaching Donne

Of all the poets that can be studied for Module 2, John Donne is an especially good choice for a number of reasons. Many sixth formers can relate to the experiences this poet depicts and the themes that recur in his work. In this section two poems by Donne have been selected. I consider how to teach them to fulfil the assessment objectives and to prepare for an examination question from an AS level examination paper. While such approaches and texts are not intended to be representative of all work at A level they do provide a useful idea of good teaching, the knowledge required at this level and the texts that can be studied. The first of the two poems is 'Twicknam Garden'. You should read the poem carefully several times before continuing to read this chapter.

Twicknam Garden
Blasted with sighs, and surrounded with tears,
Hither I come to seek the spring,
And at mine eyes, and at mine ears,
Receive such balms, as else cure everything;
But O, self traitor, I do bring

The spider love, which transubstantiates all,
And can convert manna to gall,
And that this place may thoroughly be thought
True paradise, I have the serpent brought.

'Twere wholesomer for me, that winter did
Benight the glory of this place,
And that a grave frost did forbid
These trees to laugh, and mock me to my face;
But that I may not this disgrace
Endure, nor yet leave loving, Love let me
Some senseless piece of this place be;
Make me a mandrake, so I may groan here,
Or a stone fountain weeping out my year.

Hither with crystal vials, lovers come,
And take my tears, which are love's wine,
And try your mistress' tears at home,
For all are false, that taste not just like mine;
Alas, hearts do not in eyes shine,
Nor can you more judge woman's thoughts by tears,
Than by her shadow, what she wears.
O perverse sex, where none is true but she,
Who's therefore true, because her truth kills me.

For teachers who are unfamiliar with Donne some explanation may be helpful before I explore ways of teaching this poet. These 'teacher's notes' are not designed to be given to pupils and provide only a very brief introduction to some of Donne's work, life and times so that ways of teaching this poet can be appreciated.

Teacher's Notes on 'Twicknam Garden'

AO2 states that, for English Literature, students at AS level need to be able to 'respond with *knowledge and understanding* to literary texts of different types and periods'. Some of the information that follows could help students to develop this 'knowledge and understanding'. You should not give it to students in this form and you would need to think about how students can assimilate and understand such information.

In line 2 there is reference to 'spring' and the key idea here is that moods and seasons are often related in poems. The 'spider love' in line 6 is a reference to the belief that the spider transformed everything it ate and turned it into poison. Also in line 6 the word 'transubstantiates' is used which is a reference to transubstantiation, a central doctrine of the Roman Catholic Church which teaches that during the Mass a change takes place in the bread and the wine so that although it appears to be the same, it is really Christ's presence, his body and blood. In the next line the phrase 'manna to gall' appears. It is necessary to know that gall, throughout the Bible, symbolizes bitterness or bitter experience. To give some idea of its significance it can help to know that at the crucifixion of Jesus Christ, the sponge that was held up on a stick while he was dying was soaked in gall which tastes something like our modern-day vinegar. 'Manna' is a miraculous bread-like substance that appeared each morning in the desert and fed the Jews after crossing the Red Sea during the Exodus. In Christianity, therefore, manna is proleptic of, and anticipates, the Holy Communion or Mass. The juxtaposition of 'manna' and 'gall' is highly significant. In line 9 the poet says that in order for it to be 'true paradise' he has brought a 'serpent' with him. Students will remember that in the Genesis account Adam and Eve were expelled from Eden, or Paradise, because they gave in to the temptation of the serpent, or Satan.

When, in line 10, the poet says it would be 'wholesomer' for him he means it would be more apt or fitting if his surroundings were different. In line 11, the word 'benight' means shrouded in night or darkness. A 'man-drake' is referred to in line 17 and this is a reference to a plant that was thought to scream when uprooted. A mandrake is also referred to in 'Song: Go, and Catch a Falling Star' and was considered to look like a human with two legs and two arms. The 'vials' in line 19 are actually tear vessels but most sixth formers are probably more familiar from their days of science at GCSE with a test tube, in this case used for keeping tears in. Finally, by way of explanation, 'love's wine' in line 20 may be another reference to the Mass because in Christian teaching Christ's love for the world led to his blood (symbolized by the wine) being shed in atoning sacrifice to bring about redemption and salvation. The relationship between the spiritual and the physical in Donne's poems (Halstead, 1999) is fascinating and certainly warrants further exploration with students.

Teacher's notes: the cultural context

Looking at the assessment objectives for this module it is clear that a significant proportion of marks is awarded for demonstrating an 'understanding of the contexts in which literary texts are written and understood' (AO5i). Donne's life is fascinating and it is impossible to appreciate fully either the poet or his poetry without gaining an understanding of his life and times. A few historical events relating to Donne's life and some information about his personal circumstances are an appropriate starting point. Again, these are 'teacher's notes' and it is not intended that these should be read out to a class or presented in this form to sixth formers. When studying the following notes you should look out for anything that sheds light on 'Twicknam

Garden'. You should consider how such information, together with a more detailed picture of what might be termed a seventeenth-century worldview, could inform a reading of Donne and enable students to fulfil AO5i.

Donne was born into a Catholic family in London in 1572 and his father died four years later in 1576, the year when the first playhouse was built in London. In 1584 when studying at Oxford, Donne was barred from taking a degree because he was a Catholic. The position of Catholics at this time can be appreciated when one realizes that the Catholic Mary, Queen of Scots, was executed in 1587 and in 1588 the Spanish Armada was defeated. A few years later, in 1593, John Donne's brother, Henry, died in Newgate prison, where he had been sent for giving refuge to a Catholic priest. In 1605, the Gunpowder Plot failed and the result of the Plot was that many doubted the Catholics' loyalty to England.

As well as being a time when religion was politically important it was also a time of great exploration and a growth in knowledge about the world. Between 1577 and 1580 Drake circumnavigated the world. In 1595 Sir Walter Raleigh voyaged to Guiana and in 1596 Donne joined the English expeditionary force to Catholic Spain which invaded and looted Cadiz. In 1597, Donne sailed on the 'Islands' expedition and also to the Azores. When he returned home Donne gained office and became secretary to Sir Thomas Egerton, the Lord Keeper. Such was the extent of world exploration at this time that, in 1600, the East India Company was founded.

In 1601, Donne became an MP and also secretly married Ann More who was under age, being only 17. He was sent to prison for the secret marriage but Sir Thomas Egerton saw to it that the case was dismissed. Shortly after this, in 1603–4 the Plague was particularly virulent in London but Donne survived. In 1607 he became good friends with Lucy, Countess of Bedford, who was to be his patron. Twicknam Park was her home and its elaborate garden was laid out according to a geocentric pattern of the universe (as opposed to a heliocentric pattern). In 1609, Kepler proved that the Earth revolves around the Sun and in 1610 Galileo's *Siderus Nuncias* confirmed Kepler's discovery that planets revolve around the Sun and not around the Earth. By this time Donne had become a member of the Church of England and in 1610 he wrote and published a work entitled *Pseudo Martyr* which attacked Catholics. In the same year he was awarded an honorary MA by Oxford. In 1611 the Authorized Version of the Bible, a best-seller in Donne's day, was published and by 1614 Donne was not only sitting in Parliament but serving on no less than four committees. In 1615 Donne was ordained, became a royal chaplain and gained a doctorate from Cambridge University. By 1616 Donne was preaching at court and eventually became Dean of Saint Paul's Cathedral in London.

Teacher's notes: the literary context

AO3 states that students at this level should have a 'detailed understanding of the ways in which writers' choices of form, structure and language shape meanings' and AO5i, as we have seen from the previous section, requires 'an understanding of the contexts in which literary works' were written and understood. Clearly, it is not possible to appreciate Donne's poetry fully without some understanding of Petrarchan love poetry which influenced him.

Petrarch lived from 1304 to 1374 and was an Italian poet who addressed his love poems to Laura. He established a number of conventions about how a lover who was a poet should comport himself, speak and behave. Throughout the sixteenth century many poets were influenced by Petrarch. For instance, in 1591, when Donne was 19 years old, Sir Philip Sidney published *Astrophel and Stella* which is a sonnet sequence that is written according to Petrarchan principles or conventions. Some common ideas from Petrarch are that to part and separate from one's lover is death, and that generally one's mistress could be cold and indifferent to male advances (as in 'Twicknam Garden'). Generally, one's lover was compared to the soul of the world, love was depicted as a religion and the brightness of a lover's eyes was often compared to the brightness of the Sun.

There is a lot more that an AS class should learn about Petrarchan conventions which is important if students are to see how Donne wrote in original ways while still being influenced by the Petrarchan tradition. Reading 'The Sun Rising' below after some sonnets in the Petrarchan tradition enables students to appreciate this point. To be prepared for A03 (how choice of structure, form and language shapes meanings) students need some background knowledge about the sonnet form. It is important to note from A03 that they need to be able to relate style to content – in other words, how the form influences and contributes to the meaning. For example, students need to be aware that sonnets consist of fourteen lines and that they can be either Petrarchan or Shakespearean according to the rhyme scheme they employ. The Shakespearean sonnet follows a pattern of abab cdcd efefgg whereas the Petrarchan sonnet follows the pattern: abba abba in the first eight lines (known as the octave) and then, following a shift in the poet's thought, there are two or three other rhymes such as cdecde in the final six lines (the sestet).

A level students need to be aware that the sonnet form is associated with love and that very often sonnets are a plea or lament on the part of the speaker. The speaker tends to focus on himself, on his feelings and inner state and describes the rejection, pain and anguish brought about by love. Finally, students should know that sonnets often come to a summing-up or resolution in the final couplet and end with a definitive statement or expression of feeling. Before this final summing-up and conclusion two sides of an argument or two perspectives will have been offered. Generally one side of the argument is given and then this is followed by the contrary view before the final resolution.

Although the pattern in each stanza of the following poem 'The Sun Rising' is abba cdcd ee Donne pushes the boundaries of the form as far as he can. For instance, in 'The Sun Rising' Petrarchan expectations are subverted; it is not the lover but the Sun that suffers abuse. Further, Petrarchan sonnets are reflective and the poet is self-centred but Donne takes this to the extreme in 'The Sun Rising'. As another love poem, 'The Sun Rising' helps to provide a contrast in tone to 'Twicknam Garden'. Ostensibly, the reason for the loud, aggressive outburst and anger at the start of 'The Sun Rising' is because the lovers have been disturbed. They are in bed together and the curtains in line 3 are actually the curtains around a four-poster bed, not the curtains we have today at windows. Reading the poem and the examination question that follows it from an AS level paper provides teachers with the context for attainment of the assessment objectives.

The Sun Rising
Busy old fool, unruly sun,
Why dost thou thus, through windows,
and through curtains call on us?
Must to thy motions lovers' seasons run?
Saucy pedantic wretch, go chide
Late schoolboys, and sour prentices,
Go tell court-huntsmen, that the King will ride,
Call country ants to harvest offices;
Love, all alike, no season knows, nor clime,
Nor hours, days, months, which are the rags of time.

Thy beams, so reverend, and strong
Why shouldst thou think?
I could eclipse and cloud them with a wink,
But that I would not lose her sight so long:
If her eyes have not blinded thine,
Look, and tomorrow late, tell me,
Whether both th'Indias of spice and mine
Be where thou left'st them, or lie here with me.
Ask for those kings whom thou saw'st yesterday,
And thou shalt hear, All here in one bed lay.

She' is all states, and all princes, I,
Nothing else is.
Princes do but play us; compared to this,
All honour's mimic; all wealth alchemy.
Thou sun art half as happy as we,

> In that the world's contracted thus;
> Thine age asks ease, and since thy duties be
> To warm the world, that's done in warming us.
> Shine here to us, and thou art everywhere;
> This bed thy centre is, these walls, thy sphere.

(a) What does the poem reveal of the speaker's attitude to the sun?

(b) Explore the ways in which Donne uses comparisons and contrasts in this poem.

(c) Write about the way in which, in one other poem, the speaker expresses less positive feelings about a woman (AQA, 2001).

If they are familiar with the literary context of Donne's poem students can comment on the extent to which the poem follows Petrarchan conventions. Students should point out that this poem has a rhyme scheme which is a combination of two sorts of sonnet (Petrarchan and Shakespearean). If several sonnets have been studied they will probably notice, most immediately, that this form has been manipulated by Donne as each stanza has only ten and not fourteen lines. It is important to get them thinking about the significance of such a refusal to conform to convention and the way such decisions on the part of the poet may relate to the meaning of the poem.

They need to understand that manipulating and changing something out of its recognizable form is typically metaphysical and the whole meaning of the term 'metaphysical' should be expounded. The teacher might well ask why they think the sonnet form has been shortened to ten lines from fourteen. Of course, the Sun is being 'cut down to size' and the importance of the Sun is diminished by the poet who says that he can eclipse it with a wink. A physical, tangible representation of this can be seen in the shortened structure. Donne may be making the point that the Sun does not even deserve the last four lines of a conventional and fully formed sonnet.

One way of introducing sixth formers to the idea of conventions to be followed or subverted is to talk to them about their music and to see if they are discerning enough to trace the influences on the music they listen too. This can introduce relatively inexperienced readers to the concept of an audience's expectations. In this way, a class can identify the sorts of expectations Donne's readers, at the time of publication, may have had when they first looked at this poem. A skilful A level teacher can elicit appropriate responses from a class. Ideally, students should suggest that Donne's readers would immediately notice that each stanza of the poem looked like a sonnet and that they would, therefore, have certain expectations of what they were about to read. They would have ideas about a conventional sonnet and might well assume that what they were going to read would be spoken by a rejected and scorned lover who would be lamenting his failure in love and the cruelty and harshness of his mistress. Such readers would also have assumed that what they were about to read was going to be a reasonably balanced argument where two sides are given and then resolved.

Of course, nothing of the sort happens which is one reason why Donne's poem is so pleasing. All the conventions and expectations of the audience are undermined and thwarted, the even balance and final resolution are replaced by a tirade, and the speaker appears to become even more scornful as the poem progresses. Eventually we have the dogmatic and final declaration 'Nothing else is'. Instead of the lover engaging in reflection about his beloved he simply expresses his own growing anger. The poet certainly focuses on himself with the line ending 'all princes, I' where we are left with the word 'I' rather than a reference to the Sun or the mistress.

The speaker addresses the Sun instead of his lover and the only attempt at resolution is the demand that the Sun should accept that 'Nothing else is' apart from the lovers. Finally, the device of the 'metaphysical conceit' needs to be understood by students. A 'conceit' can be described as an analogy or an extended metaphor but with an important difference. The incongruity, strangeness, even the outrageousness of the comparison are what marks out a conceit where it is 'strange but true' when understood. In this poem the sonnet form allows Donne to display his metaphysical wit. The form of the poem is easily recognized and its conventions are undermined in a way that is fitting given its content and subject matter.

Different interpretations and literary frameworks

AO4 states that students should be able to demonstrate that they can 'articulate independent opinions and judgements, informed by different interpretations of literary texts by other readers'. Students' ability to do so can be fostered by encouraging them to reflect on different readings within their own reading community, their own reading of the poem and the way different literary theories actually underpin certain interpretations and ways of reading. The ambiguity in Donne and the controversy his poems can provoke among a group of sixth formers allow the teacher to discuss different interpretations and how readers reach such diverse interpretations.

Is 'Twicknam Garden' about a distraught, rejected, bitter lover or about a poet who is being deliberately self-conscious and intending to be the centre of attention? The question usually asked of Donne's work is whether he is sincere or not. After all, so the argument often goes, he seems to be taking considerable delight in exhibiting his wit and showing off his mental ingenuity and verbal dexterity. In 'The Sun Rising' do we witness masculine possessiveness over the woman or deep devotion? In line 17 the poet describes his beloved as 'th'Indias of spice and mine'. Students at this level need to be aware that spices came from the East Indies and that the West Indies were famed as a place where gold was mined.

Class discussion can focus on whether the poet is depicting the woman as rich, alluring and sensuous or seeing her as an object to be penetrated and exploited. Rather than giving students summaries of different critical perspectives 'cold' this would be a good point to draw on Marxist, feminist and psychoanalytic approaches and readings. The same perspectives could be employed to shed light on the first line of the third stanza of 'The Sun Rising' where we read 'She is all states, and all princes, I'. Differing interpretations of this line can inject some life into an English lesson. Is this the language of domination again depicting the monarch ruling over the land as his possession or, as the identity of the prince is derived from his land which he has a duty to protect, should we interpret this as a statement of commitment to behave ethically and responsibly? One might even argue that the prince is nothing without the land. He is certainly not a prince without it. Whichever interpretation one prefers, concepts of power, wealth and gender cannot be ignored and the teacher can profitably draw on critical frameworks that foreground such issues.

A sequence of lessons for 'Twicknam Garden' and 'The Sun Rising'

How does a teacher engage a class of 16 and 17-year-olds saturated in early twenty-first-century culture, with poetry written some four hundred years ago? Clearly, teenagers today have very different preoccupations from writers such as Donne who were interested in the religious, philosophical and scientific questions of their time. How can a teacher foster enthusiasm for such poetry as well as the comprehension of it?

Such questions need to be considered in the context of hostility towards poetry. One solution is to begin where the sixth-form reader is, in the present. Drawing on Rosenblatt's transactional theory and her concept of text as 'stimulus' where readers are encouraged to look for connections between their own lives and the text is recommmended. I have called such an approach 'responsive teaching' previously (Pike, 2000c). A possible 'responsive teaching' sequence as preparation for the question on Donne above is elaborated in the following pages.

Stage 1: Introduction to literary conventions

Petrarchan and Shakespearean sonnets are studied, beginning with the Prologue to *Romeo and Juliet*. The conventions of both forms of sonnet as well as of Petrarchan love poetry in general are considered to prepare students for Donne's poems. Selected sonnets from Sir Philip Sidney's *Astrophel and Stella* are read by the class. The teacher ensures everyone understands the conventions of Petrarchan love poetry.

Stage 2: Introduction to theme

The theme of love is developed. The way lovers feel they are often the centre of the world and that nothing else is important is considered. Personal experiences can be shared of friends who are love struck and oblivious to everything else around them. A short story on this theme is read for homework.

Stage 3: Reading for relevance (text as stimulus)

No historical, literary or cultural information is given at this point. The idea of text as 'stimulus' is introduced and explained. The idea is that on a first reading readers should look for the lines, phrases or words in the poem that have something, however tenuous, to do with them. Reassure the class that any connection between their lives and the poem is a valid reaction. They should be told that they are not engaging in literary criticism during the first reading; rather they are seeing if they can find any connection between their lives and the poem. The teacher may tell the class that great literature is capable of transcending the restrictions of time. Readers are told that if the poem or simply a word in the poem reminds them of something from their experience of life or literature they should circle that phrase and write a note next to it. Readers are told that if something in the poem triggers off a memory of an advertisement, something they have watched on television, something they have read or an experience they have had they should note it down. They are searching for relevance.

Stage 4: The first reading

The teacher reads the poem to the class a couple of times. This is a well rehearsed reading. The mood in the room seems to change as it is read.

Stage 5: Initial annotation

Students annotate the text of 'Twicknam Garden' individually in silence. One student writes about the spider that has lived on the curtain rail in his bedroom for the last week. He is resisting calls from his mother that the spider should be vacuumed up. Another student writes about the day his girlfriend (they had been together for most of Year 11) 'dumped' him. He says he actually went to the park, truanting school, and sat on a park bench staring at the ducks all afternoon, feeling thoroughly miserable. He says it was a lovely sunny day but it was raining in his heart (he's a Buddy Holly fan). Another student, a girl who is taking sciences as well as English, jots down that the 'crystal vials' in line 19 reminds her of test tubes in the science lab and the way they were testing fluids last week and comparing them to the original. She says the man in the poem is so arrogant to set his tears up as the measure against which everyone else's tears should be judged. A boy is reminded of communion at church and how he's always nervous about drinking wine that is supposed to be blood. He says the new vicar has changed the wine and now it is bitter.

Stage 6: First journal entry

Still in silence, students write a first journal entry on 'Twicknam Garden' of about fifty words focusing on reading the text as a 'stimulus'.

Stage 7: Paired discussion

Now, armed with their journal entries and annotated poems, students form pairs and discuss their reactions to the poem, what it triggered off or reminded them of. They are not trying to work out the meaning of the poem or looking at style at this stage. Friendship pairs are encouraged. No one is obliged to share anything that might be too personal or uncomfortable. Paired talk ensures everyone is engaged and active. No one is a passenger in this lesson.

Stage 8: Class discussion

The teacher gathers everyone to the front away from their desks and initiates a class discussion. This discussion is not dominated by the teacher. The teacher does not fall into 'fount of all knowledge' mode. Students try out their ideas on each other. The teacher does not step in to correct what he or she considers to be an 'incorrect' interpretation. The teacher does occasionally introduce pertinent details. When the boy tells everyone about his pet spider and the conflict this is causing with his mother the teacher says 'Did you know that at the time this was written everyone thought spiders turned what they ate into poison?' One student tells his tale of rejection and how he sought solace in the park. He says the Head of Sixth Form was not very tolerant of his plight and thought Cassie's cruelty was not sufficient cause to miss double AS mathematics which he is now going to drop after AS.

Stage 9: Second journal entry

After the class discussion a second journal entry is made. Some students have modified their interpretations in the light of what their peers have said. Nothing has become 'heavy' and there has been no attempt to convey large quantities of historical information. The focus has been on making the poem relevant to modern readers and attempting to establish a 'connection' or 'live circuit' between the lives of twenty-first-century readers and the experience of a seventeenth-century poet. Responses in journal entries range from the seemingly irrelevant (spiders) to variations on the theme of rejection in love.

Stage 10: Cultural context introduced

Clearly, personal response is not sufficient preparation for their Module 2 AS examination paper. The next stage is to help students to engage with the time in which Donne lived. A film focusing on Sir Francis Drake and the defeat of the Armada is shown. The concept of Catholic Spain versus Protestant England is introduced. The difference between the Catholic mass and Protestant communion is discussed and religious symbolism is considered. Biblical references are explored and a clip from Spielberg's film *Prince of Egypt* is shown to help students see what manna is. This is contrasted with another film showing the crucifixion. It is pointed out that a gall-soaked sponge was held up to Christ and that gall is bitter like vinegar. The word 'juxtaposition' and the idea of contrasts in the poem are explored.

Stage 11: Performance reading

Next, 'The Sun Rising' is introduced. An active approach such as that employed in Year 9 with Shakespeare is employed. Students practise reading aloud simultaneously. The teacher works with individuals developing reading so that they sound sufficiently scornful.

Stage 12: (Stages 6–8 repeated with second text)

After the active reading, annotation, a first journal entry and a class discussion following the pattern with 'Twicknam Garden' takes place.

Stage 13: Application of literary context through class discussion

The teacher reminds students of the literary context (see Stage 1 above) and faciliates a reading that is informed by such knowledge. A discussion about the way Donne subverts expectations and conventions follows.

Stage 14: Intertextuality fostered

Now the two poems are compared and contrasted. First, students work in pairs and then they engage in whole-class discussion. They work on generating very different interpretations of the poems.

Stage 15: Literary theories

The teacher begins to introduce students to the critical perspectives or frameworks (the literary theories) that may be informing their interpretations. Freud, Marx and feminist writers, among others, are considered. This is supported by the reading of extracts which illustrate different literary frameworks.

Stage 16: Assessment objectives checked

The teacher reviews the teaching and learning so far to see if all the relevant assessment objectives have been covered. The teacher then assesses whether the students are sufficiently prepared for the question on 'The Sun Rising' and one other poem above.

Stage 17: Essay preparation (collaborative, guided and shared)

Preparation time is devoted to the essay. The question above is given to students which they can plan collaboratively or individually for. Quotations are located that will be used. The teacher discusses the question with the class and explains what he or she thinks should be included.

Stage 18: Teaching following formative teacher assessment

The essay is written, marked and returned. The assessment indicates the stage different learners are at and shows the teacher what needs to be revisited or covered again.

Stage 19: Essay writing (individual unassisted)

Eventually, essays will be written without collaborative preparation so that students are prepared for examination conditions.

Stage 20: Consolidation and development with further poems

Increasingly sophisticated responses develop as new Donne poems are studied. The literary conventions, cultural context and knowledge of the historical period as well as key facets of Donne's style (such as the conceit) and recurrent themes are revisited with each poem studied.

Responsive teaching at A level

The sequence of lessons described in the twenty stages above is of course only one possible approach to Donne with sixth formers. This model does, however, implement a number of important principles. The starting point is where the student is in the present and the teacher responds to, and builds on, the relevance of the poem for the individual reader. The life experience of the reader is brought to the text. Any movement into the past begins in the present; adolescent readers of seventeenth-century poems do not divorce themselves from their twenty-first-century concerns when reading. The movement towards literary criticism can only be made when sufficient motivation and enthusiasm in the present have been generated to sustain the journey into the past. Indeed, understanding literary features, style, conventions adhered to and subverted, wit, metaphysical conceits, tone, intention and mood can only be most fully developed when the reader feels the poem has something to say which is relevant to his or her own life in the present.

A common trap to fall into when teaching A level is to assume that the teacher's task is to be a lecturer and to transmit information while students take notes. The temptation can be particularly acute when challenging pre-twentieth-century works are read. It is easy to assume that modern readers will not make sense of the text unless background information is provided before an initial reading. All the techniques and active approaches practised lower down the school that enable a reader to 'connect' with a text are just as important at A level. Indeed, it is wrong to assume that sixth formers, who often exude a nonchalant and 'cool' manner, are too sophisticated for active approaches such as role play, hot-seating, performance reading or to think that they learn best through lectures and note-taking.

Skilful teaching is even more necessary in the sixth form. Very often these lessons are longer and can last ninety minutes or even two hours and there is a need to pay attention to pace, differentiation and learning activities and to foster a personal engagement with the text being studied. The sixth-form teacher sometimes needs to rouse sixth formers from party-induced lethargy, to seize the initiative and capture the class's attention. The skilful teacher can use the class discussion to teach responsively and foster 'keen' readers in both senses of the word; they are intellectually acute and also well motivated.

Differentiation

When they teach A level for the first time many teachers are surprised at the range of abilities they have within one classroom. It is possible to have one student in the class who has two A* grades at GCSE and one who has two C grades. One student may be heading for an A grade at A2 level in English literature and a place at an elite university, such as Leeds, Oxford or Southampton, to study English while another may want to drop English at the earliest opportunity as soon as the first three AS modules are completed.

For teaching A level all the excellent differentiation strategies developed lower down the school are still essential. It is not good enough to assume that at A level there is no need to differentiate, or to make the overworked excuse that differentiation occurs by outcome. Although it takes time to produce differentiated tasks matched to learners (with supporting resources) it is undoubtedly worthwhile.

When you are planning to ensure differentiation you should also be aware of the other subjects a student is taking. A teacher may have two students of about the same ability in an English literature class but one student may be studying English as well as physics, chemistry and biology while another is studying history, English language, religious studies and classical civilization. The first student may not be able to bring as much to the English lesson as the student who is studying history, religion and other subjects which inform the study of literature.

You should also remember that some students will be better at some modules than others and that a student's ability in writing, reading, speaking or listening is often not developed to the same level. There is often a wide range of ability in terms of speaking and listening within the sixth-form classroom. Watch any sixth-form class debate and you are left in no doubt about this. The teacher's task is, as usual, to 'stretch' the most able and support the least able as well as all those in between so that a challenge is provided for all and real progress is made. Some students will want to dominate conversation and others will need to be encouraged to express their views in public. The teacher needs a great deal of sensitivity and highly developed leadership skills to ensure that this happens effectively.

Significant developments in the study of English literature post-16

English has been redefined at the same time as new structures and examinations have come into force. Students of English literature at A level now need to have a far better knowledge than previous generations of two areas:

■ literary theory
■ cultural context

It is not sufficient simply to focus on the text and engage in close textual analysis. You could argue that the study of English in the sixth form is beginning to resemble the study of English at university far more than it used to. Although close textual analysis is still required it needs to be informed by perspectives that come from outside the text itself. Literary theory makes us aware of the different frameworks that can be brought to bear on the interpretation of a text and leads us to conclude that the study of the text must be about the context and the culture in which it exists as well as the text itself. These two new emphases in English teaching (literary theory and cultural context) go hand in hand. Such approaches to texts are made mandatory by AO4 and AO5. One other important difference is the synoptic assessment in the final sixth module. These developments will be evaluated in turn.

Literary theory in the sixth-form classroom

As Jenny Stevens points out 'works classed as literature will now be read within a number of contexts and in relation to a variety of other texts, and A-level teaching and learning will enter the domain of literary theory' (2000: 1). Stevens observes that 'critical theory is no longer an esoteric adjunct to our subject' and that teachers 'should not dismiss it as beyond their students' abilities, or as a diagram-ridden distraction from the study of primary texts' (ibid.: 10). It is certainly true that students can be 'energised and in some ways liberated by the ideas which underpin post-structuralist thinking' (ibid.: 2). The adolescent readers who took part in the 'Keen Readers' project (Pike, 2000a) certainly found such theory helpful as it enabled them to understand the reading process and themselves as readers in ways they were unable to before they were introduced to literary theory. The article, 'Pupils' poetics' (Pike, 2000c), gives examples of how students' reading can change as a result of making literary theory explicit in the English lesson. Although 'theory often intensifies the difficulties of reading, and constantly throws up more problems than it is capable of solving' it is worth tackling because 'the complexities it [reading] gets itself knotted up in really are there' and 'trying to unravel them is enlightening, and sometimes even fun' (Barry, 2000: 25).

Many English teachers, however, seem a little surprised to hear that literary theory at A level is new at all. They note they have always discussed concepts of gender, politics, theology, philosophy, educational theory, psychology, psychoanalysis and cultural context with their students. For instance, before the advent of the new A levels Stevens was asking her students to consider 'how far the canon is constructed and ideological?' and giving them the task of choosing which texts should be 'in' the canon. Any English teacher wishing to pursue this question may want to read 'The canon in the classroom' (Pike, 2003b) as this question of canon formation is certainly a good place to begin theory at A level. What has changed, however, is the level of explicitness with which theories are taught. An analogous case might be the teaching of grammar lower down the secondary school. Readers were using all the parts of speech before they could name them. A level students were drawing on some sophisticated literary theories when they didn't, perhaps, know the names of all the 'isms' they were drawing on. Addressing some fairly basic questions such as: 'Where do literature texts come from? How do they get there? How do I read them? Does everyone read them the way I do?' (Stevens, 2000: 3) is an effective way of introducing the literary theories that attempt to provide answers to these questions.

In a recent article in *The Use of English* (2000), Peter Barry, the author of *Beginning Theory* (1995), gives a witty, incisive and highly entertaining application of theory to the new A levels which can be recommended to any teacher wishing to see how exactly texts can be read in different ways. Barry claims the methods of literary criticism 'mostly look inwards into the text itself' and readers need to look outwards as well as inwards; indeed, the 'necessary looking outwards from the text is why we have and why we need literary theory' (Barry, 2000: 17). According to Barry, 'theory can help us especially in considering four major aspects of the relationship between literature and the world beyond, these being firstly, literature and history, secondly, literature and language, thirdly, literature and gender, and finally literature and psychoanalysis' (ibid.). Teachers wishing to prepare themselves further with a broad overview of literary theory will find *A Reader's Guide to Contemporary Literary Theory* by Raman Selden and Peter Widdowson (1993) to be one of the very best short introductions available. Other texts to recommend that have been written by English teachers are *Critical Theory and the English Teacher* by Nick Peim (1993) and *Reading Narrative as Literature: Signs of Life* by Andrew Stibbs (1991).

Reader-oriented theories at A level

Few writers who assert the importance of theory in the new A levels pay much attention, specifically, to reader response theory. It may be that this is because there is a naïve assumption that it is merely a 'hook' to get readers to engage with literature and that as such it produces personal response but not critical reading. It would, in fact, be difficult to be further from the truth. Given the insistence of assessment objective AO4 that students should 'articulate independent opinions and judgements, informed by different interpretations of literary texts by other readers' and the second half of AO5ii which enjoins readers to consider 'contextual influences on literary texts and study', it is clear that a shift in our focus of attention to embrace reader-oriented theories is long overdue. Reader response theory can be accessible and can empower students to meet these assessment objectives. Such theory also provides a relevant approach for students and ensures that the theory they study is not just more information divorced from the reality of their lives because it can begin with the way they read and a consideration of how this is different, in important respects, from the way any other individual reads.

The perspectives of Stanley Fish, Norman Holland, Jonathan Culler, Wolfgang Iser, Lousie Rosenblatt, Hans Robert Jauss, David Bleich, Michael Riffaterre, Roman Ingarden and Umberto Eco can all be drawn on in the A level English lesson. Any teacher wanting to become familiar with this important but neglected school of literary theory could gain an overview by reading the little paperback by Elizabeth Freund entitled *The Return of the Reader* (1987) or the excellent *Reader-Response Criticism* edited by Jane Tompkins (1980).

Reading extracts from *Is there a Text in this Class?* by the 'enfant terrible' of reader response criticism, Stanley Fish (1980), could be a provocative and inspiring start to theory at A level. The sort of controversy this provokes and the thought it generates about the existence of the text would be a lesson of seminal importance. This could then be followed by reference to Bleich's *Subjective Criticism* (1978) and Holland's (1975) psychoanalytic work where he claims readers operate within 'identity themes' that determine their response to a text. Even extracts from *Young Readers Responding to Poems* that Benton (1988) wrote with four Hampshire heads of English is superb for getting readers to think about the process of reading.

The famous duck/rabbit puzzle that appears in Selden and Widdowson (1993) is about the most accessible introduction to literary theory one could wish for. Consider the drawing shown in Figure 7.1. Is it a duck or a rabbit? This can introduce students to the idea that what the observer brings to the act of observation can determine what is seen. Concepts of subjectivity can be explored and asserting the impossibility of objectivity can provoke those students in the class who are studying sciences alongside English. After introducing the idea that the perceiver is entirely active rather than passive in the act of perception, Wolfgang Iser's (1971) theory of reading can be considered. The concept of gaps or blanks in a text that the reader fills in idiosyncratic and highly individual ways can provide readers with a model of the reading process to debate and problematize as they continue reading. As pre-twentieth-century texts are studied for A level, the work of Hans Robert Jauss (1982) is invaluable as this explores the way readers in different ages interpret texts. How readers read diachronically is a vital area to consider as this is the reading students engage in much of the time on their A level course.

Figure 7.1 *The duck/rabbit puzzle*

The synoptic paper – compulsory wider reading

One of the most significant changes at A level is the requirement to demonstrate the literary skill of intertextuality, which is a mark of the maturing reader, and it has been asserted, rightly, that 'the once vague and usually optional activity of "wider reading" has come of age and is expected not only of the super-bright or the super-keen student, but of all A2 candidates' (Stevens, 2002: 97). Although students may not have to study Shakespeare now for A2 they have a significant challenge to rise to. Within a specific theme, genre or period, texts have to be studied comparatively. Yet, while the synoptic paper may be just what some students need to challenge them such reading may not come naturally to those doing A2 who struggle to get a D or E grade. Considerable skill is needed on the part of the teacher to get these students to perceive the links between texts and a further challenge is provided as this skill is to be assessed in relation to 'unseen' material and a 'topic-driven approach requires considerable forethought and organization, not to mention nerve, imagination and a willingness to take risks' (ibid.: 98). Arguably, the new A levels can provide opportunities for 'more student-centred teaching and learning' (ibid.). In a sense, therefore, there is a pleasing unity to the new A levels as 'responsive teaching' (Pike, 2000b) will be required to engage students with literary theory (which addresses the act of reading) and also to foster reading itself (which allows readers to reflect back on the theory).

Extracurricular activities for English in the sixth form

A fitting note to end a chapter about A level on is that teaching English at this level is about students' lives outside the classroom as well as inside it. When a sixth former reads he or she does so with everything he or she has read and experienced previously. They should be able to bring their life experience to their reading and, therefore, the teacher of English should get involved in literary activities with students outside the classroom. The school play, theatre visits, school newspaper, school magazine, radio shows, reviews, poetry days and involvement in theatre in education all have an important place. However, an Arvon creative writing course, or something similar, is one of the very best ways in which a teacher can help sixth formers to develop their literary capabilities outside the classroom. It is important for those studying English literature, where original writing ceases at the age of 16, and such activity also helps those studying the other two versions of English in the sixth form as students work with published writers and learn about the writing process from first-hand experience.

When I taught A level English literature at a Hampshire comprehensive my sixth formers and I went on an Arvon course in Devon. Although I managed to dent the school minibus the experience was unforgettable for other reasons too. One of the sixth formers who went on the course has since attended university and is now training to be an English teacher. It is appropriate that in a chapter advocating 'responsive teaching' a student should have the last word:

> Starting the sixth form can be a very daunting experience. Not only are you expected to have transformed into an intellectual over the summer holidays but you have now become a role model for all those pupils younger than yourself. The pressures are enormous and you are expected to succeed right from the word go. From a personal point of view, I found this transition very difficult. To be able to make intellectual and personal comments, in English in particular, you need to be able to trust your fellow classmates and your teacher. For some pupils, this trust can be very thin on the ground and it also takes a long time to build. This is where Arvon saved me! At the beginning of Year 12 I was encouraged and badgered by my English teacher to go on the Arvon Creative Writing Course in Devon. I was unsure and not confident that I was the right person for it. However, I was convinced to go. Looking back on it, from a teacher's point of view, I now realise that this was the turning point in my higher education. It gave me a chance to develop the skills to make stronger relationships with my fellow classmates and the adults that ran the course. It enabled me to feel confident that my passion for creative writing was not just a silly whim. Although the course was for developing my creative writing skills, I now think that it was a lot more than this. Working with my fellow classmates, my teacher and the writers gave me a complete sense of belonging that will never leave me. I returned to my studies feeling more confident. I felt that my opinion was worthwhile and more importantly that it was respected by those around me. The Arvon Course is a definite must for all Year 12 students starting English Literature. Now that I am on the other side of the fence I can appreciate this a lot more (Bryony, student-teacher).

Further reading

Barry, P. (2000) 'The new "A" levels: tackling textuality – with theory', *The Use of English*, 52(1): 13–26.

English and Media Centre (2002) *Text, Reader, Critic – Introducing Contexts and Interpretations*. London: EMC.

Keith, G. and Shuttleworth, J. (2000) *Living Language*. London: Hodder & Stoughton.

Pike, M.A. (2000) 'Pupils' poetics', *Changing English*, 7(1): 45–54.

Pike, M.A. (2003) 'The canon in the classroom: students' experiences of texts from another times' *Journal of Curriculum Studies* 35(3) 355–70.

Selden, R. and Widdowson, P. (1993) *A Reader's Guide to Contemporary Literary Theory*. London and New York, NY: Harvester Wheatsheaf.

Stevens, J. (2000) 'The new "A" levels: critical theory in the sixth form classroom: a very very short introduction', *The Use of English*, 52(1): 1–11.

Stevens, J. (2002) 'The demands of synoptic assessment in the new English literature "A" level', *The Use of English*, 53(2): 97–107.

PART III

Challenging English

8

Making meaning: the media, ICT and drama

Reading for meaning: media, ICT and drama

What do the study of the media, ICT and drama have in common? Arguably, all three areas, when studied as an element of English, address important issues regarding meaning and are concerned with the way we make, interpret and communicate meanings. Consequently, ICT is not so much about information as interpretation; drama is more concerned with purpose than performance; and the media are above all about making and exchanging meanings. In this chapter I argue that all three areas are concerned with what it is to 'read' in its broadest sense (what it is to read our culture) and that such reading should be both critical and creative in English.

Let us take media education and ICT first. *The National Curriculum for England: English* (DfEE/QCA, 1999) contains numerous references to teaching the media and ICT within English. Within En1 (Speaking and listening), it is clear that much of the activity described can be the sort of collaborative communication that occurs around a computer. It is even suggested that group discussion and interaction 'may be face-to-face or by electronic means' (ibid.: p.33 Note for 10). Within En3 (Writing), we are reminded that pupils 'could make choices of font style and size and whether to use bold, italics or bullets in presenting their work' (ibid.: 37) and that they can 'use a variety of ways to present their work, including using pictures and moving images as well as print' (ibid.: 38). By far the most detailed and extensive coverage of ICT and the media in English, however, comes within En2 (Reading), where within a section entitled 'Media and moving image texts' we read that pupils should be taught:

a) how meaning is conveyed in texts that include print, images and sometimes sounds

b) how choice of form, layout and presentation contribute to effect (for example, font, caption, illustration in printed text, sequencing, framing, soundtrack in moving image text)

c) how the nature and purpose of media products influence content and meaning (for example, selection of stories for a front page or new broadcast)

d) how audiences and readers choose and respond to media (ibid.: 35).

Then, just over the page, in a section entitled 'Non-fiction and non-literary texts' we learn that the range of texts our children read should include 'print and ICT-based information and reference texts' and also 'media and moving image texts (for example, newspapers, magazines, advertisements, television, film, videos)' (ibid.: 36).

ICT and media study in English are, rightly in my view, mainly located within En2 (Reading), because these areas of study, although ostensibly technological, are fundamentally about meaning, interpretation and the reader's response. In dealing with students' cultural experience, reading in its broadest sense, we are engaging in a vital aspect of English as we are enabling learners to see that we *ascribe* meaning and do not passively *receive* meaning. When we read and respond to media, moving image and digital texts we actively construct our world. Media and ICT study, rightly conceived, is not just concerned with language and communication as is often thought but with the exchange and construction of meanings, beliefs and values by which to live.

Teaching ICT and the media in English is about *interpretation* as well as *information*. Media images and digital texts provide information but the task of the English teacher is a hermeneutical one. Although computers 'provide the data' the challenge is how we 'create explanations, arguments and new configurations which will make sense of that data in human and social terms' (Andrews, 2000: 9). Media education in English addresses how meanings are 'made', 'sustained' and 'contested' and should focus on 'what those meanings and beliefs are, where they came from, who makes them and why' (Davies, 1996: 60). We might well add 'how' and 'when' to the 'what', 'where', 'who' and 'why' questions we ask to help us understand the way meanings and beliefs are constructed. Media education concerns who communicates, why they do so, the text type they have chosen, how it is constructed (its content and style), the subject of the communication, how it is represented and how the intended audience responds.

Media and ICT study fits well within the development of English as a school subject in the UK at the start of the twenty-first century. At its best, English is becoming more socially and culturally aware as a result of the emphasis upon literacy with 11–14-year-olds (where audience and purpose are seen to determine text-type) and with the introduction of new courses for

16–18-year-olds at A level (where background knowledge regarding the context of works informs interpretation). Media education and the discriminating and skilful use of ICT are concerned to promote social and cultural awareness and understanding and are an example of the way Cox's 'cultural analysis' model can work in English (see Chapter 1).

Drama within English is also concerned with meaning and interpretation. Children engaged in drama in the English lesson collaborate in a search for meaning for 'the drama invites them to speculate, create and reflect together' (Grainger, 1998: 30) and the underlying 'cognitive and affective similarities between reading and drama' are that both are engaged in a 'common search for meaning' (ibid.: 29). As 'meaning-making in drama encourages children to go further than a literal reading of the text' (Winston, 1999: 33) the challenge for the English teacher teaching drama is how to 'make better use of drama as an active method of thinking about meaning' (ibid.: 35).

In drama, pupils learn to 'use a variety of dramatic techniques to explore ideas, issues, texts and meanings' (Grainger, 1998: 32) and because it offers role adoption, drama fosters the 'ability to consider what has been read from various stand points' (Winston, 1999: 34). Clearly, when assuming different roles the 'variety of stances adopted provide children with opportunities to develop their understanding of the issues and meanings in the drama, in the book and in their own lives' (ibid.). Drama, like the study of the media and ICT in English, addresses important issues about the way we live and provides a range of opportunities for learning activities that are directly relevant to learners' lives.

Media education in English

Media education enables children to interpret the texts, images and sounds their culture saturates them in. Texts that have had an impact on learners' lives can be studied in order to engage their interest and after initally generating personal opinions and responses we can move on to develop in readers an awareness of values, beliefs, points of view, bias, opinion and so on in order to foster a more culturally and socially informed response. Key areas include representation, audiences, language, narrative, genre, values and media institutions. Creativity and the notion of the media as art fit well within the overall theme of this book and the opportunities to create are almost limitless. Media education can also motivate some boys who often fail to achieve their potential in other areas of English and reluctant readers often surprise their English teacher by being able to read popular culture critically.

Advertising

Eleven-year-olds always seem to enjoy thinking up new names and slogans for chocolate bars and love to design the wrapper and draw a cross-section of the bar (labelling caramel, toffee, chocolate, nuts and biscuit and making you feel hungry in the process). The connotations and associations of names can be discussed and after such teaching one of your Year 7 pupils is always sure to come up with the 'Rhino' bar to communicate how big, tough and chewy his or her chocolate bar is. The same approach can be taken with products such as perfumes and cars with older learners and whole advertising campaigns can be designed which lead pupils to consider where and when to place adverts in order to appeal to particular audiences. Pupils can pick accents or famous actors for voice-overs and can create a range of media products apart from advertisements including game shows, headlines, sit coms or holiday brochures, to name just a few.

Pupils and teachers can enjoy classroom games designed to promote learning about advertising slogans that employ rhyme, alliteration, onomatopoeia or word puns. All you need do is to sit in front of your television one evening and jot down all the slogans you hear. The next day simply call out the start of the slogan and your class will chorus in unison the ending. Pupils can then come up with their own, put them into categories according to the linguistic device employed and consider why certain advertising techniques have been chosen. Public information leaflets such as those produced by the Health Education Authority can be a superb resource and teachers can easily obtain thirty copies of these. One such leaflet, designed to raise awareness about the dangers of sunbathing, reads 'If you worship the sun . . . don't sacrifice your skin' and employs other puns such as 'throwing light on sun rays'. What is important here is that the way image and text work in conjunction is understood and that pupils comment on the significance of design features (why the leaflet is orange, for example), where you would find it and how it seeks to persuade a particular audience. Pop-music videos and DVDs, CD covers, radio and television news programmes, documentaries, soaps, sit coms, dramas, magazines and fanzines, pop lyrics, billboards, text and picture messaging on mobile phones, websites, emails, posters, pizza boxes, chocolate bar wrappers – can all be profitably analysed by the skilful teacher within English.

Literature and the media

The relationship between literature and the media can be explored and television adaptations of plays and novels can be compared with the original text and other adaptations. Opening sequences of well-known film versions can be viewed repeatedly to look at how an audience's expectations are manipulated, how atmosphere is created and the effect of the soundtrack as well as how characters are portrayed. Children can produce a storyboard of key episodes in a class novel and can compare the way different camera angles and sequences are employed. Classes can also produce the opening sequence for a new soap, film or drama and come up with a title, characters and so on. How the classroom television can be used to teach literature is described in Chapter 10.

Reading the news

It is especially important to cultivate critical responses to and readings of the news for being able to deconstruct film clips used on the television news is a necessary life skill. Take, for instance, footage of a violent clash between rioters and police. The viewer needs to be aware of where the camera is and from whose perspective we are seeing the action and this is a valuable exercise to try in class. Are we behind the riot shields or the throwers of petrol bombs? Camera angle, cropping and an awareness of what is not seen, as well as what is, all require analysis. Such material can be topical as all you have to do is to record a minute or so of footage one evening to play the next day as a stimulus for discussion. The coverage and perspective provided by different television channels can be compared as can that of different newspapers. Teachers can buy a copy of *The Guardian*, *The Times*, *The Daily Telegraph*, *Sun*, *Mirror* and *Daily Mail* on the same day in order to compare the way particular events are depicted and represented in different papers. After students have become aware of the characteristic differences between papers you can take headlines from each paper and set your pupils the task of deciding which headline belongs to which paper. This can be developed and headlines can be matched to stories.

Sequencing the news for television, radio or newspaper can be especially rewarding and all the teacher has to do is to provide short paragraphs giving the main details of news stories and leave pupils to argue, persuade and negotiate regarding prioritization as they evaluate the importance and appeal of different stories. There is considerable scope here for the development of speaking and listening skills and for using such activities for En1 Assessment. Media study is, of course, compulsory at GCSE and the staging of a press conference (as described in Chapter 6) can be a valuable way to help pupils understand the media reporting process. Putting on a Media Day (also described in Chapter 6) can be one of the highlights of the school year and one such day I organized was especially memorable (and provided an insight into how news is created not simply reported) because the BBC decided to report on the reporting skills of our cub-reporters. That pupils become aware of the differences between fact and opinion is especially important if they are to 'read' the news and become well informed citizens.

Television viewing

Critical reading is the aim of media education and representations of gender, families and relationships are all legitimate topics as are stereotyping and censorship. Readers whose critical skills are developing need to become aware of the way television channels compete and undertake strategic programming to maximize viewing audience figures and need to debate the difference between the BBC's public service remit and the aims of commercial channels. Discussing where revenue comes from and the cost of advertising is often an 'eye-opener' for many adolescents. One of the best ways of enabling pupils to become media analysts is to photocopy a schedule of one evening's viewing so they can see the offerings of different channels side by side. They can then guess which night of the week the programming is for and discuss strategic timing and why particular programmes start at certain times so that stations maintain viewer loyalty throughout the evening. Once pupils are sufficiently aware they can even design an evening's viewing for different target audiences.

The challenge of media education in English

Despite the opportunities for innovative, interactive, critical and challenging reading of media texts, the teaching of the media within English can be done badly, if it fails to focus on interpretation and neglects to foster cultural and social understanding. It is all too easy to *test* rather than *teach* understanding and to use a media text (such as a newspaper article) for a comprehension exercise without engaging in specifically media education. Teachers and classes can watch a television version of the novel they are reading without exploring the way it is 'a particular kind of text for the particular medium of television' (Hart, 2001: 75). It is also possible to treat advertisements as 'explorations of the skill and subtlety of advertising agencies' with 'no reference to social context' (ibid.: 74).

Although media education is inherently concerned with values and ideology recent research reports of that English teachers 'tended to talk of the media as manipulators whom children needed to be taught to read' but actually 'seemed uncomfortable about discussing *who* was manipulating and for what purpose' (ibid.). Equally, it is 'by no means certain that exposing an advertiser's means of exploiting our fantasies in any way reduces our susceptibility' especially if 'teachers no longer feel that they have an alternative set of values to offer in their place' (ibid.). Indeed, recent research has shown that when teachers of English were asked 'to indicate their own ideological positions' they 'tended to refer to issues of gender, race and equal opportunity; the agenda set and sanctioned by the media' and made 'no reference to approaches to ideology in terms, for example, of manipulative, hegemonic or pluralist models' (ibid.), thereby demonstrating a lack of awareness of ideological debate which resulted in some media work lacking a 'meaningful context' (ibid.).

Understanding the commercial and ideological context of media texts is of central importance yet, in recent research, many teachers 'described their unease at the idea of teaching about media institutions' and generally felt this topic was rather 'dry' suggesting such knowledge was 'boring and even irrelevant' as it concerned 'factual knowledge about current ownership and profits' (ibid.). Encouraging students to see the relevance of profit margins and circulation figures and the way in which quantitative data can only be interpreted and understood adequately by reference to ideology and values is essential. Take the following figures, for instance, of daily newspaper sales from December 2002: *Sun* (3,447,108), *Daily Mirror* (2,031,596), *Daily Mail* (2,327,732) *Daily Express* (916,055) *Guardian* (378,516), *Daily Telegraph* (923,815) and *The Times* (619,682) (Greenslade, 2003: 4). Knowing the political sympathies and ownership of papers, as well as their target audiences and readerships can be fascinating and is about empowering inexperienced readers to become culturally and politically aware. The ability to interpret such figures can also provide the justification for numeracy in English.

Information and communication technology (ICT) in English

Like the study of the media, ICT in English should be concerned with the *interpretation* and analysis of information, communication and technology as well as its use. English teachers are presented with the opportunity to help children engage in critical and creative rather than merely functional computer literacy and ICT must be seen as providing additional cultural tools requiring interpretive skills. The interactive nature of CD-ROMs and websites can also provide immediate feedback when learning grammar so pupils become more independent learners.

Reading digital images and texts leads us to synthesize, recreate and develop new understandings. Clarke, for instance, suggests that using ICT with a Shakespeare play facilitates 'comparative readings' and can help children understand a play's 'cultural relativity' (2000: 103). With 'a play as the imaginative centre' different texts can be 'assembled and constructed around it' in order to encourage 'the comparative study of different media and text types' (ibid.: 104). It has even been suggested that a key creative act occurs when a 'student literally "puts together" elements of image and text that he/she has researched; representing them, and hopefully transforming them for a different purpose or audience' (Andrews, 2000: 9).

Both Clarke (with regard to literature) and Andrews (in relation to literacy) draw our attention to the importance of writing in the English/ICT lesson. Clarke points out that Shakespeare has been 'used, exploited, honoured, adapted and transformed' over time and that with access to a computer we should 'invite the students to see themselves as heirs to the process of interpretation and transformation' (2000: 111). In this way they can work as directors of the play and not merely read digitized images and texts but also write them. The ability to 'create multimedia texts' may well be one of the 'inevitable consequences of engaging in on-screen learning' (Andrews, 2000: 9) in a multimedia environment.

Using ICT to teach English

A multimedia learning environment also gives English teachers the opportunity to be creative. Take, for instance, the following scene. I am sitting at the back of a classroom observing a student at a school in Bradford. My PGCE student, Alison, is teaching a Year 10 class and the text today is a poem from their GCSE anthology. Not only does the poem appear on the interactive whiteboard at the front of the room but at key moments in the lesson images or background information is displayed as the stimulus for short five-minute tasks designed to help pupils think about themes in the poem and its cultural context. The technology alone did not make this a good lesson and Alison still had to find resources (images and texts) prior to the lesson. Similarly, pupils need to learn how to access the information they want from the Internet and it is good practice to help students to recognize a 'good' website that matches their needs as this skill can save them (as we all know) many valuable hours in the future. What made Alison's a good lesson was the sensitive and discriminating application of the technology.

Interactive whiteboards are especially valuable for whole-class literacy teaching where modelling and guided writing are undertaken. It is easy to highlight word classes or parts of a text in colour for discussion. Programmes such as Clicker, Publisher and PowerPoint are useful and when software such as Notebook is used 'the screen can be written on with fingers or with special pen-shaped plastic tools' so that 'what has been handwritten can be converted to word-processed text or moved around the screen' (Branson, 2002: 21). It is this ability to change a text and manipulate it that is so valuable in English. A simple starter activity on word roots, for instance, lends itself well to whiteboard use because of the focus on 'word formation and word relationships' which is brought home to pupils when they see 'the constituent parts of words as moveable and flexible' (ibid.: 22). We should also give pupils opportunities to develop their communication and presentation skills and they need to be taught how to deliver effectively a PowerPoint presentation which is a skill they will certainly need in the future.

It is important to note that poems, narratives and plays (works of literary art), can be found on websites and that ICT can be used to access far more than information. Indeed, whole websites are dedicated to English teaching. Facsimiles of Blake's poems can be found, the British Library can be visited and drafts of famous texts can provide insight into the creative writing process. Although pupils can develop their ability to read non-literary and information texts and can produce the front page of a newspaper and other media texts, they can also use ICT to engage with literary texts. Writing a poem is different on a computer but one of its advantages is that text can be so easily manipulated. Line lengths, for example, can be changed by simply tapping the return key. A literary text can, therefore, be issued to pupils who can organize, restructure, complete, parody or transform it in a variety of ways.

The challenge of ICT in English

The rapid pace of development in ICT is evidently a challenge and it has been pointed out that 'ICT is developing too fast for research – especially longitudinal research to keep up with it' (Andrews, 2000: 11), although the government's Best Practice Research Scholarships scheme does invite teachers to undertake small-scale research into the impact of ICT on learning. Professional bursaries are also available for those with four or five years' experience. Indeed, while it is 'one thing to be trained; it is another to have the power to continue developing and learning from ICT' (ibid.). Arguably, that is precisely why more than 'training' is required; English teachers have a very real developmental need and must be encouraged to develop innovative applications of ICT. The way ICT will develop and come to be routinely used in English has the potential to alter the nature of the subject and it is important that while the technology changes the creative and critical heart of English is preserved.

It is especially important that ICT is effectively integrated into an English lesson and is seen as one teaching and learning tool among many. Pupils need to be adequately prepared for such work and should review their progress. We should certainly avoid the situation where we notice they have not 'done' any ICT for a while and 'plug them in' for this reason or because we are tired and it is the last lesson of the day. We must not see ICT as separate from the usual learning that takes place in our classroom for if it is not effectively integrated into lesson planning (with aims and objectives that fit the sequence – see Chapter 2) it will be ineffective.

Studying ICT and the media can also play a part in teaching citizenship and thinking skills when pupils learn about 'the social, historical, political and cultural contexts which shape and influence the texts' they read and view and as they pay attention to 'explicit and implied meanings, bias and objectivity, and fact and opinion' (DfEE/QCA, 1999: 9) and develop critical capabilities. English must retain its vital function within the curriculum and should foster an understanding of what it is to be human and to struggle to interpret one's world where beliefs and values are contested.

Drama in English

Drama 'commonly explores moral dilemmas, injustices of various kinds and will consider the implications of specific human actions within a range of ordinary and extraordinary situations' (Winston, 1999: 460). Like ICT and the study of the media it is concerned with interpretation and the reader's response. Within English, pupils 'participate in a range of drama activities' and learn to 'evaluate their own and others' contributions' (DfEE/QCA, 1999: 32). They employ different ways of conveying 'action, character, atmosphere and tension' and when they are 'scripting and performing in plays' need to be helped to 'appreciate how the structure and organisation of scenes and plays contribute to dramatic effect' so they can 'evaluate critically' the dramas they watch and perform in (ibid.).

The range of experiences provided by the drama curriculum is extensive. Children 'might improvise or work from script; they might invent their own work or study play texts; they might create drama, perform it, read it or watch and respond to it; they might work physically, through representation, or through talk' (Winston, 1999: 460). Yet, the focus in this activity will also be on making meaning and understanding beliefs, values and attitudes. Anton Franks considers drama to have three dimensions. First, 'drama as art, text and performance selects, shapes, frames and actively materialises aspects of personal social and cultural life'; secondly, 'involvement in drama is to engage the personal with wider social concerns and interests'; and, thirdly, 'modes, structures and forms of drama, as text and performance' have 'particular values' attached to them (1999: 44). Essentially, then, drama is concerned with meaning and values and has this in common with the study of the media and ICT in English where creative and critical reading and the exchange of meanings are at the core.

In a sense, every English lesson should be a drama lesson for 'the fields of English and drama are inextricably intertwined' (ibid.: 41). Indeed, in America and Canada, both subjects fall within the category 'language arts' and it is important to consider 'what drama contributes to the study of English as an arts subject' (ibid.: 39). Certainly, approaching texts through dramatization, extempore improvisation and reading aloud (Newbould and Stibbs, 1983) is a valuable way of generating enthusiasm and engagement in English (see Chapters 10 and 11 for examples). When we read in English we need drama 'for its techniques and conventions which facilitate children's engagement in, and response to, texts' (Grainger, 1998: 29).

Both drama and English involve prediction regarding narrative action and the adoption of roles. In story drama, for instance, an 'aesthetic' reading is possible because gaps are left for the child to fill imaginatively and these 'gaps in the tale' are what drama attempts to 'investigate, to shape, construct and pack with meaning' (ibid.: 30). Story drama is so valuable because students can bring their whole experience of literature and life to the lesson, and Grainger (ibid.) provides examples of this approach at work. Arguably, the 'search for meaning links reading and storydrama' (ibid.: 30) and living with uncertainty in drama ensures that 'options can be left open and multiple meanings accepted' (ibid.: 33). In this way, drama in English provides children with an additional store of experience as it 'deeply engages children', 'involves a high degree of social interaction' and allows 'feelings to be foregrounded and explored' (Winston, 1999: 35). By focusing on meaning drama can be experienced alongside the study of the media and ICT as part of the art of English.

Further reading

Andrews, R. (2000) 'Learning, literacy and ICT: what's the connection?', *English in Education*, 34(3): 3–18.
Clarke, S. (2000) 'Changing technology, changing Shakespeare, or our daughter is a misprint', in A. Goodwyn (ed.) *English in the Digital Age*. London: Cassell.
Grainger, T. (1998) 'Drama and reading: illuminating their interaction', *English in Education*, 32(1): 29–36.
Hart, A. (2001) 'Awkward practice: teaching media in English', *Changing English – Studies in Reading and Culture*, 8(1): 65–81.

9

Differentiation and the individual: gender ethnicity and special needs

Differentiation

A 'one-size-fits-all' approach is not to be recommended in English teaching. You simply cannot take all children through the same material at the same pace in the same way. You certainly cannot teach successfully if you believe you have a homogeneous group sitting in front of you because no such group exists. English teachers recognize that each child has differing needs and learns in different ways from other children. The differentiation advocated by the TTA (2002) focuses on differences of gender, ethnicity and ability. Student-teachers should 'differentiate their teaching to meet the needs of pupils, including the more able and those with special educational needs' (ibid.: 12, 3.3.4) and should also 'take account of the varying interests, experiences and achievements of boys and girls, and pupils from different cultural and ethnic groups' (ibid.: 3.3.6).

Differentiation is a constant challenge for all teachers of English but we have at our disposal a range of strategies and approaches that enable us to vary our teaching to help a variety of learners. We can differentiate by task, topic or text and can also differentiate by the language we use (for instance, the sorts of questions we ask as well as the vocabulary we employ) and the resources and level of support we provide. The momentum and pace of activities can be varied and the structure and organization of a lesson can be adapted for different pupils. Every lesson plan you write should have a section headed 'Differentiation' to ensure this vital aspect of teaching English is planned for.

Although it should never be your primary way of differentiating, most tasks in English do differentiate between learners as a wide variety of different outcomes can be the result of the same activity. If you ask different children to write short stories or poems no two will ever be quite the same. Differentiation should, properly understood, be about a focus on the individual and the English teacher has a responsibility to challenge 'stereo-typed views' (ibid.: 12, 3.3.14). I argue in this chapter that individuals cannot be adequately understood or taught simply by applying an understanding of their ethnic origins, gender or ability to the task of teaching English which is relational in that it involves establishing relationships with individuals and responding to their individuality.

To illustrate the reality of the 'relational' in differentiation, the tale of 'Mickey, the Tractor and the Motorbike' may help. Mickey was an under-achieving boy with special educational needs in my Year 9 English class who was constantly in trouble. He wrote just five words in his Key Stage 3 test (which I shall not reprint here), put down his biro and placed his head in his arms. Mickey often forgot his school bag, rarely completed homework and was deeply frustrated with teachers' organizational expectations and his own perceived lack of ability. Mickey looked the part too and one morning when he arrived looking particularly dishevelled I found out why. He had not been home but had spent the night in a farmer's tractor.

Mickey's sartorial inelegance, uniquely abrasive social skills and police record did not endear him to many colleagues. It was decided that when Mickey felt he was about to do something rash (and 'explode' physically or verbally or both in a particular lesson) he should excuse himself and make his way to my room where he had a desk waiting and could talk about the situation later on. Mickey's reason for choosing me as his trusted member of staff began with a motorbike. Both Mickey's dad (whom he rarely saw but talked much about) and I were motorcyclists although we rode quite differ-ent machines and were rather different types of biker. When I mentioned I rode a metallic grey, retro, Honda CB750 F2N we had a 'point of contact'. The conversation about bikes turned to family, being beaten up by his brother, cooking family meals, bullying and being bullied and so on. I am not suggesting that every English teacher should risk life and limb in order to bond with difficult pupils. What I am advocating is that we find a 'point of contact' for each of our pupils and get to know them as individuals. If a girl is interested in horses, discuss horses with her. Showing an interest is more important than expert knowledge and you can learn a great deal about a child in the process that will make teaching him or her far easier.

In English, Mickey especially enjoyed *Buddy* by Nigel Hinton (differentiation by text) where the central character has a biker dad who goes to prison for theft. We discussed the racial taunts and verbal bullying endured by Charmian and Jules (differentiation by topic) and Mickey engaged in shorter, more highly structured and time-specific activities than some of his peers for which I provided a pen and English book, so we did not argue about lost or missing equipment at the start (differentiation by task). The level of support and nature of resources were adjusted in relation to the challenge Mickey faced in different tasks. The language of teacher questioning and explanations was modified to remove barriers to learning and extensive use was made of class discussion. Pace and momentum were adjusted in response to Mickey's learning (and that does not imply the pace always slowed down) and the structure and organization of lessons were planned with differentiation (and especially Mickey) in mind. My point, though, is that this could not have been successfully achieved in any mechanistic fashion as the differentiation derived from knowledge of an individual and the understanding that comes from a relationship. Mickey had to be taught not as a 'boy' and not as a pupil with certain 'special needs' but as the one and only, totally unique, 'Mickey'. While gender, ethnicity and ability are all relevant we cannot base our teaching solely on an understanding of these. People are more complex than that and do not easily fit the categories we sometimes use to describe them.

Boys and English teaching

While individuals like Mickey are cause for concern so too are specific groups and although we must beware of stereotyping it is clear that 'boys' are one such group. Overall, boys' results are far lower than girls' in English at GCSE and for the last few years the 'discrepancy between the numbers of girls and boys achieving grades A–C in English has varied annually between 13 and 18%, (Daly, 2000a: 227). This is a pressing issue for schools and especially for English. One year, as a curriculum manager, looking at the gender makeup of a Year 11 cohort I was dismayed because out of a year group of 200 in the school we had 90 girls and 110 boys; if the gender distribution had been reversed I knew GCSE results would have been higher. The issue of boys' attainment has led to numerous studies into reading preferences and learning styles which have suggested how boys can do better in English. You might like to evaluate the following statements in the light of your experience of teaching English:

Boys need clear short term targets and a structure within which to work (QCA, 1998: 21).

Boys are generally more competitive in discussion. They value the element of performance in talk and delight in displaying their verbal skills' (ibid.: 12).

Boys find it difficult to talk about their own feelings . . . and in particular to relate them to their own experiences' (ibid.).

Boys respond well to clearly set tasks with well defined outcomes (ibid.: 10).

Boys work best when given tightly structured tasks which channel their speaking and listening energies and skills in purposeful directions (ibid.).

Boys are often more concise than girls in their writing and what may be perceived as a lack of commitment may be more efficient selection of key ideas and illustration (ibid.: 11).

While it is important to bear in mind such generalizations we must be careful not to impose a too simplified view of our learners on our classrooms as 'it is not difficult to find evidence which challenges the stereotype or individual classes whose aptitudes and preferences do not match the norm' (Myhill, 1999a: 238). Many boys fit the description above but many do not. There is also the danger of generating self-fulfilling prophecies (explored in Chapter 4) where students conform to our expectations and we perpetuate inequalities. Like Myhill, I am keen to promote the view that we should focus on learners as individuals; the boys I studied reading poetry (Pike, 2000a) certainly read in remarkably different ways to each other. It is also important that we do not alter our teaching and curriculum to improve boys' attainment to the detriment of girls. If strategies designed to improve the performance of many boys is also beneficial for girls that is a different matter but we need to be aware that teaching English must always be ethically justifiable.

Reluctant readers?

Daly notes that the central issue 'is boys' resistant attitude towards a fundamental aspect of literacy development: reading' (2000b: 30) and Elaine Millard (1997) makes a number of suggestions for improving boys' attitudes to reading, suggesting it could be given a higher profile in school with male reading being rewarded more than is currently the case. Local football clubs, policemen and others can promote reading and 'male members of families should be specifically targeted in school initiatives to promote book buying and an interest in reading' (ibid.: 169). Readathons, marathon reading events where children are sponsored to read books for a good cause, can be great fun as time is made for extended, sustained reading of whole books.

A boy-friendly English curriculum?

Millard suggests there is an 'over-emphasis on narrative, particularly fictional narrative' which could be revised so that more 'boy-friendly' reading is promoted (1997: 166–7). As we have seen (from Chapter 5) the National Literacy Strategy at Key Stage 3 has brought about a greater emphasis on non-fiction and the long-term effects of this on boys' attainment remain to be seen. Millard also suggests that 'more of the range of books that capture boys' narrative attention' should be read (ibid.: 169) and advocates 'an introduction of material that has direct relevance to children's interests and which build on real, rather than imposed, textual pleasures' (ibid.: 173). Millard also suggests that we should cater for boys' tastes far more by 'changing the balance of texts selected for class or group work to include action and humour' (ibid.: 174). We must, of course, recognize that relevance is not necessarily synonymous with contemporary culture and that, approached in an appropriate way, some pre-twentieth-century texts (see Chapter 11) can be more relevant than contemporary ones. The ways we teach and how we select texts certainly need careful consideration if many boys are to be motivated.

Gender stereotyping and the individual

Myhill, however, argues that Millard's book is founded upon 'a premise that boys and girls are literate in different ways, a premise which obscures and glosses over the ways in which we are all differently literate' from each other and argues that there is a pressing need to recognize that 'girls and boys are not two discrete and homogeneous groups' (Myhill, 1999a: 238). After surveying a hundred teachers Myhill observed that their 'responses suggest that the cause of male underachievement in English does not rest in the curriculum, or with teachers, and is not genetic in origin' and there is 'significant agreement amongst English teachers that the root of the gap between boys' and girls' achievement in English' can be attributed to 'the poor motivation of boys' (ibid.: 230). Myhill argues that the improvement in girls' performance in maths and science in the 1980s was due to a positive construction of female capability which involved the dismantling of negative female stereotypes whereas with the issue of boys and English today the reverse is true as we have a stereotype of boys as reluctant, difficult and disinterested. Indeed, a discourse encompassing 'a biological explanation' risks 'naturalising boys' literacy "underachievement" by framing it as a biological imperative' (Barwood, 2001: 71).

Blaming the text or suggesting the English curriculum is somehow 'feminine' and not 'boy-friendly' can simply exacerbate the problem as it provides an excuse for underperformance and legitimizes underachievement on gender grounds and condones failure. Instead of providing excuses we should promote the importance of individual responsibility. It is also problematic to suggest that an English curriculum focusing on 'feelings and character' or 'relationships and feelings' (Millard, 1997: 176) is somehow inappropriate for boys and a contributory cause of their failure because boys (as well as girls) need to understand relationships. To suggest than an interest in human feelings is somehow inappropriate for adolescent males can perpetuate the stereotyping which has contributed to, or even created, the problem in the first place. If we expect boys to be a problem they will be; what we have faith for and believe in becomes our reality.

My own research into disaffected boys' reading of poetry suggests that when the 'personal reading styles of pupils are allowed to flourish' (Pike, 2000d: 41) significant gains in attainment can be achieved. Boys who showed antipathy to poetry initially became keen when they were required to be problem-solvers and active constructors of meaning rather than passive recipients. Evidently, a 'premium should be placed on active reading' and 'the generation of ideas and alternative hypotheses' (ibid.: 52). We also need to be realistic and understand that 'boys respond with greater perception and emotional openness in some situations than others' and that everything from 'private journals to public debate' should be employed (ibid.). The emphasis on text as 'stimulus' (Rosenblatt, 1985) where memories and experiences of life as well as literature are brought to the reading event is so valuable because it 'enables boys to bypass empathy while bringing their own experiences to the literary work' (Pike, 2000d: 52). Providing a progressive challenge so that boys do not become bored is also essential. Skilful teaching that is not based on undifferentiated assumptions about 'what boys need' ensures we avoid 'the futility of a curricular approach which attempts to minimise the deeper differences between learners' (Daly, 2000b: 31). The teacher and the strategies he or she employs can have a dramatic impact on boys' performance.

Ethnicity and the individual

It is appropriate that issues of gender and ethnicity are explored together in one chapter because narrow stereotyping on the basis of either detracts attention from the individual. It is especially important, as teachers of English, that we do not fall into the trap of assuming we can understand a learner on the basis of his or her membership of an ethnic group as there is 'far more diversity within each so-called group than between groups' (Naidoo, 1995: 7). An anthropologist who had lived with a remote tribe in Africa explained to me recently that he had realized, after spending some time with the tribe, that he actually had more in common (in terms of personality, disposition, outlook, sense of humour and so on) with a member of the tribe, who became his friend, than with his own brother back in England. In the politically charged debate surrounding multicultural education we must never lose sight of the individual.

While privileging personal response and individuality, it is also undeniable that English is a peculiarly social and cultural activity. We should, therefore, be aware of the contrast between 'different ethnic groups with culturally different expectations of schooling' (Glenn, 2000: 9) and teachers of English should learn about the different cultures represented in the school community within which they teach. A key theme in this book is that English teaching is an ethical activity and has social obligations and responsibilities to fulfil. Both language and literature need to be taught in ways that honour the rich complexities of our ethnically diverse classrooms. Consequently, we need to teach literature that: (1) comes from different cultures; (2) is about multicultural Britain; and (3) deals with racism. We need also to teach language so that children's bilingualism is supported and is a distinct advantage rather than a disadvantage.

Bilingualism

Bilingual children do not necessarily learn in any peculiar way compared to other children, they just learn in two languages and 'learning through two languages is intellectually challenging and broadens a child's horizons' (Glenn, 2000:. 17). As I happen to live in a bilingual home and my wife and I are attempting to bring up bilingual children I am acutely aware of the power of the dominant language and the effort it takes to ensure that the language which is not culturally dominant does not become marginalized or even extinct. Yet, there are not only cultural reasons for supporting bilingualism; there is research evidence to suggest that thinking skills may be enhanced if a child is bilingual.

The challenge for English teachers is how to help bilingual children, who are not proficient in English, to improve in this language while valuing the literature and language of their home culture. As English teachers we need to be able to answer Sujata Bhatt's question from 'Search for my Tongue':

> I ask you what would you do,
> if you had two tongues in your mouth,
> and lost the first one, the mother tongue,
> and could not really know the other,
> the foreign tongue'

Important lessons can be learnt from Joanna Eade's report (1997) of her work on improving the English of bilingual learners at a multilingual and multi-racial school in London. Eade alerts us to the fact that although a reader needs a knowledge of the sound system of English, a phonics approach often poses a problem. Whereas a competent English speaker can tell if something sounds right a bilingual learner cannot always tell. If children cannot distinguish between pairs of English sounds (such as *s* and *sh* or *ee*) and 'do not make such distinctions in their speech' they are also 'unlikely to hear them when the teacher tries to drill them' (ibid.: 34).

A context for language work is so important because 'formal English exercises which take language out of context' have the tendency to 'make little sense to bilingual children' (ibid.). As context clues can help children's word attack skills to improve bilingual learners need texts with the 'best possible cues' such as those which have a 'strong sense of pattern and rhythm' (ibid.) which presents English teachers, in particular, with a significant opportunity. Group discussion is also vital because children gain confidence from listening to each other, and being asked to write without prior discussion is 'particularly daunting for bilingual children' who need 'an opportunity to rehearse orally what they want to write, to test the language out' (ibid.: 39). Here again context is important.

As an English teacher, it is also necessary to conduct an audit of a bilingual child's current language skills. If the child has a learning support assistant, who may be a member of the child's home community, it is essential to liaise effectively with him or her. You need to communicate well with this adult about the aims and objectives of your lesson; your resources should be passed on in advance and, ideally, the literacy requirements of the lesson should be made explicit so this adult is fully involved and can be as helpful as possible to the child. Clearly, there is a pressing need to differentiate according to the bilingual learner's current level of attainment and linguistic competence.

Multicultural literature and reading against racism

The *National Curriculum for England: English* (DfEE/QCA, 1999) clearly stipulates that children in the 11–16 age range should read texts from different cultures and traditions and should understand their 'values and assumptions', 'subject matter and language', 'distinctive qualities', 'familiar themes' and learn to 'make connections and comparisons between texts from different cultures' (ibid.: 34). Children should read 'drama, fiction and poetry by major writers from different cultures and traditions' (ibid: 36) and examples of such writers include, to name just a few, Wole Soyinka, Athol Fugard, Chinua Achebe (see Chapter 12 for examples of work at GCSE with this poet), Maya Angelou, Ngũgĩ wa Thiong'o, Brathwaite and Derek Walcott.

Many GCSE anthologies now include a section on literature from a range of different cultures. The AQA *Anthology* (2002a), for instance, has a section of 'Poems from different cultures' which includes 'Blessing' by Imtiaz Dharker, 'Half-caste' by John Agard, 'Presents from my Aunts in Pakistan' by Moniza Alvi, 'Hurricane Hits England' by Grace Nichols and 'Nothing's Changed' by Tatamkhulu Afrika. Although this ensures children now read literature from different cultures, which extends children's experience in important ways and can help them reflect on their own culture, it has been argued that to 'allocate so called "multicultural literature" a separate place on a curriculum chiefly dedicated to "our literature" is to marginalize it' (Naidoo, 1994: 42). It would also appear that such literature is relatively rare in undergraduate degrees because many PGCE students still feel daunted by the prospect of having to teach literature they are unfamiliar with from cultures they know little about. Filling such gaps in one's subject knowledge can, however, be easily undertaken prior to a PGCE course and the study guides that come with GCSE anthologies provide some helpful background information about these texts.

English departments can organize visits from writers to promote multicultural reading and talk about their work. Beverley Naidoo's visit to the school where I was Head of English to conduct writing workshops based on novels such as *Journey to Jo'burg* was important for all children. When children from ethnic minorities read literature about children who are also from ethnic minorities they often identify with them and such reading is also healthy for students who do not belong to ethnic minorities because they can develop empathy for characters and understand their lives and the challenges they face. Naidoo notes that the 'vast majority of the responses I receive suggest that readers – black and white – have at least experienced some form of empathy with my characters' (1995: 11).

Naidoo suggests that Rosenblatt's transactional model can provide the framework for understanding multicultural reading because it acknowledges 'both writer and reader and their social contexts in the production and reproduction of texts' (ibid.: 7) as Rosenblatt sees the reader and the writer bringing to the literary work 'past experiences in literature and in life' (1985: 35). This model informs my own notion of 'responsive teaching' (see Chapter 1) and provides a focus on the individual's response which is so important when reading cross-culturally. Ensuring attention is paid to the individual rather than the group, which literature can facilitate, is also a key element in understanding and combating racism, and *Reading against Racism* (Evans, 1992) shows how literature education can be part of an overall anti-racist strategy.

English teachers and researchers of English teaching will also be particularly interested in the approach termed 'narrative multiculturalism' of Joann Phillion (2002a; 2002b) recently published in the *Journal of Curriculum Studies*. Just as the immersion of the reader in a story has been shown to be of value in the professional development of teachers (see Chapter 4) a narrative approach can also be a means of yielding understandings about multicultural teaching. Phillion describes her 'narrative approach to understanding multicultural teaching and learning' as 'understanding derived from a starting point in experience' which 'involves passionate, intensive, up-close participation rather than distanced objectivity' and depends upon 'close relationships with participants' who are from 'different cultural, ethnic and language backgrounds' (2002b: 536). Phillion's articles 'document successful strategies in working with immigrant and minority students' (2002b: 535). While Naidoo defines the 'coastline' of literature and suggests geographical boundaries only limit our common global literary heritage, Phillion's narrative multiculturalism is 'a way to think, do research and represent understanding' which is located 'in an intellectual landscape between theory and practice' (2002a: 300).

English and special educational needs

As a teacher of English you may have in your class children who have dyspraxia, dyslexia, ADHD (attention deficit hyperactivity disorder) or a whole host of other special educational needs. Nearly all these needs will have specific implications for the teaching of language and literature and you will need to differentiate accordingly. It is essential that you are fully aware of the special needs of individual children in your care and you need to find out about the precise nature of these needs. Liaison with the special needs department is essential and you should go to talk to the special needs teachers during a free lesson, a break or after school. Normally you will be given helpful summaries about particular needs and strategies for teaching children with them. It is especially important that you do not forget to liaise with learning support assistants who work with children in your lessons as you need to discuss in advance with them the challenge your lessons may present to the children they help (see Chapter 2). Just because a child has adult help does not mean that you are not primarily responsible for the child's learning as you (and not the adult assistant) are his or her English teacher.

Inclusion and IEPs

Every English teacher should differentiate and must read and refer to 'Inclusion: providing effective learning opportunities for all pupils', the detailed inclusion statement at the end of the programmes of study and before the level descriptors at the back of *The National Curriculum for England: English* (DfEE/QCA, 1999: 42–50). Teachers should plan with 'barriers to learning' in mind and should provide an 'appropriate challenge'. However, over and above planning for this routine differentiation some children have needs that are 'additional to' and 'different from' those a teacher might ordinarily differentiate for. These children will either be the focus of 'school action', 'school action plus' or will have a 'statement of special educational need'. If you are preparing to teach, *Introducing Special Needs – a Companion Guide for Student Teachers* by Garner and Davies (2001) will also be especially useful. Children who are covered by 'school action', 'school action plus' or a 'statement' have an IEP. An IEP is an Individual Education Plan that has a maximum of three or four targets on it. Normally at least one of these targets will be specific to a child's literacy although there may well be social targets as well that, as an English teacher, you need to be aware of. You need to plan lessons with children's IEPs on the desk next to you. If there are thirty children in a class and two of them have IEPs your planning for English lessons must take account of the agreed targets of these two children, especially those related to literacy.

Literature about special needs

English literature can be especially beneficial for understanding children with special needs. Reading literature that portrays characters with special needs is especially important and there are a number of excellent books that provide positive images of children or young people with special needs. English teachers may like to read the children's books shortlisted for the tenth Special Educational Needs Book Awards in 2002:

- *Ghost Writer* by Julia Jarman (Anderson).
- *Lisa and the Lacemaker* by Kathy Hoopman (Jessica Kingsley).
- *Running on Empty* by Anna Patterson (Lucky Duck).
- *Return of the Mad Mangler* by Susan Gates (Puffin Books).
- *Falling for Joshua* by Brian Keaney (The Watts Group).

Adapting texts: participation, simplification and enrichment

All teachers of English would appreciate *Literature for All* (Grove, 1998) as it contains numerous suggestions for using images, group writing, games (such as a *Pilgrim's Progress* board game), narratives and creative writing with children who have a wide range of special needs. Nicola Grove describes specific ways of adapting literary texts for students with special educational needs within English lessons and argues that doing so is not just about improving literacy skills but, more importantly, addresses the need to provide children with an experience of literature. Grove suggests that when we are working with students who have difficulties with language and learning we can compensate for the child's difficulties by simplifying and enriching experience.

Our guiding principle should be 'partial participation' which 'can enable students to experience something of the essence of a text, even if they cannot grasp everything' because access to literature does not always depend on access to literacy as students who 'cannot decode meaning' may often be able to 'apprehend meaning through repeated associations and inference' (Grove, 1998: 20). Consequently, enrichment offers more than simplification can. Whereas simplification 'involves providing input at a level appropriate to the child's ability to decode language, simplifying or explaining vocabulary' it is clear that 'this approach will be inadequate if we want to provide children with real experiences of literature' (ibid.: 26). Grove gives an example of a speech from *Macbeth* and notes that the passage is 'fraught with difficulty' if you try to simplify it. English teachers will be aware of how well active approaches (see Chapter 11 and Chapter 5) can work across the ability range.

Instead of working at the literal level and decoding into a simpler version, Grove suggests we must consider subtext, context and allusions and 'translate these into sensory associations which can illustrate and embody the feeling in which the text is grounded'; we can use sound, rhythm and 'whole phrases, which function as "scripts" associated with particular events' (ibid.). Grove's suggestions are principled, ethically justifiable and grounded in a belief that the personal responses of children with special needs should be fostered as literature is an art for everyone.

■ Further reading

English and gender

Millard, E. (1997) *Differently Literate*. London: Falmer Press
Myhill, D. (1999) 'Bottom set boys: a deficit model of male achievement', *The Use of English*, 50(3), 228–40.
Pike, M.A. (2000) 'Boys, poetry and the individual talent', *English in Education*, 34(3): 41–55.
QCA (1998) *Can Do Better: Raising Boys' Achievement in English*. London: HMSO.

English and ethnicity

Eade, J. (1997) 'Using a core text with bilingual children', *English in Education*, 31(3): 32–9.
Evans, E. (ed.) (1992) *Reading against Racism*. Buckingham and Philadelphia, PA: Open University Press.
Glenn, C. (2000) 'Rethinking bilingual education', in R.P. Porter (ed.) *Educating Language Minority Children*. New Brunswick, NJ, and London: Transaction Publishers.
Naidoo, B. (1995) 'Crossing boundaries through fiction: a personal account', *English in Education*, 29(1): 4–13.
Phillion, J. (2002) 'Becoming a narrative inquirer in a multicultural landscape', *Journal of Curriculum Studies*, 84(5): 535–56.

English and special needs

Garner, P. and Davies, J. (2001) *Introducing Special Needs – a Companion Guide for Student Teachers*. London: David Fulton.
Grove, N. (1998) *Literature for All – Developing Literature in the Curriculum for Pupils with Special Educational Needs*. London: David Fulton.

10

Firing the canon

The challenge of the canon

The *National Curriculum for England: English* (DfEE/QCA, 1999) specifies the writers that are included in a canon for secondary English. Between the ages of 11 and 16, children are required to study texts by authors included in a prescribed list. They must study *two major prose writers published before 1914* (from Jane Austen, Charlotte Bronte, Emily Bronte, John Bunyan, Wilkie Collins, Joseph Conrad, Daniel Defoe, Charles Dickens, Arthur Conan Doyle, George Eliot, Henry Fielding, Elizabeth Gaskell, Thomas Hardy, Henry James, Mary Shelley, Robert Louis Stephenson, Jonathan Swift, Anthony Trollope and H.G. Wells) and works by *four major poets published before 1914* (from Matthew Arnold, Elizabeth Barrett Browning, William Blake, Emily Bronte, Robert Browning, Robert Burns, Lord Byron, Geoffrey Chaucer, John Clare, Samuel Taylor Coleridge, John Donne, John Dryden, Thomas Gray, George Herbert, Robert Herrick, Gerald Manley Hopkins, John Keats, Andrew Marvell, John Milton, Alexander Pope, Christina Rosetti, William Shakespeare (sonnets), Percy Bysshe Shelley, Edmund Spencer, Alfred Lord Tennyson, Henry Vaughan, William Wordsworth and Sir Thomas Wyatt). Across Key Stage 3 (11–14) and Key Stage 4 (14–16), children should also read *two plays by Shakespeare* (one at each key stage) and 'should be taught' both 'how and why texts have been influential and significant' (ibid.: 34, 2a) as well as 'the appeal and importance of these texts over time' (ibid.: 34, 2c) and also 'the characteristics of texts that are considered to be of high quality' (ibid.: 34, 2b). The three examples of such texts given are the Greek myths, the King James Authorized Version of the Bible and the Arthurian legends (ibid.: 34).

Such lists can appear daunting to the new and experienced teacher alike. The very thought of one's most difficult class (who struggle to comprehend simple and straightforward contemporary texts) reading the classics can simply beggar belief. The challenge such writers pose to pupils should not be underestimated. Canonical authors inhabited a very different world from our own and to read them is to read diachronically, across time. There are a number of challenges to meet as the 'genres and styles' of important pre-twentieth-century poets 'tend to be different from those that are popular today' and the 'allusions [to classical mythology and Christian theology] have little resonance for most of our students' (Protherough, 1986: 125). It has even been suggested that readers today are at a serious disadvantage when they attempt to read the works of writers from the great tradition because according to Delaney (1972), the experiences of these writers (fearing Hell, observing nature closely, dying of love, dying of consumption, dying of the pox, going to church and going to prostitutes) are so alien to the experiences of the modern reader. Yet, it is not only unnecessary but also harmful (to their reading as well as their health) for today's readers to have had precisely the same experiences as the canonical writers they study. Experience is, however, the key to enabling children to enjoy and appreciate canonical works and to perceive the relevance of such texts to their own lives. Reading classic works can even fulfil the aims of the 'personal growth' model of English. At the start of a chapter like this one it is helpful to provide a series of snapshots to show how children can have fun with the canon through active approaches and responsive teaching.

Firing the canon

The following are some of the ways the canon can be 'fired':

- Year 7 are giving a loud clap every time the word 'what' occurs in Blake's 'Tiger' to signify the chink of the hammer on the anvil in the blacksmith's forge – they compare the colours of the fire in the forge to the markings on the tiger and learn about the juxtaposition of the fire and the night.
- Another Year 7 group are performing extracts they have selected from Tennyson's 'Charge of the Light Brigade' in groups of four. Later on they discuss the effect of the rhythm in the poem. This is related to a history project they are doing on the Crimean War.
- Year 8 are stomping around their classroom reciting 'they banged the drum, they turned the dusty drill' from Oscar Wilde's 'The Ballad of Reading Gaol'. Every now and then the teacher stops them and sends them off to find, highlight and circle rhymes, personification, alliteration, imagery and so on.
- Another Year 8 group are finishing off their sketches based on 'How are the Mighty Fallen' from the Authorized Version of the Bible. Each sketch

is divided into light and dark and words related to goodness, health and power are justaposed with those associated in the text with death and destruction.

■ Another Year 8 group are designing a cartoon strip based on 'The Rime of the Ancient Mariner' by Coleridge so they can explore the structure of the poem.

■ Year 9 have just played a literary version of *Who Wants to be a Millionaire* to revise plot, character and theme in *Silas Marner*. Last lesson they thought about how they would spend their fortune if they won the lottery. After the game show they focus on Marner's gold and the theme of what brings happiness.

■ Another Year 9 group are working in the school's learning resources centre in groups of four at computers. They are doing research on selected scenes for their Key Stage 3 test. Some are using CD-ROMs and others are using the Internet with a worksheet that specifies helpful sites.

■ Year 10 are writing one side of a telephone conversation based on the dramatic monologues of Robert Browning's 'Porphyria's Lover' and 'My Last Duchess'. Gender, voice and power relations are being explored as a result of thought tracking the character of the Count in the second monologue.

■ Another Year 10 group are designing adverts for Farfrae and Henchard's respective business enterprises based on *The Mayor of Casterbridge*, which they have watched the film of. They have already designed the front page of the *Casterbridge Chronicle* with a lead story about a trade war.

■ Year 11 are writing their own satires for GCSE coursework based on Swift's *A Modest Proposal*. Some outrageous ideas are being described and everyone knows that satire ridicules vice and folly as a result of watching a popular contemporary television satire. They are setting the world to rights.

■ Another Year 11 group have just finished reading Jane Austen's *Northanger Abbey* and are talking about gothic horror. They already have a plan to help them write their own short piece of gothic horror for GCSE coursework.

■ A Year 12 group have been looking at personification in Donne's 'Death be not Proud' (their set author for AS English literature) and have written their own poems to go with images of the hooded Grim Reaper. They are discussing whether Donne is sincere or is just displaying his wit.

■ Year 13 are exploring the character of Satan in Book IX of 'Paradise Lost' with the book of Revelation as a source. They are also learning about Milton's political views on law, order and rebellion in society.

The relevance of the canon

The examples above may be reassuring for the teacher with reservations about how canonical works can be successfully taught. Studying pre-twentieth-century texts with a difficult class might not appear to be as suicidal as at first thought. Many effective approaches to teaching classic authors have been developed (Atkinson, 1995) and there are a number of tried, tested and exciting ways of teaching texts from other times. Before describing such approaches and examining *how* to teach pre-twentieth-century texts it is important to consider *why* we should teach such texts in the first place.

Such a question is important because many have argued for a more diverse and multicultural canon in the belief that the dominance of classical writers perpetuates social and cultural injustice (Blackledge, 1994; Richardson, 1998). Ethnocentric and gender considerations result in calls for a more inclusive and culturally representative canon that reflects the diverse identities and cultural backgrounds of readers. Yet, arguments such as these betray a fundamental misunderstanding of the way adolescent readers read literary works. Paradoxically, it is the very *difference* (be it social, cultural, ethnic, religious, moral or linguistic) between the world of the text and that of the reader which can provide a justification for pre-twentieth-century works being part of the curriculum for ethnically and socially heterogeneous schools in the twenty-first century.

It is entirely misguided to assume that only texts written in the late twentieth or early twenty-first century can be relevant to today's adolescents as Blake and Donne 'can have a good deal more relevance to life today than contemporary poems which foreground the ephemeral preoccupations of the present' (Benton and Benton, 1998: vii). Further, reading can result in a 'change of horizons' through the 'negation of familiar experiences' and by 'raising newly articulated experiences to the level of consciousness' (Jauss, 1982: 25). Works that force no 'horizonal' change are merely for entertainment (rather than education) because 'no turn toward the horizon of yet unknown experience' (ibid.) is demanded. If the reading diet in school becomes restricted to immediately accessible texts with predictable subject matter (Fleming, 1996: 39), as works are misguidedly chosen that are 'relevant' to pupils' concerns, there may be little possibility of 'horizonal' change.

A literary text, by definition, 'diverges from the ordinary experience of the reader in that it offers views and opens up perspectives in which the empirically known world of one's own personal experience appears changed' (Iser, 1971: 7). The literary work does not reside entirely with the reader's own experiences for then it would not be indeterminate and would not have gaps in it that readers can use their imaginations to fill. The indeterminacy of literary texts means they are resistant to the course of time 'because their structure allows the reader to place himself in the world of fiction' (ibid.: 29). The literary text created in the past can be experienced and recreated in the present for 'one of the chief values of literature is that by its very indeterminacy it is able to transcend the restrictions of time and the written word and to give people of all ages and backgrounds the chance to enter other worlds' (ibid.: 30).

Although the relevance of pre-twentieth-century literature to the lives of young people growing up in a multicultural society is often considered to be limited (Grimes and Belote, 1994), relevance is not dependent upon writer and reader residing within the same culture or having a similar background because 'we recognize in literature so many elements that play a part in our own experience' although, significantly, 'they are simply put together in a different way – in other words, they constitute a familiar world reproduced in an unfamiliar form, (Iser, 1971: 7).

The nature of a literary text is especially pertinent when some of the objections to classic literature being read in schools are considered. It has been argued that pre-twentieth-century literature (Gabler and Gabler, 1982; Davis, 1992) can perpetuate anachronistic values and prejudice in the hands of governments wishing to engineer a certain sort of social cohesion. Yet, it is the very difference between today's experience and the world portrayed in such texts that can result in the work 'outlasting its historical genesis' (Iser, 1971: 29). A text's indeterminacy requires a reader to bring personal experience, cultural background, imagination, predisposition and even idiosyncratic knowledge with him or her so that a co-construction of meaning with its author is achieved.

In our decisions about how learning should occur we need to ensure that 'the reading of literature becomes a collaborative venture in the re-making of meaning through personal, and shared, responses to a text' (Webb, 1992: 101). In this way, students' horizons are broadened by the study of canonical texts because any cultural difference between readers and between readers and texts can become a resource for aesthetic reading that broadens horizons. Studying pre-twentieth-century texts can provide readers with valuable experiences that cannot be gained from later works. The justification for pre-twentieth-century literature in today's classrooms lies in its power to enable twenty-first-century readers to understand themselves in the present and to play an important role in the future.

The emphasis on teaching literature from the past in schools with children who have diverse backgrounds is justified when teachers use such literature to 'address the needs and realities of the world our young people actually inhabit' (Davies, 1996: 9). When such an approach is adopted, active and exploratory reading of pre-twentieth-century texts provides opportunities for pupils to explore themselves as readers and to consider human experience in other times (and other places if they live outside the UK). With appropriate pedagogy such works can 'take on meaning in relation to the very different ideological conditions of contemporary life' (Easthope, 1991: 57). In this way, the diachronic transaction can be potentially richer, in certain respects, than a synchronic one. It is worth reminding ourselves of the purpose of studying literature:

The fundamental aim of such an area of study is to help readers discover what texts are trying to reveal, in a spirit of good faith. This form of study aims to give young people access to what different generations and cultures are trying to tell each other about their lives; it aims to give them access to the excitement or amazement of hearing such things, and thus to enlarge the scope of their lives (Davies, 1996: 141).

It is important to consider how, in such a spirit of good faith, teachers can help readers discover the literature of other generations. How readers, saturated in early twenty-first-century culture, can derive pleasure from texts that are reproduced trans-historically requires skilled teaching.

The practicalities of teaching texts from other times

Several questions should be asked when planning work with texts from other times: How should the text be introduced? How can personal response be fostered? How will young readers be empowered to perceive the relevance of this text to their lives? How will background information be conveyed? How will the difficulties of language be overcome? How will unfamiliar vocabulary be dealt with? These questions will be answered under three headings: 'Pre-reading', 'Mid-reading' and 'Post-reading'.

Pre-reading

Theme, character, setting, situation, period, genre and style can all be introduced before reading the text. For example, in order to demonstrate the relevance of the text children can read contemporary newspaper accounts and stories or watch extracts from films and documentaries on the same theme as the text to be studied: lottery-winning millionaires and fortunes gained and lost before reading about the miser's gold in *Silas Marner*; voyages around the world and shipwrecks before 'The Rime of the Ancient Mariner' and *Gulliver's Travels*; accounts of life in prison on Death Row in the USA before 'The Ballad of Reading Gaol'; descriptions of battles and extracts from war films before the biblical 'How are the Mighty Fallen'; accounts of cloning and genetic engineering before Mary Shelley's *Frankenstein*.

Creative writing can also be undertaken on the theme to be explored in the text; for instance, children's own depictions of a battle normally provide a contrast to 'How are the Mighty Fallen'. Familiarizing children with contemporary television satire before reading Swift's *A Modest Proposal* can prepare them for the classic text and also arouse their curiosity. Telling a gripping story before reading is always a good way to begin. If the text to be read was 'The Ballad of Reading Gaol', the story of CTW (Charles Thomas

Wooldridge), to whom the poem is dedicated, can ensure young readers, who have empathized with the character, are desperate to read the poem to find out what happened to him after he committed the murder that resulted in his time in Reading Gaol.

Many pre-twentieth-century works are not as short as those referred to above and 'cutting the classics' is essential before reading many texts. Contemporary novels written specifically for children and teenagers do not need the sort of modification required by many pre-twentieth-century works. Victorian novels, for instance, are generally quite long and it is impossible to teach *Little Dorrit* in quite the same way that one teaches *Roll of Thunder, Hear my Cry*. The constraints of time and the need to sustain children's motivation mean that this must be done skilfully. A selection process is required where the teacher chooses key passages. These can be:

- those where decisive developments occur which cannot easily be missed out;
- passages you have selected for further study and discussion after reading;
- those chosen for reading aloud as they lend themselves to such activity.

These key passages form the core of the text that will be shared in the classroom. As they are reading texts during the school holidays, teachers often mark passages for special attention and select others for cutting. Having a teacher's copy of a text like this is an invaluable tool for teaching. The parts of the text, usually a novel, that are missed out need to be familiar to pupils somehow so either the teacher can summarize the events and developments in these passages or children can read on their own. Although you can read all of *Animal Farm*, *Z for Zachariah* or *Flowers for Algernon* fairly rapidly as a class these texts can also benefit from such treatment. Even short novels such as *Silas Marner* can be cut to good effect so that you focus on the arrival of Eppie, Silas counting his gold, Dunsey's death or Eppie's decision to stay with Silas at the end.

The passages that will not be read as a whole class benefit from differentiation strategies especially if they are set for homework and there are a range of abilities within the class. Atkinson suggests 'for those who would find unaided reading difficult, activities to consolidate work on the novel so far, for example a contribution to a time-line wall chart or to a class comic-strip version of the book' is appropriate whereas 'for those able or keen to read on, a task to report back in some way to the rest of the class about the intervening narrative' (1995: 58) is often best. When 'cutting the classics' it is important to calculate timing carefully as there is little worse than reaching the end of a term and only being half way through a book. Equally, taking too long with a text so that it drags and becomes tedious is to be avoided. The pace and momentum, especially with the key passages, have to be challenging.

Exactly the same approach can be taken with longer narrative poems such as 'The Rime of the Ancient Mariner'. With such poems there will be portions the teacher will want to read aloud to the class and many poems need to be heard as children appreciate listening to them. English teachers need to practise such passages and hear themselves read to ensure a polished performance. When reading aloud, especially during a first reading, it is wise not to stop to provide too much explanation as this can cause the overall impact of the passage to be lost. The reason for reading is to foster an appreciation of the effect of the language and to cultivate enjoyment. Explanation should, ideally, be reserved for the time before or after the reading. Children can be told that they do not have to understand every word and should focus on what they do understand rather than what they do not understand. Film versions of pre-twentieth-century texts can be used before starting a text to familiarize readers with period, setting and character. A recent study of how teachers taught Shakespeare revealed that 'nearly half said they used the video beforehand' (Stibbs, 1998: 245) although 'they were more likely to use video earlier rather than later with less able or younger pupils' (ibid.: 246).

Mid-reading

A very wide range of activities are possible to promote response to texts (Newbold and Stibbs, 1983) and many can be adapted for use with pre-twentieth-century texts. Many of the active approaches devised for use with Shakespeare by Rex Gibson can be adapted for use with pre-twentieth-century texts as can DARTs. Diagrams, pictures, illustrations, interviews with characters, hot-seating, narratives from different viewpoints and characters can all be used. Stories can be transformed into a variety of media (radio, web pages, home pages of a character, newspapers, films, production scripts of scenes and so on). Prediction exercises focusing on the next chapter, the next scene or the end of the text can be employed. Work on language can include activities to foster close textual analysis (taking words out, cloze, sequencing, reordering and so on). Class discussion about events, characters and themes as well as other speaking and listening activities such as hot-seating and thought- tracking can be used. Journals, commentaries and annotation can be used to help children to relate a text from another time to their own experience. Prediction, improvisation and short role plays (sometimes based on dialogue in a novel) can maintain motivation by providing active approaches during reading.

CD-ROMs of Shakespeare (Clarke, 1995) and other classic texts can help children acquire background information, learn details of social and cultural context and understand how variations in the text can prompt inquiry. Comparing and contrasting different productions is a great way to get children to think about the different possibilities for a whole play, a scene or even how you say a few lines. Although children are not leaping around the room shouting Shakespearean insults at each other when they are doing this and are sitting in front of computers, it does not have to be a solitary activity as often they work in threes. Working on a literary text, while sitting at a computer, can certainly prompt collaborative discussion.

Even viewing the film of the book should be active. Most of the teachers in Stibbs' research 'had pupils analyzing dramatic or filmic features' and required them to comment on 'settings, costumes, choreography, music or camera angles' (1998: 246) or on different openings to the same play. The conclusion reached was that 'these teachers were using video to explore dramatic staging (or filming) of the texts rather than to support treating the text as character study or poetry'; in other words, they were focusing on Shakespeare as a 'social and physical activity' (ibid.).

Post-reading

Some tasks can only be completed with a full knowledge of the text, including how it ends, although nearly all the above activities could work equally well after reading the whole text. Performing dialogues is superb for getting children into a text and experienced teachers often have an eye for what can be transformed into dialogue. Confrontation scenes always seem to be good as are those where there is a fairly rapid exchange. After reading a whole text students can produce a study guide for it, story board the final sequence (long-shot, close-shot, middle-shot, etc.), adapt parts of it for film, construct diagrams of plot and relationships between characters and draw tension graphs throughout the text. Writing inspired by the text can be undertaken and one text can be compared with another to foster skills of intertextuality. In my view, watching the whole film of the book is best left until the end of class reading. Watching a recording always gives children the opportunity to talk about the adaptation after their reading when different television or film versions can be compared. All the teachers in Stibbs' research 'used clips or whole plays or films in some way or another' (1998: 245) and all who taught Key Stage 3 used video with Shakespeare. Almost all these teachers used more than one version and sometimes three or four versions of the same play.

Top of the canon: the Bible versus Shakespeare

Some canonical texts are more influential than others and it is interesting to consider which classic texts have exerted the greatest influence on subsequent literature. Looking at the relative space allocated to different authors in the *Oxford Dictionary of Quotations* is revealing as it gives an indication of the cultural, linguistic and literary importance of various authors. Less than a page is given to Anthony Trollope, Henry James or Jane Austen whereas over fifty pages are devoted to the Bible and to Shakespeare. Some of the most quoted authors are Tennyson, Milton, Johnson, Browning, Kipling, Dickens, Byron, Wordsworth, Pope, Keats and Shelley. While there are around two *hundred* quotations from the leading prose-writer Charles Dickens, there are around two *thousand* quotations from each of the Bible and Shakespeare.

Shakespeare's works and the King James (Authorized) Version of the Bible are considered by scholars to be the most important and influential works in the English language and, remarkably, they were written at about the same time. Shakespeare was beginning work on *The Tempest*, his last play, when the Authorised Version was published in 1611. Whereas Shakespeare 'ransacked the lexicon' the King James Bible employs 'barely eight thousand words' and, consequently, the 'Shakespearean cornucopia and, the biblical iron rations represent, as it were, the North and South Poles of the language, reference points for writers and speakers throughout the world' (McCrum et al., 1986: 113).

While the study of Shakespeare is virtually universal in English lessons in secondary schools the Bible rarely makes an appearance on the English curriculum. There is a rich supply of material on how to teach Shakespeare but very little on how to use the Bible within English. Yet, as a literary work, many consider the Bible to be far more influential even than Shakespeare. It is 'probably the most important single source for all our literature' (Alter and Kermode, 1987: 2) and may well have inspired more poetry, music and works of art than any other single text. Certainly, no other book 'has left so strong a mark upon the mass of our literature' (Newbolt, 1921: 341) as the Bible is 'the most formative influence on Western literature' (Jasper, 1999: 12–13) and a 'major element in our own imaginative tradition' (Frye, 1982: xviii). While this may be so, the Bible is not, generally, part of the imaginative life of the English lesson which is where we are getting it wrong. The high status of great literary works can lead to a too reverential attitude among readers who can become passive as they feel they need to be told the text's meaning rather than construct their own interpretation of it (Pike, 2003e). The teaching of the Bible and other classic works should therefore focus on the potential of such texts for fostering the aesthetic, imaginative and creative lives of students (Pike, 2002b) and we should not exempt the Bible from the sort of treatment we give Shakespeare however irreverent some may find this.

A good example of a text that works well at Key Stage 3 is David's lament for Saul and Jonathan in 2 Samuel 1: 17–27 found in *Poems from other Ages* (Merrick and Fox, 1993: 26):

And David lamented with this lamentation over Saul and over Jonathan his son:

The beauty of Israel is slain upon thy high places: how are the mighty fallen!
Tell it not in Gath, publish it not in the streets of Askelon lest the daughters
of the Philistines rejoice, lest the daughters of the uncircumcised triumph.
Ye mountains of Gilboa, let there be no dew, neither let there be rain, upon
you, nor fields of offerings: for there the shield of the mighty is vilely cast
away, the shield of Saul, as though he had not been anointed with oil.
From the blood of the slain, from the fat of the mighty, the bow of Jonathan
turned not back, and the sword of Saul returned not empty.

Saul and Jonathan were lovely and pleasant in their lives, and in their death
they were not divided, they were swifter than eagles, they were stronger than
lions.

Ye daughters of Israel, weep over Saul, who clothed you in scarlet, with
other delights, who put ornaments of gold upon your apparel.

How are the mighty fallen in the midst of battle. O Jonathan thou wast slain
in thy high places.

I am distressed for thee, my brother Jonathan: very pleasant hast thou been
unto me: thy love to me was wonderful, passing the love of women.

How are the mighty fallen, and the weapons of war perished!

Children can write their own descriptions of a battle before coming to this
passage and can then have their attention drawn to the way the power of
this passage does not rely on graphic depiction. Eventually, children who are
used to media images of violence are surprised when they recognize the dignity of this passage where the exploits of Saul and Jonathan in battle are not
depicted with words like 'hack', 'maim', 'slice' or 'stab' but where fighting is
described in terms of harvest or of reaping where 'the sword of Saul returned
not empty' and the 'bow of Jonathan turned not back'. One initial approach
is for children to divide a page and to pick out words on one side under the
heading 'Death, suffering and loss' (e.g. 'fallen', 'vilely', 'cast away', 'slain',
'perished') and on the other side under the heading 'Life, happiness and
strength' ('delights', 'mighty', 'pleasant', 'wonderful', 'triumph', 'rejoice').
Such an activity helps children to engage with the language and is also fun;
they can then illustrate the two sides of their page to demonstrate the contrast and juxtaposition in the piece.

After focusing on the repetition of 'how are the mighty fallen!' teachers
can draw their students' attention to the imperatives 'Tell it not' and 'publish
it not' and can discuss the merits of 'Tell it not' over 'Do not tell it', 'Do not
mention it' or 'Don't talk about it'. The writer's wish for barrenness and deso-
lation (no dew, no rain, etc.) at the scene of death is an opportunity to
discuss the important relationship between setting and mood in literature.
The use of hyperbole in the description of Saul and Jonathan as 'swifter than
eagles' and 'stronger than lions' can be studied and children can have a go at

making up their own. At the same time the appropriateness of such language for this context can be considered. The power of the repetition 'How are the mighty fallen' and 'thy high places' can also be discussed before children write their own laments. The repetition of 'mighty' and the use of the adverb 'vilely' to describe death can stimulate further discussion. When they think of the vocabulary they should use children are often struck by the use of 'pleasant' and 'distressed' and wonder why stronger vocabulary was not chosen. This is, of course, an opportunity for students to discover that words invariably lose power over time and that while 'pleasant' indicates mild appreciation or enjoyment today it represented stronger feelings in 1611.

David's lament is only one of many passages that can be approached using active approaches and DARTs. We should never be reluctant to cut, paste and sequence or to use such passages as a stimulus for imaginative and creative writing. Active approaches can be used with the Bible as well as with Shakespeare and we must not allow ourselves to be robbed of a great literary work and resource in English lessons simply because it is the subject of strongly held religious beliefs. The Bible is a rich source of literary material for the English lesson. Take, for instance, St Paul's depiction of love as charity in 1 Corinthians 13:

> Though I speak with the tongues of men and angels,
> And have not charity, I am become as sounding brass,
> Or a tinkling cymbal.
> And though I have the gift of prophecy, and understand
> All mysteries, and all knowledge; and though I have all faith,
> So that I could remove mountains, and have not charity,
> I am nothing.
> And though I bestow all my goods to feed the poor,
> And though I give my body to be burned, and have not charity,
> It profiteth me nothing.
>
> Charity suffereth long and is kind, charity envieth not;
> Charity vaunteth not itself, is not puffed up,
> Doth not behave itself unseemly, seeketh not her own,
> Is not easily provoked, thinketh no evil;
> Rejoiceth not in iniquity, but rejoiceth in the truth;
> Beareth all things, believeth all things,
> Hopeth all things, endureth all things,
> Charity never faileth.

I have an abiding memory of reading this passage as a schoolboy at a school service to a packed Salisbury Cathedral but it is not for that reason it is included here. This text (and the rest of it) offers the imaginative English teacher a host of opportunities. Another passage of similarly remarkable quality can be found in Isaiah 53:

> Surely he hath borne our griefs, and carried our sorrows:
> Yet we did esteem him stricken of God, and afflicted.
> But he was wounded for our transgressions,
> He was bruised for our iniquities:
> The chastisement of our peace was upon him:
> And with his stripes we are healed.
> All we like sheep have gone astray;
> We have turned every one to his own way;
> And the Lord hath laid on him the iniquity of us all.

Many other extracts hold similarly rich literary and linguistic possibilities. All should, of course, be read in the quite unsurpassable Authorized King James Version of 1611 (DfEE/QCA, 1999: 34). Among many of such passages are 'The Lord is my Shepherd' (Psalm 23), 'By the Rivers of Babylon' (Psalm 137), 'To Everything there is a Season' (Ecclesiastes 3: 1–8), 'War in Heaven' (Revelation 12: 7–11), 'The Mark of the Beast' (Revelation 14: 9–11), 'Take no Thought for your Life' (Luke 12: 22–8) and 'Every Valley shall be Exalted' (Isaiah 40). The poetry of 'The Song of Solomon' may be of interest to sixth formers who can pause to consider the ethnicity of the woman in this most famous of love songs who declares 'I am black, but comely O ye daughters of Jerusalem' (1: 5). Just one of many passages younger children can enjoy representing visually is the description of the 'Alpha and Omega' in Revelation 1:

> And I turned to see the voice that spake with me.
> And being turned, I saw seven golden candlesticks;
> And in the midst of the seven candlesticks
> One like unto the Son of man,
> Clothed with a garment down to the foot,
> and girt about the paps with a golden girdle
> His head and his hairs were white like wool, as white as snow;
> And his eyes were as a flame of fire;
> And his feet like unto fine brass, as if they burned in a furnace;
> And his voice as the sound of many waters.
> And he had in his right hand seven stars:
> and out of his mouth went a sharp two-edged sword:
> and his countenance was as the sun shineth in his strength.
> And when I saw him, I fell at his feet as dead.
> And he laid his right hand upon me, saying unto me,
> Fear not; I am the first and the last:
> I am he that liveth, and was dead;
> And, behold, I am alive for evermore, Amen;
> and have the keys of hell and of death.

Narratives, such as the one depicting the six days of creation in Genesis or the story of Joseph can also be fruitful resources in English lessons and the Bible is an important intertextual resource for studying Shakespeare and other canonical texts. Patterns of imagery (light, darkness, washing, water, blood) found in *Macbeth* echo those found in the Bible and 'reference to biblical sources, with their distinctive patterns of imagery, can give a fuller understanding of the play and of the times in which it was written and first performed' (Smith and Shortt, 2002: 166–7). Macbeth's pursuit of the witches' occult knowledge parallels King Saul's visit to the witch of Endor in the biblical narrative (1 Samuel: 28) and it is hard to imagine teaching *Measure for Measure* without reference to the biblical passage which the title is a quotation of (Luke 6: 38). In one school *The Tempest* is introduced with a unit entitled 'Bother with brothers' that includes the reading of the Genesis narrative about Cain and Abel. The effect of biblical echoes and extracts in contemporary works also needs to be understood. Briggs' satire in *When the Wind Blows* includes biblical fragments from the 23rd Psalm ('Lay me down in Green Pastures') recited by Jim and Hilda as they enter the 'Valley of the Shadow of Death' induced by radiation poisoning. The reasons for, and effects of, including these biblical echoes is worth discussing. Equally, it is important to understand the influence of the biblical imagery upon works such as 'The Wasteland' by T.S. Eliot.

Students need to read the Bible to understand the works of writers who have been influenced by what it says. Fifteen-year-olds, who participated in the 'Keen Readers' (Pike, 2000a) research, noticed the biblical symbolism in Blake's 'A Poison Tree' and the way the poem is redolent of Adam and Eve in Eden. One able reader drew on the Bible and noted in her GCSE English literature examination that 'The Lamb' is 'about salvation (redemption) and also creation' because when 'John the Baptist saw Jesus coming to him to be baptized in the river Jordan he said "Behold the Lamb of God which taketh away the sin of the world"'. Line 13 of the poem states 'He is called by thy name' (Pike, 2000e: 185). Reference to the Bible was necessary to understand Blake's poem although this reader struggled to comprehend how a God of love could sacrifice the Lamb, Christ, because, in her words, 'what happens to Jesus is horrific (nailed to a cross etc.)' and yet God 'gave the lamb referred to in verse 1 all these beautiful qualities' (ibid.).

Similarly, those who study Milton, Donne or Herbert (currently set authors for AS level English literature) or plays by Shakespeare such as *Macbeth* or *Measure for Measure* require a degree of biblical knowledge. Indeed, *Paradise Lost* is often taught with extracts from the biblical book of Revelation as a parallel text. An AS level English language course could well begin with a study of John 1 ('In the beginning was the Word'). Further, the number of versions of the Bible provide English teachers with a valuable resource for teaching about language change over time which is an important element of the *National Curriculum*. Teachers of A level can use 'The Lord's Prayer' in six versions (Old English *c*. 995, Middle English 1200, Wycliff 1388, Tyndale 1526, Authorized Version 1611 and *New English Bible* 1961) to enable students to see how language has changed. Very well-known passages in different versions encourage children to consider word choices and word order and can foster close textual analysis.

The 'Keen Readers' project

Recent research which sheds light on adolescents' experiences of pre-twentieth-century texts is the 'Keen Readers' project (Pike, 2000b), also referred to as the 'Bournemouth case study' (Pike, 2003b). This three-year longitudinal case study focused on the attitudes and attainment of readers between Year 9 and Year 11 with special attention being devoted to their responses to canonical texts. Students were closely monitored during approximately four hundred hours of English lessons and teaching strategies were developed by means of action research (see Chapter 4). Responses to texts and teaching techniques were the focus of attention. The 'responsive teaching' methods described elsewhere in this book (Chapters 1 and 7) were employed and both the motivation and attainment of all students increased significantly during the three years of the research project. Some dramatic progress was evident and one boy I taught who had a particular loathing of poetry at the end of Year 9 and gained a very modest level 5 in his Key Stage 3 test (roughly equivalent to an E grade at GCSE) gained an A* at the end of Year 11. On the evidence of his attainment in Year 9 he could have been expected to attain a C grade. Even accounting for some underachievement at Key Stage 3 an A* represented remarkable value-added progress. Significant value-added progress was, in fact, evident in all the readers.

While affirming the efficacy of the 'responsive teaching' methodology (described in more detail in the next chapter) certain findings are of particular relevance in a chapter devoted to the teaching of canonical literature. These adolescents read and responded to the fifteen pre-twentieth-century poems in the 1998/1999 GCSE English/English literature anthology (NEAB). Five poems by William Blake were studied as well as ten other poems from various authors. 'What is our Life?' by Sir Walter Raleigh, 'The Latest Decalogue' by Arthur Hugh Clough and 'Jordan' by Herbert were among those studied. A wide range of contemporary poetry was also studied, such as 'Daily London Recipe' by Steve Turner and 'Life Doesn't Frighten Me At All' by Maya Angelou. The same responsive teaching methods were employed with works regardless of time of publication and students were encouraged to relate texts to their own experience by reading the texts as a 'stimulus' (Rosenblatt) initially.

This ensured that teenagers perceived the relevance of pre-twentieth-century texts. One of the most striking findings to emerge from the research was that after a poetry-rich diet, especially throughout Year 10 and Year 11, five out of six readers actually preferred certain pre-twentieth-century works to many contemporary works that, on the face of it, appeared more relevant and accessible. A fairly typical comment was made by one of the readers during an interview about his reading: 'I prefer pre-twentieth-century poems. With pre-twentieth-century poems you have to go into them and try and find things, get really into the poem and see what the poet is trying to say. Twentieth-century poems seem to be more just text on the page'.

While it would be unfair to many challenging contemporary works to equate Iser's indeterminacy with older texts, it appears that these readers preferred some pre-twentieth-century texts to more recent works because the ostensibly more relevant works did not supply as much indeterminacy for them and they could not make the work their own to a comparable degree. The indeterminacy in Blake was an especially valuable resource for meaning-making. Sometimes readers even reordered and shaped such pre-twentieth-century texts to their own familiar world. One boy interpreted the conflict between the speaker and the foe in 'A Poison Tree' in terms of a rivalry within the comprehensive school. He read the lines 'I sunned it with smiles/And with soft deceitful wiles' and explained to the boy sitting next to him: 'I think he doesn't show his enemy he's fearful of him, sort of thing . . . like at school, he's like, you know, "soft deceitful wiles", trying to keep it all to himself and not show anybody.'

It was generally only after a 'live circuit' of response had been established between present-day reader and pre-twentieth-century text (and after the poem was perceived to be relevant) that teaching about style, language, original meaning and so on was possible. This is because 'a major criterion of the usefulness of background information' is that 'it will have value only when the student feels the need of it and when it is assimilated into the students' experience of particular literary works' (Rosenblatt, 1968: 123).

Reading canonical texts from the past enabled these readers to interpret their own situations in the present more perceptively because of the 'aesthetic distance' the classic text provided. An extract from one girl's answer illustrates the way readers can understand 'the appeal and importance of these texts over time' (DfEE/QCA, 1999: 34) in a way that reflects their present context. She wrote, in response to 'The Latest Decalogue' by Arthur Hugh Clough, that the speaker in the poem was 'being cynical about the way the people seemed to follow the letter of the law but not the spirit or ethos' of it and suggested that the poem 'causes the reader to look at themselves and the way they live'. After pointing out that Clough was 'showing up the immoral newest decalogue everyone seems to be following' she went on to compare

Victorian society with her own and wrote: 'I feel that in today's society we live in a more multi-cultural, pluralistic world, there is less hypocrisy as people are very frank and open about themselves.'

The pre-twentieth-century text gave this student the vantage point from which to reflect upon her own views and the world in which she lived. This reader reflected upon her own beliefs and values and her own multicultural society in response to this pre-twentieth-century text; a justification for studying such canonical works is that doing so can help young people live in the present and prepare them for the future.

Further reading

Atkinson, J. (1995) 'How do we teach pre-twentieth-century literature?', in R. Protherough and King, P. (eds) *The Challenge of English in the National Curriculum*. London: Routledge.

Benton, M. (2000) 'Canons ancient and modern: the texts we teach', *Educational Review*, 52(3): 269–77.

Pike, M.A. (2000) 'Keen readers: adolescents and pre-twentieth-century poetry' *Educational Review*, 52(1): 13–28.

Pike, M.A. (2002) 'The most wanted text in the West: Rewards offered for reading the Bible as literature', *The Use of English*, 54/(1): 29–42.

Pike, M.A. (2003) 'The canon in the classroom: students' experiences of texts from other times', *Journal of Curriculum Studies* 35(3) 355–70.

Popularizing poetry

The unpopularity of poetry

Poetry needs popularizing. According to *The National Curriculum for England: English* young readers should read for 'pleasure' as well as 'study' and should become 'enthusiastic, discriminating and responsive' (DfEE/QCA, 1999: 34). Many pupils, however, experience anything but enjoyment when reading poetry. Andrews reports that poetry provokes the 'most groans' from pupils (1991: 2) and O'Brien suggests that most teachers prefer to teach novels or plays as they have 'little confidence' they possess the 'strategies and techniques to make it (poetry) enjoyable and absorbing' (1985: 1). In particular, evidence of 'boys' antipathy to poetry' especially from the age of 14 'has stubbornly persisted while a variety of curriculum documents have come and gone' (Pike, 2000d: 41). Various descriptions of the widespread antipathy of pupils to poetry have been reported (Benton, 1984; O'Brien, 1985; Dias and Hayhoe, 1988; Andrews, 1991; OFSTED, 1993; QCA, 1998). Studies of how pupils' antipathy has been transformed into enthusiasm are not quite so plentiful. This chapter, therefore, relates key findings and strategies from a recent school-based project and shows how an English teacher can foster enthusiastic and perceptive readers when faced with negative attitudes at the outset. Practical strategies and theoretical perspectives are synthesized to enable teachers and pupils to enjoy poetry in the English lesson.

What's the point of poetry?

A fundamental problem many pupils have with poetry is that they do not understand the nature of the genre or how to adopt an appropriate reading stance. Pupils often understand the point of reading and writing letters, newspapers or adverts and even enjoy novels and plays but poetry poses an entirely different problem. 'What's the point of poetry?' is a question many pupils ask. Many are baffled by the whole notion of poetry. The following conversation illustrates the point. After an English lesson, my student-teacher and I were standing outside the dining hall supervising the queue. Steve, an extrovert boy from the Year 10 English class, struck up a conversation with the student-teacher about the lesson he had just had where she and I had engaged in team teaching a lesson on poetry. A brief extract from their conversation will suffice. I heard Steve argue 'Poetry is pointless – it's not like a novel, poems are too short . . . I just think that anyone who sits at home reading poems can't have much to do!' Sagely, the student-teacher replied: 'But why aren't plays or novels pointless then, Steve?' It was a good question but Steve's reply intrigued me: 'It's all just in one short few lines. I mean, why? I can see the point of a book because you go back to it and it's a story and you find out what happened'. Steve continued to explain that a poem was 'just too concise' and remarked 'it's not like a book where you find out what happens next – you read a poem and it's all there – you've read it!' (Pike, 2000d: 45). He was perplexed by poetry. Steve's lack of a plausible, working definition of what poetry is and how it should be read prevented him from functioning as positively as he might in poetry lessons.

What is poetry?

For Steve, a rationale for poetry was entirely lacking; he simply did not understand what it was all about and he may not be alone because, in the rush to study poems, many of us have never paused to discuss what they are or how they should be read. A friend of Steve's in the same English class, Josie, later confessed that at the start of her GCSE course she did not 'understand what the point of poems was' and wondered 'why doesn't a person write simply what they mean instead of writing in a way that confuses everyone?' Many readers of poetry in school do not understand the nature of the genre they are reading and this may be especially true as children begin to study different sorts of poetry from Year 9 onwards in most schools. We need to think about children's experience of poetry. At an early age children read poems that amuse or which they find interesting but then, later on, when more serious poetry is studied at GCSE, many do not have an adequate working definition of what a poem *is* or what it is *for*.

We need to make sure that young readers do not expect poems to mean in the same way as prose and that they realize they cannot treat poems as comprehension exercises. We need to ensure that they know the appropriate stance to adopt and cultivate a tolerance of ambiguity so they are not frustrated if they do not find one single, correct interpretation to a poem.

Evidently, a 'prerequisite for reading poetry . . . is to have some sense of what it means to say one is reading poetry rather than some other type of written discourse' (Fleming, 1992: 34). Directly addressing pupils' personal theories of poetry can provide a foundation for more positive reactions to the genre (Pike, 2000c) and a greater understanding of its reading requirements for 'it would seem desirable that specific consideration of the genre itself as part of pupils' experience of poetry would enhance their understanding' (Fleming, 1992: 40).

For Rosenblatt, poems, as literary works of art, come into being through the 'reader's attention to what the text activates' within him or her' (1985) and are not to be confused with the print on the page for the poem is an 'event' that only the reader can bring about. According to Rosenblatt, the reader brings past experiences of life and literature as well as memories, present preoccupations, values and aspirations to the reading and all these enter into a 'relationship with the text' (1978). In other words, literary works of art come into being through the readers' 'attention to what the text activates' (1985). After talking about this theory with a Year 8 class one boy summed it up particularly well: 'Poetry is an event – this event happens when something in the text connects with something inside the reader – when this happens it becomes a poem . . . When the reader and text connect it becomes a poem. Before that it is just black squiggles on white paper'.

Allied to this notion of the poem as event is Rosenblatt's concept of the text as a 'stimulus' that activates 'elements of the reader's past experience' both 'with literature and with life'. Following Steve's conversation with the student-teacher we encouraged Steve's class to see the poem as an event that only they could stage as the poem could only exist if they brought their experiences to the poem they read. In other words, the active role of the reader in the creation of meaning was taught to help readers understand the process they were involved in. The way 'stimulus' was explained to them was that if the poem sparked off a memory, association or an experience, even something they had watched on television, such as an advert, it was a connection between the world of the poem and that of the reader. Readers were introduced to the idea that until they made the poem live it had no life and was merely 'text' not a living 'poem'.

The notion of poem as event certainly worked with Steve who concluded some time later 'a poem only becomes a poem when you apply your own experience to the poem, it's not actually poetry when it's on the page but when a reader reads it and thinks of events that have happened to him or her, it becomes a poem' (15-year-old Steve quoted in Pike, 2000d: 51). Originally, standing outside the dining hall, Steve was unclear about 'what it was he was reading or how he was supposed to be reading it' but he made progress by gaining 'an increasing conscious awareness of the particular reading requirements of different discourses' (Fleming, 1992: 40). Rosenblatt's notion of poem as event can be introduced to younger children with the use of Venn diagrams (see Figure 11.1).

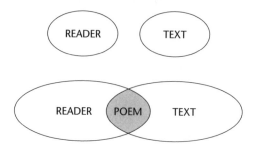

Figure 11.1 *Venn diagrams to introduce the notion of poems*

These diagrams, drawn on the board, can be used to illustrate Rosenblatt's theory that a poem only occurs when there is a transaction between reader and text. The diagrams are usually a huge success and, in the words of one Year 8 girl, 'poetry is really hard to explain, if I think of the diagram it's easy'. Another Year 8 pupil was equally convinced and explained, 'I think the diagram is a brilliant way to explain poetry'. One bright Year 8 boy observed that 'if a reader hates the poem, or does not understand it, the poem cannot get out of the text; if the reader likes the text, the poem sees it as an invitation, and leaps into the reader's mind, that is when the text becomes a poem'. When readers understand that what they bring to the poem is as important as what the author brings, personal response and active reading are fostered because they understand that no one else can read the poem for them. Children also tend to be entirely comfortable with the idea that a poem is like a piece of art. After a class discussion with one group one boy remarked 'someone said a poem's artwork and this really seemed to me to be a very good definition' and another boy explained 'I used to think that a poem was in a separate world from other things, but it is not'.

How to read poetry

Once the foundation has been laid that the poem is an event and is art, the way is prepared to teach children how to adopt an appropriate reading stance. According to Rosenblatt there are two sorts of reading: 'efferent' and 'aesthetic'. Efferent reading is like reading the back of a cereal packet, a medicine bottle or a mortgage document where you read to carry away (from the Latin verb *effere* – meaning 'to carry away') information. Such reading is for comprehension and its purpose is to extract information (how many tablets to take how many times a day or how much money is owed when or how much fibre or how many calories are in our breakfast). We expect exact, pre-cise information and clarity so that we can easily understand what we need to do. For Rosenbaltt, the opposite of 'efferent' reading is 'aesthetic' reading and any reading occurs on a continuum between efferent and aesthetic poles. If a reader knows that poems cannot be treated as comprehension exercises, they can develop a tolerance of ambiguity. This is so important because such readers do not then become frustrated if a poem has several competing interpretations. When the difference between reading a home-work diary and a poem is explained to children they are more likely to develop positive attitudes to the genre. If 'young readers become aware that an efferent stance is not appropriate with this genre then their knowledge about language and of the reading requirements of different genres will have developed considerably' (Pike, 2000c: 50).

Although the binary division in Rosenblatt's model has been problema-tized (Pike, 2003d) because children take away a great deal as a by-product of an aesthetic encounter (what they enjoy they remember), aesthetic reading can certainly be fostered by focusing on the text as a stimulus. Rosenblatt's concept of the poem as 'event' can help young readers understand the nature of the reading process they are engaged in and empower them to resist the 'temptation to rely on secondary understanding' where they only parrot 'the opinions of teachers, textbooks or critics' (Brumfit, 1991: 34).

Practical approaches

A number of approaches to reading poems are available to teachers. A helpful resource is '36 things to do with a poem' by Geoff Fox and Brian Merrick (1981). Just some of these excellent ideas are: jotting down five minutes of instant reactions, listening to a tape recording, each child finding and read-ing a poem each day to the class, presenting poems in dramatic form in pairs or groups, making taped versions of poems, the all-class chorally spoken ver-sion, choosing photographs to accompany a reading, displaying episodic poems as a frieze around the room, personal anthologies, learning poems by heart, group discussions, giving a poem to a class untitled so titles can be proposed, including 'wrong' words in a poem to be spotted, parodying or imitating a poem, inventing the story behind the poem (what has happened before and what will happen after?), reworking a poem in a different genre, fac-tual and open-ended questions to ask, collecting favourite poems and, last but not least, having a visiting poet in school to give workshops.

The *New Touchstones* poetry books for pupils by Michael and Peter Benton (1998) are a resource every English department should have as is the beauti-fully produced *Double Vision* by Benton and Benton (1990) where poems are presented alongside works of art. It is also important that pupils should be given the opportunity to write their own poems, and Sue Dymoke's *Drafting and Assessing Poetry* (2002) is a comprehensive guide to such activity that includes innovative approaches to creative writing and examples that show how the writing process works. Courses organized by the Arvon Foundation at centres in Devon and Yorkshire where pupils and teachers get to work with published poets cannot be recommended highly enough. There are, of course, many ways to encourage pupils to write poems. Just a few of the most successful are collecting public language (from adverts, notices, classrooms, magazines, etc.) as the raw material of poems; taking words (one from each line) from novels which capture the mood of a passage; making new poems from scattered words of cut-up poems; writing haikus and cinquains; writing ballads based on news stories; using postcards as a stimulus, activities with metaphors and similes like the 'furniture game'; or any one of a number of similar activities described in Sandy Brownjohn's *Does it Have to Rhyme?* (1980), *What Rhymes with 'Secret'?* (1982) or by Cliff Yates in *Jumpstart: Poetry in the Secondary School* (1999).

A 'responsive teaching' sequence for poetry

English teachers frequently bemoan the fact that the older children get the less original work they produce. As they move up the school they write more and more about what other people have written rather than producing their own imaginative writing. When writing poetry children often draw upon personal experience but when they read students often 'do not see the significance of literature in relation to their own lives' (Wade and Ball, 1983: 7). Active approaches are, therefore, most valuable when they legitimate personal response. Although pupils enjoy 'doing things to texts', for a poem to have significance the reader has to perceive how it relates to his or her own life and experience so that a 'live circuit' of relevance is set up. The approach termed 'responsive teaching' can be especially useful for reading poetry (Pike, 2000b: 20) as it enables readers to 'connect' with the text but such teaching necessarily requires a shift in the locus of control from teacher to pupil. A possible sequence at GCSE is as follows.

Individual to paired response

In the UK, at GCSE, an anthology is provided and a choice from a range of poems is possible. Many teachers encourage students to read a wide range of poems before choosing which ones will be studied in greater depth as it can be best to see which poems pupils have the most positive reactions to in order to decide what to spend most time on. It is especially important for young, inexperienced readers to hear the poem being read and new English teachers should not underestimate the impact that a good reading can have. Reading the poem twice to the class is often best as much can be missed when reading a poem for the first time. After this first reading the class can be encouraged to allow the text to act as a 'stimulus' and to spend five minutes adding their initial annotations around the poem. Readers focus on particular words, phrases or lines that spark off connections or evoke memories, moods, experiences and so on. In order to elicit personal response children can be steered away from technical features, such as similes and metaphors at this stage when the focus is on text as 'stimulus'. After such impressionistic and personal annotation five or ten minutes can be spent writing a brief first journal entry. Children can be allowed to do this individually in silence so they are not distracted by others' views and interpretations.

The individual journal entry is preparation for speaking and listening as children often feel more secure and confident talking about a poem if they have had sufficient opportunity to develop their response and to jot something down first. Discussion that immediately follows a reading can lead to domination by those who respond most rapidly. Launching straight into a whole-class discussion at this stage can often lead to only the most vocal, confident individuals voicing their opinions. Therefore, after the journal entry pupils can discuss the poem in pairs which is especially valuable because it allows no passengers and every children is propelled into a dialogue.

Whole-class discussion (with a difference)

Following this paired talk, a whole-class discussion can take place where different pupils volunteer their responses and interpretations. The teacher should not, at this stage, employ a rapid succession of comprehension-style questions as this can encourage reactive and dependent learners. The objective is to create the 'forum' described by Trelawny-Ross (1998). The teacher might begin by saying 'Who's going to start?' or 'What did you make of that?' Considerable effort should be devoted to avoid the all too common situation where those 'who ask questions – teachers, texts, tests – are not seeking knowledge; those who would seek knowledge – students – do not ask questions' (Dillon, 1988: 197). Instead, pupils can be encouraged to take the initiative and be encouraged to come up with their own questions as well as tentative answers to them. Children should be prompted to reply to others and engage with their views so that exchange develops. After the whole-class discussion a second journal entry can be made by each reader who records his or her reactions to views quite different from his or her own that have emerged in the class discussion. Some may already have developed their initial response by engaging in the paired and whole-class discussion. The sequence from paired to whole-class discussion enables readers to try their ideas out on a partner before expressing their views more publicly. Most importantly, pupils are likely to try out *their own ideas* rather than repeating the teacher's. Subsequently, it is *their* ideas that are the subject of revision or modification. After the class discussion a second journal entry can be made. It is important to note that so far the teacher has not given a lecture and readers have not passively listened and taken down notes. Pupils are encouraged to take the initiative and become active thinkers and readers rather than passive recipients of information. The 'locus of control' has begun to shift.

Teaching based on pupils' reading

Clearly, if the poem is chosen for further study and is to be written about in the examination, considerably more work is needed on it. Specific information will need to be acquired by pupils about the social and cultural context and about the literary techniques employed. The author's beliefs and important themes need to be explored. This information can be introduced by the teacher but pupils will need to relate this new knowledge to their understanding of the poem. Allowing pupils to 'make their own sense of a poem may mean they miss some of the important ideas expressed in it' (Trelawny-Ross, 1998: 45) but, at the same time, teaching about background information is only of value when the reader 'feels the need of it and when it is assimilated into the student's experience' (Rosenblatt, 1968: 123). Consequently, we can 'base the acts of teaching upon the act of reading' (Benton, 1995: 336) as reader-response criticism suggests.

One way of going about this is to photocopy contrasting statements from journal entries (these can be anonymous if necessary) and circulate them among the class, to provoke further debate. Internally publishing students' views, in this way, means that any teaching is founded on an already-healthy debate which has developed from readers' ideas and not those of the teacher. Teaching can take place at the point where students' responses and interpretations indicate it is required. Such an approach takes a little more time but is ultimately far more interesting. It is, of course, the antithesis of an approach where children are told by the teacher what the poem means and take notes so they can repeat their teachers' views in the examination. The latter, more traditional approach, is not even the way to produce the best results as attainment derives from pupils' enthusiasm and such a didactic style militates against the development of such enthusiasm; evidently, 'children cannot learn things simply by being told; they need to be able to relate such principles to their own actions, experience and conceptions' (Edwards and Mercer, 1987: 95). The approach just described was employed in the 'Keen Readers' (Pike, 2000a) research project where the transformation of readers from apathy to enthusiasm was marked. What is important is that there is a connection between the poem and the life of the reader. The following approach to 'The Ballad of Reading Gaol' by Oscar Wilde demonstrates another way of teaching responsively where active approaches are employed that are combined with an attempt to foster the personal connection between reader and text.

Teaching 'The Ballad of Reading Gaol' by Oscar Wilde

Pupils can be introduced to the poem by telling them the story of CTW, Charles Thomas Wooldridge, the character the poem is based on. The idea is to make the children (probably Year 8) desperate to read the poem in order to learn of Wooldridge's fate. The story goes something like this. In 1896 when our story is set Charles was 30 years of age. He was handsome and intelligent and could write a better letter than his lawyer. He was also an officer in the Royal Horse Guards and was stationed at a barracks in London. He was married and totally devoted to, and in love with, his wife. Their home was in Windsor but due to the nature of his employment they were separated much of the time. One day he received a letter from his wife saying that she never wanted to see him again, and asking that he never attempt to contact her. She had found another man. As you can imagine Charles was devastated.

English teachers are good at elaborating with some poetic licence upon the story and can stop and ask questions to enable readers to empathize with Charles. How do you feel when you receive a letter in handwriting you know? How would you feel if you were in love and this happened to you? What would you do? Would you try to see her? Why do you think she has ended the relationship in this way? And so on. The class can then be told, by teacher in storyteller mode, that Charles took his cut-throat razor (this may need describing) and boarded a train to Windsor which is a great opportunity for another prediction exercise. What will he do with it? They can then be told that he found his wife walking up the High Street in the middle of the day and that he murdered her in broad daylight. At this point, the teacher can explain that the poem they are about to read was written by a famous writer who was in prison with Charles. The teacher can prompt children to remember occassions when they got to know someone and became close friends in a matter of a couple of weeks. They can be told that the two men were in prison together for six weeks and that the poem they are about to read tells the story of CTW, to whom it is dedicated.

After a reading (the whole poem can be reduced to fit on one side of A4 paper) children can be asked to pick out their favourite group of lines. This forces even the most trenchant poetry-hater to say something positive. They can then be asked what they liked and why although this should be brisk and must only take a couple of minutes. Quite a few normally choose the first four lines of stanza 19 'We sewed the sacks, we broke the stones/ We turned the dusty drill;/ We banged the tins, and bawled the hymns/ And sweated on the mill'. The whole class can then stomp and chant these lines around the room with the teacher in role as prison warder. This can be repeated at periodic intervals throughout the lesson. The children can be given a series of DARTs to do in a short space of time (such as identifying and marking with arrows or highlighting the internal and external rhymes, alliteration, onomatopoeia, imagery, personification, repetition and so on). They can work in pairs on one task at a time and have fun seeing how many devices they can spot and in between tasks can stomp 'we sewed the sacks . . .'.

Class discussion can follow where they consider the nature of love and rejection. Can you kill what you love? Is it love if you do? Why does he look wistfully upon the sky? Why can't he pray? Why does he drink the sun 'as though it had been wine'? Why was he glad the 'hangman's day is near'? What do they think of the way his burial is described as warders 'stripped him of his canvas clothes and hid him in a hole'? It is normally possible to evoke personal responses to the poem and children often remember their experience of it long after much that is learnt in English is forgotten. Combining active approaches with personal response is the key. An appropriate note to end on is the reaction of a Year 8 girl to the poem which sums up the key themes of this chapter regarding 'stimulus', the poem as 'event' and the need for personal relevance and significance as well as active approaches. After the activities she wrote:

> When I read 'The Ballad of Reading Gaol', I felt sad and sorrowful and my brain looked like :

One PGCE student, who participated in the same lesson (in a workshop I ran) by taking on the role of the pupil, recounts his experience of learning to teach poetry below:

> I'm marching up and down a crowded classroom chanting the words of a poem by Oscar Wilde at the top of my voice. 'There really isn't room for this,' I think, as I crash into a colleague for the second time. Next I have 30 seconds to identify all the internal rhymes. Then the external ones. This isn't a lesson plan gone awry. The emphasis of today's seminar is on learning innovative ways of

getting children interested in older poetry without swamping them with obscure contextual detail that will alienate them. It's worked with us. A large part of starting to teach English is about losing your inhibitions – to know what it's like to be a 12-year-old, you've got to act like one. We listen attentively to our tutor as he bombards us with task after task. We've got to think quickly so we never get bored. We're repeating a lot of things, it's all going in – and the poem's brought to life. This is a distilled version of a lesson, but the PGCE has so much to cram in we have to move at this pace. You don't get much opportunity to read aloud as an undergraduate, and now I've got to learn to ham it up in front of a class of children I don't know. It's daunting, but you throw yourself into it. Every Friday, one person from our tutor group reads in front of us as practice. If you can do accents, the children will love you. I always avoided poetry in favour of prose as I found novels easier to write about. Friends who also read English were the same. As a nervous trainee, it might seem easier to 'go with what you know' when choosing texts for a class, but the PGCE requires you to know a bit about everything, so I think I'll try some of that poetry I'm unfamiliar with. (Struan Bates, *The Times Educational Supplement*, 2002).

Further reading

Andrews, R. (1991) *The Problem with Poetry*. Milton Keynes: Open University Press.
Benton, M. (1988) *Young Readers Responding to Poems*. London: Routledge.
Pike, M.A. (2000) 'Pupils' poetics', *Changing English*, 7(1): 45–54.
Pike, M.A. (2000) 'Boys, poetry and the individual talent', *English in Education*, 34(3): 41–55.
Pike, M.A. (2001) 'Adolescents as active readers', in NFER (ed.) *TOPIC (Practical Applications of Research in Education)* 26. Slough: NFER.
Pike, M.A. (2003) 'From personal to social transaction: a model of aesthetic reading in the classroom', *Journal of Aesthetic Education*, 37(2): 61–72.

12

Spiritual and moral development through English

Spiritual, moral, social and cultural development

In the first chapter of this book different models, or emphases, within English teaching were presented and the importance of the 'personal growth' model for English teachers was considered. It is fitting, therefore, that this final chapter should return to the subject of personal development through English. This is acknowledged at the beginning of *The National Curriculum for England: English*, for even before the programmes of study, a statement is included about the sort of personal development an education in English can provide and a whole section is devoted to the promotion of 'pupils' spiritual, moral, social and cultural development through English' (DfEE/QCA, 1999: 8). Often known as SMSC, English teachers have a statutory obligation to promote such development and as OFSTED inspectors now report on children's progress in these areas many English departments have an SMSC policy.

English teachers generally feel confident that they are fulfilling their obligation to nurture children's *social* and *cultural* development. After all, 'social' development is described in terms of 'helping pupils collaborate with others' (ibid.) as well as enabling them to think of the effects their talk and writing has on the intended audience and studying texts where relationships are depicted. Teachers of English also tend to feel well prepared to educate children culturally especially as 'cultural development' is described as 'helping pupils explore and reflect on the way cultures are represented in their stories and poems' (ibid.). Indeed, cultural development includes 'learning about language variation' and 'how language relates to national, regional and cultural identities' (ibid.). Social and cultural development are undoubtedly the province of English teachers who could be considered specialists on such matters.

English teachers do not, however, feel so well equipped to take responsibility for children's spiritual and moral development. This chapter, therefore, shows how English teachers can promote children's spiritual and moral development in a way that is true to the aims of the 'personal growth' model and is itself morally justified. English teachers are often as much spiritual and moral specialists as they are social and cultural experts. With reference to a number of texts and activities, how English teachers can foster the spiritual and moral development of their pupils will be explored. The current definitions are broad and English teachers have opportunities to promote:

■ *spiritual development*, through helping pupils represent, explore and reflect on their own and others' inner life in drama and the discussion of texts and ideas
■ *moral development*, through exploring questions of right and wrong, values and conflict between values in their reading of fiction and non-fiction, in their discussions and in drama (ibid.)

Ethics and English

In *Moral Education through English 11–16*, Ros McCulloch and Margaret Mathieson make a bold claim and assert 'Literature, more than any other subject in the curriculum, offers the fullest possible picture both of the complexities of the moral situation and the consequences of action' (1995: 30). Clearly, English teachers are uniquely placed as moral educators. A good example of the way children in English lessons grapple with 'the complexities of the moral situation' is provided by pupils' readings of 'Vultures' by Chinua Achebe, a poem that currently appears in the AQA *Anthology* for GCSE English (2002a). In this poem, Achebe explores the nature of evil and the capacity of humans for both warmth and human kindness and also incomprehensible brutality and inhumanity.

The poem draws upon Achebe's experiences of war and particularly the aftermath of war as he wrote it when he was working for the Biafran government at the time the region declared itself an independent state. Biafra was starved into submission by the Nigerian army and the resultant carnage is apparent in the first stanza where Achebe describes how a vulture and its mate 'picked the eyes of a swollen corpse in a water-logged trench and ate the things in its bowel'. Although the behaviour of the vultures causes revulsion Achebe recognizes that they are companions who have great affection for each other. Although incomprehensible, this is not uncommon as many heinous crimes, such as those of Myra Hindley and Ian Brady, have been committed by people who appeared to be in love. It is in the second stanza of 'Vultures' that we are rendered speechless though. The Commandant of Belsen, a Nazi concentration camp, buys chocolates for his children on the way home from work; to them he is a loving, thoughtful, caring and generous father. One Year 10 boy had a disturbing encounter with the poem and could not get away from the fact that the man who bought sweets for his children had the smell of 'human roast clinging rebelliously to his nostrils'. He explained, 'this line is quite disturbing . . . it describes how incredibly disgusting and evil he can be and then the poet writes that he buys his children some chocolate at a sweet shop . . . the children think of their father the Commandant as "Daddy"'. Clearly, such evil and paradoxical behaviour is not something that is easy to come to terms with.

Works like 'Vultures' have the power to extend pupils' moral understanding as they can be provoked to formulate their own moral responses as a result of their reading. Achebe asks a question and poses a moral dilemma for readers. Another Year 10 boy summed it up: 'Do we have evil hearts with a kind, loving part to it or a kind heart in which is "lodged the perpetuity of evil"?' Such questions address the fundamental nature of the human condition. Achebe does not resolve the difficulty in any simple, easy or straightforward way for readers. The final ambiguity remains and readers are required to finish the poem for themselves as they have to provide their own moral interpretation. The Year 10 boys I worked with acquired far more than skills or knowledge and their interpretation was undeniably 'personal'; no one else could come up with the answer for them.

For me, this is why English concerns ethics and is 'about the good (that is, what values and virtues we should cultivate) and about the right (that is, what our moral duties may be)' (Holmes, 1984: 10). Ethical discussion does not merely describe a situation for it 'is less interested in what people in fact do than in what they ought to do, less in what their values presently are and more in what their values ought to be' (ibid.). Yet, literary texts do not necessarily show us *the* way to live but rather *a* way of living. Literary texts are so powerful because they enable us to reflect upon the way we live. How 'Vultures' enabled my Year 10 boys to think about their lives and about moral issues is particularly interesting. The text did not overtly tell them how to live or how humans should behave and yet it fostered moral development. We should always be ready to point out that 'works of art are artificial (and therefore not necessarily authoritative and truthful)' (Stibbs, 2001: 42) and it is perfectly valid for Harold Bloom, therefore, to point out that 'we do not live by the ethics of the *Iliad* or by the politics of Plato' (1994: 40). In the case of 'Vultures' it was the difference between the moral order the boys in Year 10 believed to be right and the Commandant's actions that was the stimulus for moral development. Reflecting upon the behaviour of the Commandant provoked them to think about their own values.

The extent to which English is a morally educative discipline has been the subject of some debate. Some argue that reading great literature 'will not make one a better or a worse person, a more useful or more harmful citizen' (ibid.: 30) as texts are merely the product of cultural forces rather than of genius. Others, such as F.R. Leavis (1948), who had a profound influence on English during the middle decades of the twentieth century, believed that great authors bring a rare degree of honesty to their depiction and understanding of humanity and that such writers turn us into discerning *people* not just discerning *readers* and empower us to sift the true from the false in the *world* as well as in the *text*. The perspective that has been so influential upon this book, namely reader-response theory, is of value in resolving the question about the morally educative power of literature. It is how the reader reads and responds to what is read that can determine the extent to which it is morally educative.

English is morally educative because readers can become involved in moral situations through reading literary works. Readers can empathize and can enter into situations vicariously so that they can learn without having to experience those same situations themselves in life. Reading fiction can be one of the best ways to learn about human character; we learn, for instance, how it is possible for goodness and wickedness to exist together in a single individual and as pupils learn such things their understanding of human character becomes increasingly discriminating and subtle. Literature is rich in action, decisions, feelings, relationships, characters and themes. Literature is about how people treat each other, the motivation for their actions, why they do what they do and how they feel about what they have done. In English most teachers would agree that they educate pupils' emotions as well as their minds and in doing so pupils' moral awareness and understanding deepen. Indeed, many of the activities explored throughout this book (hot-seating, thought-tracking, predictions, interviews and diaries to name but a few) foster a knowledge of others as young readers respond to characters and situations in literature. If 'a large sense' is to be given to the term 'moral', as Arnold believed, whatever 'bears upon the question "how to live" comes under it' (1879/1988: 499). Literature is concerned with morality as it is concerned with life 'and human life itself is in so preponderating a degree moral' (ibid.). Literature as art is bound up with our moral sense of ourselves, others and our world. In 'Religion and Literature' when T.S. Eliot considers 'literature from an ethical viewpoint he is surely right that the greatness of literature cannot be judged by literary standards alone' (Pike, 2000e: 179) because it 'affects us as entire human beings, it affects our moral and religious existence' (Eliot, 1935: 396) and the author of a work of imagination is trying to affect us 'wholly, as human beings' (ibid.: 394) which necessarily includes more than rational or cognitive faculties.

English teachers are also aware that children need to have models of legitimate and honourable behaviour to follow and need to select texts skilfully. Clearly, we do not want to choose narratives that legitimate wrongdoing and promote evil characters as models of behaviour. Consequently, whether a narrative viewpoint endorses certain characters is important to consider.

Class discussion in response to a text is also central as the teacher will necessarily legitimate certain actions and values and condemn others. Teaching English is to engage in moral education and it is important to examine our key beliefs and values so that we are agreed about the moral lessons children should learn through what they read. There is broad agreement concerning moral values in schools in the UK. We want to emphasize the importance of honesty (telling the truth), justice and fairness, keeping promises and contracts as well as the moral obligation to respect others and their property. We want children to respect the beliefs of others and to be tolerant of them even when they do not agree with them. We help children to take responsibility for their own actions rather than shifting the blame on to others. We want children to learn that it is more important to do what is right than what is popular and to have the moral fibre to resist peer pressure and the power of 'the group'. At the same time we want children to learn to co-operate with each other and to work together. We work hard in English to ensure children can read advertisements and media texts with discernment and can identify bias and prejudice and the difference between fact and opinion.

Through literature we seek to teach children about rights and responsibilities (both their own and those of others). As English teachers, we work to enable children to identify with and respect other people. English is unique because 'in making possible a significant degree of identification with characters, literature encourages pupils to involve themselves closely in the problems these characters are facing' (McCulloch and Mathieson, 1995 p. 36). Our discipline engenders attention to values through the engagement that comes about with the development of sympathy and empathy and much of what we want to teach is summed up in the biblical Golden Rule 'all things whatsover ye would that men should do to you, do ye even so to them' (Matthew 7: 12). Indeed, Judeo-Christian morality founded upon the Ten Commandments continues to provide a moral framework for society in the West. If we abide by the Golden Rule we will clean our environment rather than pollute it, we will seek to include those who are marginalized rather than excluding them still further and we will be sure to temper justice with mercy. We will also love and defend the values we believe in as they ensure a tolerance of diversity and make for a peaceful society. It is hard to imagine an English teacher who would not entirely subscribe to and wholeheartedly endorse such core values. As Kant realized others are ends and not means.

Opportunities for moral development at Key Stage 3 and Key Stage 4

Many popular texts in English lessons provide opportunities for moral development. There are the obvious examples such as *Friedrich* by Hans Peter

Richter and *The Diary of Anne Frank* that deal with extreme forms of prejudice and evil under the Nazis in Europe in the 1930s and also classic texts such as *The Lord of the Flies* by William Golding where the power of 'the group' is explored. But there are also other texts that do not immediately spring to mind when thinking about moral education which still provide the stimulus for moral reflection. Just a few examples will illustrate how it is possible to foster moral development through a variety of texts as the English stockroom is bursting with resources for moral education.

At Key Stage 3, stealing and lying are dealt with in *Buddy* by Nigel Hinton and *The Turbulent Term of Tyke Tyler* by Gene Kemp. Buddy shoplifts and also steals five pounds from his mother's purse and lies to her about it and Buddy's dad is enmeshed in crime after losing his job. Similarly, in *Tyke Tiler* when Tyke's friend, Danny, steals from a teacher's handbag Tyke sets out to replace it. Tyke and Danny also 'lose' the leaflets they were supposed to deliver in a river but never tell anyone about it. The place of science is dealt with in *Mrs Frisby and the Rats of NIMH* by Robert O'Brien, in *Frankenstein* by Mary Shelley (the adaptation into a play script for Key Stage 3 by Philip Pullman is especially good) and also in *Flowers for Algernon* by Daniel Keyes, the remarkable account of a person's mental and emotional transformation. Such novels can be used to explore issues such as cloning, genetic modification and stem-cell research. *Sumitra's Story, My Mate Shofiq, Welcome Home Jellybean* or *The Pearl* all teach important moral lessons. Even Roald Dahl's *Boy* offers opportunities for moral reflection as does *Holes* by Louis Sacher, which is set in a camp for young offenders.

For Key Stage 4 (14–16), gender, power and the right to a voice are key themes in Browning's dramatic monologues 'My Last Duchess' and 'Porphyria's Lover'. *Roll of Thunder, Hear My Cry* by Mildred D. Taylor opens with the wrecking of the white children's bus, and the justification for this. Similarly, *To Kill a Mockingbird* by Harper Lee examines issues of justice, honesty (telling lies), respect for others as well as racial prejudice. Injustice is explored in *A Kestrel for a Knave* (for instance, McDowell is picked out by Mr Crossley and victimized) and collective responsibility can be explored in relation to the group punishment in response to graffiti appearing on a wall.

■ Morality, the media and ICT

Texts are not the only starting point for moral development in English. Topics such as abortion, the death penalty, the fur trade, animal experimentation, terrorism, war, prejudice and policing are all common. Studying the media is an integral part of English and debates take place on such subjects as journalistic impartiality and objectivity, weighing people's right to privacy against the public's right to know, censorship, as well as the link between violent films and antisocial behaviour. When considering censorship, students necessarily consider how people's rights should be respected and the impact on other people and society of blasphemy, profanity, vulgarity and indecency. ICT is also an integral element of English and the use and abuse of the Internet can provide a way of discussing the link between pornography and sexually related crimes such as rape. It also provides a way into a discussion about freedom of information, slander, defamation of character and the rights of individuals.

When engaging with the moral issues described above students may well ask some fundamental questions about human nature, the meaning of life and the reason for existence. These are the sorts of questions which foster spiritual development. Spirituality is not simply about abstract, other-worldly, religious themes but about experiences (so central to the 'personal growth' model) in the here and now. Certainly, spirituality as discussed in this chapter is the sort that has its feet firmly on the ground as it is about the experience of pupils in the literature lesson which cannot be explained rationally or cognitively as it concerns the child's 'inner life'.

Spiritual development through English

Spirituality is not confined to religious belief but is concerned with matters of fundamental significance and is often associated with awe and wonder in English. At the end of a first reading of *King Lear*, for instance, readers often wish to *be* rather than to analyse for what they experience cannot be put into words. David Hay, one of the UK's foremost authorities on children's spiritual development, has suggested that one way of viewing spirituality is to see it as referring to 'sensitive awareness' (1998: 11) which is what the literary encounter seeks to foster. In the discussion paper *Spiritual and Moral Development* (SCAA, 1995), 'spirituality' is defined, most helpfully, in the following way:

> The term needs to be seen as applying to something fundamental in the human condition which is not necessarily expressed through the physical senses and/or expressed through everyday language. It has to do with relationships with other people and, for believers, with God. It has to do with the universal search for individual identity – with our responses to challenging experiences, such as death, suffering, beauty, and encounters with good and evil. It is to do with the search for meaning and purpose in life and for values by which to live (ibid.: 3).

Hans Robert Jauss, a famous literary theorist, defines 'aesthetic distance' which is a feature of the literary encounter as 'the disparity between the given horizon of expectations and the appearance of a new work, whose reception can result in a "change of horizons" through negation of familiar experiences or through raising newly articulated experiences to the level of consciousness' (1982: 25). Arguably, the 'aesthetic distance' travelled by learners, when they read and respond personally to literary works, can be the territory across which spiritual journeys are made. Literary works that deal with 'challenging experiences, such as death, suffering, beauty, and encounters with good and evil' have the potential to bring about profound 'horizonal' change as they can enable readers to 'search for meaning and purpose and for values by which to live' (SCAA, 1995: 3). Such 'horizonal' change, appears to be related to Wolfgang Iser's view of the nature of a literary work as something which 'opens up perspectives in which the empirically known world of one's own personal experience appears changed' (1971: 7). Evidently, spiritually and morally educative experiences are often closely bound up with aesthetic response for 'aesthetic distance' provides the possibility of especially significant long-distance travel (Pike, 2000b; 2002c) whereby young readers encounter new horizons as a work helps them augment or reconfigure their experience.

John Dewey reminds us in *Art as Experience* (1934/1980), one of the twentieth century's most influential texts on aesthetic education, that writers on spirituality, such as James (1902), often argue that the spiritual need not be confined to places of worship. Dewey explicitly links the spiritual and the aesthetic in his plea for both these fundamental aspects of human experience to be integrated with everyday life. It is important to emphasize that, far from being an escape from the world of experience, spirituality is inextricably bound up *in* everyday experience. It is certainly bound up with the everyday art of English teaching.

What does spiritual development look like in English?

Spiritual development through reading rarely takes the form of angels riverdancing on the duvet. Nor does it entail teenagers gazing beatifically heavenwards as they are lost in the silvery shimmering light of transcendence. The children who experience spiritual development in English lessons are usually far from angelic. In English, teachers often deal with a robust, down-to-earth, practical sort of spirituality rather than the airy, abstract, transcendent variety. When children ask the really fundamental questions about the purpose of life, the search for meaning, values by which to live, the nature of being human, the nature of evil, where we live after we die and whether God is there, they are engaging in spiritual matters. If they discuss whether humans have a spiritual dimension, whether there is a rational explanation for everything or even whether spiritual development is possible in English they are becoming spiritually aware.

A group of my GCSE students who recently read the poignant poem 'What is our Life?' by Sir Walter Raleigh, written while he was awaiting execution in the Tower of London, experienced spiritual development (Pike, 2000a). The poem enabled teenagers to consider the meaning and purpose of life because in the poem Raleigh fails to find any higher meaning in human existence. Raleigh's nihilism is provocative and these young readers reacted to it. The poem made them consider their own existence and the nature and meaning of life. One boy found it perplexing that 'the poet fails to find any sense of purpose for life on earth' and explained that the phrase 'short comedy' that Raleigh uses to describe our lives had a profound impact upon him. He wrote in an essay 'Raleigh is saying that our life is just a comedy, designed to amuse "Heaven the judicious sharp spectator"' and the idea Raleigh presents of God as a detached onlooker was disconcerting. Later on, the same boy wrote that Raleigh's experiences 'caused him [Raleigh] to question life and reading the poem made me do the same; it left me in a confused, depressed mood'. For this student, in particular, to express such feeling was rare indeed. It is interesting that it was a text that posed philosophical and theological questions about the nature of human existence that prompted such a response.

Another text that fostered spiritual development was the unlikely 'Daily London Recipe' by Steve Turner. The poem is a satire of daily life in modern society in which people are reduced to the ingredients of a recipe. The poem contains instructions to 'push', 'take' and 'scrape remainder off' with reference to commuters on the London underground. The impersonality of the subject is striking as people are dehumanized and many adolescent readers saw Turner's work as a warning to them. One boy argued that Turner is attacking 'the way people are robbed of individuality and are unable to be creative at what they do'. Essentially, he saw the poem as a Marxist critique of society where the workers are reduced to cogs in the economic machine and derive little or no satisfaction from their labour, although he did not use quite these terms. A girl in the class was struck by people's 'lack of dignity' in the poem and reflected 'we shouldn't end up in a lifestyle which is repetitive and meaningless'. Another girl related the poem to her own life and individual career plans and explained 'I have become determined not to lose my individuality and creativity to a job when I am older'. Such comments are examples of a clear, down-to-earth type of spiritual development as readers recognized the need for non-material well-being, self-respect and creativity which fall within the QCA's definition of the 'spiritual'. We should not underestimate the degree to which the literature we read with classes has the power to provoke them to consider issues of spiritual significance.

■ The English teacher as poet, prophet and priest?

The call or vocation which teaching is often considered to be (whereby the English teacher enables children to have new experiences and to discover spiritual, moral and aesthetic significance for themselves) is closely related to the role of the prophet or priest. The English teacher as mediator between art and life, curriculum and learner, text and reader, is of importance because such a teacher brings *significance* as well as *coherence* to learning encounters and turns a given curriculum 'into a dynamic series of learning experiences with a sense of cumulative purpose' (Stables et al., 1999: 450). Learning of this sort is a significant event (ibid.) and can bring about spiritual development by 'helping pupils represent, explore and reflect on their own and others' inner life' (QCA, 1999a: 8) but it is the English teacher who mediates such significance. The English teacher is vital because the 'formal curriculum is rarely if ever, framed in these terms' as it 'is atomistic, with related elements linked thematically but not in terms of building towards significance' (Stables et al., 1999: 450). Just as the poet could be said both to 'function as priest' (Long, 2000: 149) and as prophet, so too can the English teacher who similarly brings about new ways of seeing.

English teachers (like prophets and priests) mediate significance for groups as well as individuals. Cultivating experience is generally acknowledged to be the way forward in both spiritual and aesthetic education and what makes English invaluable for spiritual and moral development is that 'all reading is experience – an indirect form of experience, but a peculiarly powerful one, and for many minds the most varied and fruitful in the whole of life' (Newbolt, 1921: 336). While, 'spiritual development occurs when a reader responds personally to a written work of art when this is an aesthetic experience' (Pike, 2000e: 179), spirituality is not only personal and individual it is also shared. When focusing on the individual's personal and spiritual growth through experience it is important to remember that, as Schleiermacher believed, each individual carries in him or her a minimum of all others. John Donne's 'Mediatation XVII' (1627) is in a similar vein: 'No man is an Island, entire of itself; every man is a/ Piece of the continent, a part of the main . . . any man's death/ Diminishes me, because I am involved in mankind/ And therefore never send to know for whom the bell/ tolls; It tolls for thee.' The emphasis on human relatedness is singularly appropriate here for children live in a social world and the responses, interpretations and experiences of others are required to augment the child's own. Consequently, an essential element of spiritual development is the growth of 'relational consciousness' which Rebecca Nye, a leading researcher on spiritual development, has observed to be characterized by an 'unusual level of perceptiveness' in the way children 'felt related to things, especially people, including themselves and God' (1998: 5). What is being described is a 'relational orientation toward people or symbols at a spiritual level' (Reimer and Furrow, 2001: 15).

The English teacher is also a poet. Spiritual development is necessarily mediated by language as 'language provides access to spiritual processes of thought and experience that are potentially co-constructed between the individual and his/her context' (ibid.: 10). The importance of the English teacher as a language-user is hard to overestimate as language is the most advanced symbolic system known to humanity. Spiritual development can occur as children have the opportunity to 'balance and reconcile different ideas and feelings through collaborative effort' (Bell, 1988: 93). Teaching that fosters spiritual growth is typified by exchange rather than transmission because it is founded upon children's experiences. Articulating and expressing experience through language is a first step and spiritual development often occurs by encouraging the child to participate in an exchange of meaning with others. When pupils grapple with issues of fundamental significance they often come to reflect upon their own reflections and engage in metacognition. Spirituality is central to education because it emphasizes the importance of such 'reflexiveness' (Bruner, 1986: 361). This is essential as the 'process of education consists of being able to distance oneself in some way from what one knows by being able to reflect on one's own knowledge' (ibid.: 127). The value of developing spiritual awareness lies, partly, in the vantage point it gives children from which they can interpret their own experiences and those of others.

Spirituality, morality and the art of teaching English

I want to suggest that there is a link not just between literature and spiritual growth but also between pedagogy and the deepening of spiritual and moral awareness. Teaching influenced by reader-response theory has the capacity to foster spiritual growth because attention is paid to the reader's response; evidently, 'spiritual and moral development does not simply result from the text studied but is also a result of *how* it is studied' (Pike, 2000e: 180). Such teaching acknowledges the 'life experience of the reader' as the 'source of the most significant guiding factors during reading' (Benton, 1988: 14) and recognizes that children do not 'read literature in a vacuum or in a generalized kind of academic setting' (Dias and Hayhoe, 1988: 22). As we have seen, the reader 'brings to or adds to the non-verbal or socio-physical setting, his whole past experience of life and literature' (Rosenblatt, 1978: 8) and this necessarily includes the reader's spiritual and moral faculties. Classroom activities, subject ideology and the nature of aesthetic learning ensure that literature lessons can be particularly good points of departure for embarking upon spiritual journeys and especially significant everyday places in which children can learn to travel (Pike, 2000b). Such an approach to English ensures people do not live 'starved existences' and guarantees that through literature 'one of the richest fields of our spiritual being' (Newbolt, 1921: 257) is cultivated.

Further reading

McCulloch, R. and Mathieson, M. (1995) *Moral Education through English 11–16*. London: David Fulton.

Pike, M.A. (2000) 'Spirituality, morality and poetry', *International Journal of Children's Spirituality*, 5(2): 177–91.

Pike, M.A. (2002) 'Aesthetic distance and the spiritual journey: educating for morally and spiritually significant experiences across the art and literature curriculum', *International Journal of Children's Spirituality*, 7(1): 9–21.

Pike, M.A. (2004) 'Aesthetic distance and the spiritual journey', in C. Erricker, J. Erricker, C. Ota (eds) *Issues in Spiritual Education: Literary, Aesthetic and Empirical Approaches*. Brighton: Sussex Academic Publishers.

Smith, D. (1999) *Making Sense of Spiritual Development*. Nottingham: The Stapleford Centre.

References

Alter, E. and Kermode, F. (eds) (1987) *The Literary Guide to the Bible*. Cambridge, MA: Harvard University Press.

Altrichter, H., Posch, P., Somekh, B. (1993) *Teachers Investigate their Work – an Introduction to the Methods of Action Research*. London and New York, NY: Routledge.

Andrews, R. (1991) *The Problem with Poetry*. Milton Keynes: Open University Press.

Andrews, R. (2000) 'Learning, literacy and ICT: what's the connection?', *English in Education*, 34(3): 3–18.

AQA (2001) *AQA GCE A level English Literature Specification B 2003*. Leeds: AQA.

AQA (2002a) *AQA GCSE English/English Literature Anthology 2004*. Oxford: Oxford University Press.

AQA (2002b) *AQA GCSE English/English Literature Specification A 2004*. Leeds: AQA.

Arnold, M. (1879/1988) 'Preface to Wordsworth's poems (1879)', in R. Selden (ed.) *The Theory of Criticism – from Plato to the Present*. London and New York, NY: Longman.

Atkinson, J. (1995) 'How do we teach pre-twentieth century literature?' in R. Protherough and P. King (eds) *The Challenge of English in the National Curriculum*. London: Routledge.

Barry, P. (1995) *Beginning Theory*. Manchester: Manchester University Press.

Barry, P. (2000) 'The new A levels: tackling textuality – with theory', *The Use of English*, 52(1): 13–26.

Barwood, G. (2001) 'Boys and reading: clues to gendered social practice', *New Zealand Journal of Educational Studies*, 36(1): 71–9.

Bell, R. (1988) 'Four readers reading', in M. Benton (ed.) *Young Readers Responding to Poems*. London: Routledge.

Benton, M. (ed.) (1988) *Young Readers Responding to Poems*. London: Routledge.

Benton, M. (1995) 'From "A Rake's Progress" to "Rosie's Walk": lessons in aesthetic reading', *Journal of Aesthetic Education*, 29(1): 33–46.

Benton, M. (2000) 'Canons ancient and modern: the texts we teach', *Educational Review*, 52(3): 269–77.

Benton, M. and Benton, P. (1990) *Double Vision*. London: Tate Gallery and Hodder & Stoughton.

Benton, M. and Benton, P. (1998) *New Touchstones 14–16*. London: Hodder & Stoughton.

Benton, P. (1984) 'Teaching poetry: the rhetoric and the reality', *Oxford Review of Education*, 10(3): 115–34.

Blackledge, A. (1994) 'Poetry and bias in the primary school', *Educational Review*, 46(1): 39–46.

Bleich, D. (1978) *Subjective Criticism*. Baltimore, MD, and London: Johns Hopkins University Press.

Bloom, H. (1994) *The Western Canon – the Books and School of the Ages*. New York, NY: Harcourt Brace.

Bousted, M. (2000) 'Rhetoric and practice in English teaching', *English in Education*, 34(1): 12–23.

Branson, J. (2002) 'Learning to whiteboard', *The Secondary English Magazine*, 5(5): 20–1.

Brindley, S. (ed.) (1994) *Teaching English*. London: Routledge.

Britton, J. (1993) *Literature in its Place*. London: Cassell.

Brownjohn, S. (1980) *Does it Have to Rhyme?*. London: Hodder & Stoughton.

Brownjohn, S. (1982) *What Rhymes with 'Secret'?*. London: Hodder & Stoughton.

Brumfit, C. (1991) *Assessment in Literature Teaching*. London: Macmillan.

Bruner, J. (1986) *Actual Minds, Possible Worlds*. London: Harvard University Press.

References

Bryant, I. (1996) 'Action research and reflective practice', in D. Scott and R. Usher (eds) *Understanding Educational Research*. London: Routledge.

Bullock, A. (1975) *A Language for Life*. London: HMSO.

Byatt, A.S. (1998) 'Hauntings', in B. Cox (ed.) *Literacy is not Enough: Essays on the Importance of Reading*. Manchester: Manchester University Press.

Clarke, S. (1995) 'Is "N C" English never changing? Shakespeare and the new information technologies', *English in Education*, 29(2): 12–19.

Clarke, S. (2000) 'Changing technology, changing Shakespeare, or our daughter is a misprint', in A. Goodwyn (ed.) *English in the Digital Age*. London: Cassell.

Cockcroft, W.H. (1982) *Mathematics Counts*. London: HMSO.

Cox, B. (1991) *Cox on Cox: An English Curriculum for the 1990s*. London: Hodder & Stoughton.

Cox, B. (1995) *The Battle for the National Curriculum*. London: Hodder & Stoughton.

Cox, B. (ed.) (1998) *Literacy is not Enough*. Manchester: Manchester University Press.

Crystal, D. (1996) *Discover Grammar*. Harlow: Longman.

Crystal, D. (2001) *Language and the Internet*. Cambridge: Cambridge University Press.

Daly, C. (2000a) 'Gender difference in achievement in English', in J. Davison and J. Moss (eds) *Issues in English Teaching*. London: Routledge.

Daly, C. (2000b) 'Gender and English: three studies offer important reading', *The Secondary English Magazine*, 3(3): 30–1.

Davies, C. (1996) *What is English Teaching?*. Buckingham: Open University Press.

Davis, M. (1992) 'Censorship update', *The (NCTE) Council Chronicle*, 2(1): 13.

Davison, J. and Dowson, J. (eds) (1998) *Learning to Teach English in the Secondary School – a Companion to School Experience*. London: Routledge.

Day, C. (1998) 'Working with the different selves of teachers: beyond comfortable collaboration', *Educational Action Research*, 6(2): 255–75.

Dean, G. (2002) *Teaching English in the Key Stage 3 Literacy Strategy – a Practical Guide*. London: David Fulton.

Dearing, R. (1996) *Review of Qualifications for 16–19 year olds*. London: School Curriculum Assessment Authority.

Delaney, S. (1972) 'Up against the great tradition', in L. Kampf and P. Lauter (eds) *The Politics of Literature*. New York, NY: Random House.

Derewianka, B. (1990) *Exploring how Texts Work*. NSW, Australia: PETA.

Dewey, J. (1934/1980) *Art as Experience*. New York, NY: Perigree.

DES (1989) *English for Ages 5–16* (the Cox report). London: DES.

DES (1995) *English in the National Curriculum* (the Dearing report). London: HMSO.

DFE (1990) *English in the National Curriculum (No. 2)*. London: HMSO.

DfEE (1998) *The National Literacy Strategy*. London: HMSO.

DfEE (2001) *Key Stage 3 National Strategy: Framework for Teaching English: Years 7, 8 and 9*. London: HMSO.

DfEE (2002) *Transition from Year 6 to Year 7 English – Units of Work*. London: HMSO.

DfEE/QCA (1999) *The National Curriculum for England: English Key Stages 1–4*. London: HMSO.

DfES (2001) *Year 7 Spelling Bank*. London: HMSO.

DfES (2002a) *Key Objectives Bank: Year 8*. London: HMSO.

DfES (2002b) *Key Objectives Bank: Year 9*. London: HMSO.

DfES (2002c) *Transition from Year 6 to Year 7*. London: HMSO.

Dias, P. and Hayhoe, M. (1988) *Developing Response to Poetry*. Milton Keynes: Open University Press.

Dillon, J. (1988) 'The remedial status of student questioning', *Journal of Curriculum Studies*, 20(3): 197–210.

Dunn, J. (1988) *The Beginnings of Social Understanding*. Oxford: Blackwell.

Dymoke, S. (2002) *Drafting and Assessing Poetry*. London: Sage/Paul Chapman Publishing.

Eade, J. (1997) 'Using a core text with bilingual children', *English in Education*, 31(3): 32–9.

Easthope, A. (1991) *Literary into Cultural Studies*. London: Routledge.

Edwards, D. and Mercer, N. (1987) *Common Knowledge*. London: Routledge.

Eisner, E. (2002) *The Educational Imagination* (3rd edn). Upper Saddle River, NJ: Prentice Hall.

Eliot, G. (1866/1967) 'Letter to Frederic Harrison', in F.R. Leavis *Introduction to Silas Marner*. Harmondsworth: Penguin Books.

Eliot, T.S. (1935) 'Religion and literature', in *Selected Essays*. London: Faber & Faber.

Elliot, J. (1991) *Action Research for Educational Change*. Buckingham: Open University Press.

English and Media Centre (2002) *Text, Reader, Critic – Introducing Contexts and Interpretations*. London: EMC.

Erben, M. (1998) *Biography and Education – a Reader*. London: Falmer Press.

Evans, E. (ed.) (1992) *Reading against Racism*. Buckingham and Philadelphia, PA: Open University Press.

Feagin, S. (1996) *Reading with Feeling – an Aesthetics of Appreciation*. Ithaca, NY, and London: Cornell University Press.

Fernandez, C., Chokshi, S., Cannon, J. and Yoshida, M. (2001) 'Learning and lesson study in the United States', in M.E. Sharpe (ed.) *New and Old Voices in Japanese Education*. New York, NY: Amonk.

Fish, S.E. (1978) 'Normal circumstances, literal language, direct speech acts, the ordinary, the everyday, the obvious, what goes without saying, and other special cases', *Critical Inquiry*, 4: 625–44.

Fish, S.E. (1980) *Is there a Text in this Class? The Authority of Interpretive Communities*. Boston, MA: Harvard University Press.

Fleming, M. (1992) 'Pupils' perception of the nature of poetry', *Cambridge Journal of Education*, 22 (1): 31–41.

Fleming, M. (1996) 'Poetry teaching in the secondary school: the concept of difficulty', in L. Thompson (ed.) *The Teaching of Poetry*. London: Cassell.

Fleming, M. and Stevens, D. (1998) *English Teaching in the Secondary School – a Handbook for Students and Teachers*. London: David Fulton.

Fox, G. and Merrick, D. (1981) '36 things to do with a poem', *The Times Educational Supplement*, 20 February.

Franks, A. (1999) 'Where the action is: how drama contributes to the art of the teaching and learning of English', *English in Education*, 33(2): 39–49.

Freund, E. (1987) *The Return of the Reader – Reader Response Criticism*. London: Methuen.

Frye, N. (1982) *The Great Code – the Bible and Literature*. London: Routledge & Kegan Paul.

Gabler, M. and Gabler, N. (1982) 'Mind control through textbooks', *Phi Delta Kappan*, 64(2): 96.

Garner, P. and Davies, J. (2001) *Introducing Special Needs – a Companion Guide for Student Teachers*. London: David Fulton.

Gibson, R. (1994) 'Teaching Shakespeare in schools', in S. Brindley (ed.) *Teaching English*. London: Routledge.

Gibson, R. (1998) *Teaching Shakespeare*. Cambridge: Cambridge University Press.

Glenn, C. (2000) 'Rethinking bilingual education', in R.P. Porter (ed.) *Educating Language Minority Children*. New Brunswick, NY, and London: Transaction Publishers.

Goodman, S., Lillis, T., Maybin, J. and Mercer, N. (2003) *Language, Literacy and Education: A Reader*. Stoke-on-Trent: Trentham Books/Open University.

Goodwyn, A. and Findlay, K. (1999) 'The Cox models revisited: English teachers' views of their subject and the National Curriculum', *English in Education*, 33(2) 19–31.

Grainger, T. (1998) 'Drama and reading: illuminating their interaction', *English in Education*, 32(1): 29–36.

Greenslade, R. (2003) 'Reading problems', *Media Guardian*, 13 January: 4–5.

Grimes, M.L. and Belote, S.B. (1994) 'Reclaiming the canon: the case for adolescent literature', in M. Hayhoe and S. Parker (eds) *Who owns English?*. Buckingham and Philadelphia, PA: Open University Press.

References

Grove, N. (1998) *Literature for All – Developing Literature in the Curriculum for Pupils with Special Educational Needs*. London: David Fulton.

Halliday, M. (1978) *Language as Social Semiotic*. London: Edward Arnold.

Halstead, J.M. (1999) 'John Donne and the theology of incarnation', in L. Gearon (ed.) *English Literature, Theology and the Curriculum*. London: Cassell.

Hannon, P. (2000) *Reflecting on Literacy in Education*. London: Routledge/Falmer.

Hart, A. (2001) 'Awkward practice: teaching media in English', *Changing English – Studies in Reading and Culture*, 8(1): 65–81.

Hattersley, R. (1998) 'Reading to make us glad', in B. Cox (ed.) *Literacy is not Enough – Essays on the Importance of Reading*. Manchester: Manchester University Press.

Hay, D. (1998) 'Why should we care about children 's spirituality?', *Pastoral Care*, March.

Hay McBer (2000) *Research into Teacher Effectiveness – Report to the DfEE*. London: DfEE.

Hegel, G.W.F. (1997) 'Introduction to aesthetics', in D.E. Cooper (ed.) *Aesthetics: The Classic Readings*. Oxford: Blackwell.

Heidegger, M. (1934/1993) 'Being and time', in D. Krell (ed.) *Martin Heidegger: Basic Writings*. London: Routledge.

Heidegger, M. (1936/1993) 'The question concerning technology', in D. Krell (ed.) *Martin Heidegger: Basic Writings*. London: Routledge.

HMI (2001) *Good Teaching, Effective Departments. Findings from a HMI Survey of Subject Teaching in Secondary Schools, 2000/01*. London: OFSTED.

Holland, N. (1975) *5 Readers Reading*. New Haven, CT, and London: Yale University Press.

Holmes, A.F. (1984) *Ethics – Approaching Moral Decisions*. Leicester: InterVarsity Press.

Huebner, D.E. (1962/1999) 'The art of teaching', in V. Hillis (ed.) *The Lure of the Transcendent*. Hillsdale, NJ, and London: Lawrence Erlbaum Associates.

Huebner, D.E. (1979/1999) 'Developing teacher competencies', in V. Hillis (ed.) *The Lure of the Transcendent*. Hillsdale, NJ, and London: Lawrence Erlbaum Associates.

Iser, W. (1971) 'Indeterminacy and the reader's response in prose fiction', in J. Hillis Miller (ed.) *Aspects of Narrative: Selected Papers from the English Institute*. New York, NY: Columbia University Press.

James, W. (1902) *The Varieties of Religious Experience*. London: Fontana.

Jasper, D. (1999) 'How can we read the Bible?', in L. Gearon (ed.) *English Literature, Theology and the Curriculum*. London: Cassell.

Jauss, H.R. (1982) *Toward an Aesthetic of Reception*. Minneapolis, MN: University of Minnesota Press.

Keith, G. and Shuttleworth, J. (2000) *Living Language – Exploring Advanced Level English*. London: Hodder & Stoughton.

Kress, G. (1989) *Linguistic Processes in Sociocultural Practice*. Oxford: Oxford University Press.

Knight, P. (2002) 'A systemic approach to professional development: learning as practice', *Teaching and Teacher Education*, 18: 229–41.

Kyriacou, C. (1998) 'Planning and preparation', Chapter 2 in *Essential Teaching Skills*. Cheltenham: Nelson-Thornes.

Leavis, F.R. (1948) *The Great Tradition: George Eliot, Henry James, Joseph Conrad*. London: Chatto & Windus.

Littlefair, A. (1991) *Reading All Types of Writing*. Milton Keynes: Open University Press.

Littlefair, A. (1992) 'Reading and writing across the curriculum', in C. Harrison and M. Coles (eds) *The Reading for Real Handbook*. London: Routledge.

Lomax, P. (ed.) (1990) *Managing Better Schools and Colleges: An Action Research Way*. Clevedon: Multilingual Matters.

Long, J. (2000) 'Spirituality and the idea of transcendence', *International Journal of Children 's Spirituality*, 5(2): 147–61.

Lunzer, E. and Gardner, K. (eds) (1979) *The Effective Use of Reading*. London: Heinemann Educational Books for the Schools Council.

Marshall, B. (1998) 'English teachers and the third way' in B. Cox (ed.) *Literacy is not Enough.* Manchester, M.U.P.

Marshall, B. (2000) 'A rough guide to English teachers', *English in Education,* 34(1): 24–41.

May, P. (1981) *Which Way to Teach?.* Leicester: InterVarsity Press.

Maybin, J. (1996) 'An English canon?', in J. Maybin and N. Mercer (eds) *Using English from Conversation to Canon.* London and New York, NY: The Open University and Routledge.

Maybin, J. and Mercer, N. (eds) (1996) *Using English: From Conversation to Canon.* London and New York, NY: The Open University and Routledge.

McCrum, R., Cran, W. and MacNeil, R. (1987) *The Story of English.* New York, NY: Viking Penguin.

McCulloch, R. and Mathieson, M. (1995) *Moral Education through English 11–16.* London: David Fulton.

McNiff, J. (1993) *Teaching as Learning – an Action Research Approach.* London: Routledge.

McNiff, J., Lomax, P. and Whitehead, J. (1996) *You and Your Action Research Project.* London: Routledge.

Meek, M. (1985) 'Play and paradoxes: some considerations of imagination and language', in G. Wells and J. Nicholls (eds) *Language and Learning – an Interactional Perspective.* London: Falmer Press.

Mercer, N. (2000) *Words and Minds.* London: Taylor & Francis.

Mercer, N. and Swann, J. (1996) *Learning English: Development and Diversity.* London and New York, NY: The Open University and Routledge.

Merrick, D. and Fox, G. (1993) *Poems from other Ages.* London: Collins.

Millard, E. (1997) *Differently Literate.* London: Falmer Press.

Muijs, D. and Reynolds, D. (2001) *Effective Teaching.* London: Paul Chapman Publishing/Sage.

Myhill, D. (1999a) 'Bottom set boys: a deficit model of male achievement', *The Use of English,* 50(3): 228–40.

Myhill, D. (1999b) 'Writing matters: linguistic characteristics of writing in GCSE English examinations', *English in Education,* 33(3): 70–81.

Naidoo, B. (1994) 'The territory of literature: defining the coastline', *English in Education,* 28(1) 39–44.

Naidoo, B. (1995) 'Crossing boundaries through fiction: a personal account', *English in Education,* 29(1): 4–13.

Newbolt Committee (1921) *The Teaching of English in England.* London: HMSO.

Newbould, A. and Stibbs, A. (1983) *Exploring Texts through Reading Aloud and Dramatization.* London: Ward Lock Educational.

NFER (1996) *GCSE Grade Predictions Based on Levels C and D CAT Scores in Years 6 and 7.* Slough: NFER-Nelson Education.

Nye, R. (1998) 'Relational consciousness: a key to unlocking psychological facets of children 's spirituality ', paper presented at the International Seminar on Religious Education and Values, 15–16 July.

O'Brien, V. (1985) *Teaching Poetry in the Secondary School.* London: Arnold.

OFSTED (1993) *Boys and English.* London: DFE.

OFSTED (1994a) *Spiritual, Moral, Social and Cultural Development: An OFSTED Discussion Paper.* London: HMSO.

OFSTED (1994b) *Framework for the Inspection of Schools* (revised edn). London: OFSTED.

Open University (2002) *Language and Literature in a Changing World* (MA course E844). Milton Keynes: Open University Press.

Ousbey, J. (1991) 'Reading and the imagination', in C. Harrison and E. Ashworth (eds) *Celebrating Literacy, Defending Literacy.* Oxford: Blackwell.

Palmer, C. (1992) 'African slave trade: the cruellest commerce', *National Geographic Magazine,* September: 62–91.

References

Palmer, P.J. (1993) *To Know as we are Known: A Spirituality of Education*. New York, NY: HarperCollins.

Paxman, J. (1998) *The English – a Portrait of a People*. Harmondsworth: Penguin Books.

Peim, N. (1993) *Critical Theory and the English Teacher*. London: Routledge.

Phillion, J. (2002a) 'Classroom stories of multicultural teaching and learning', *Journal of Curriculum Studies*, 34(3): 281–300.

Phillion, J (2002b) 'Becoming a narrative inquirer in a multicultural landscape', *Journal of Curriculum Studies*, 34(5): 535–56.

Pike, M.A. (1996) 'A whole new perspective – a media day', *Northcliffe Newsdesk*, 12 (Winter): 1.

Pike, M.A. (1999) 'Reading the writer, reading the reader: pre-twentieth century literature in the English literature examination', *The Use of English*, 51(1): 41–52.

Pike, M.A, (2000a) 'Keen readers: a study of communication and learning in adolescents' reading of pre-twentieth century poetry', unpublished PhD thesis, Research and Graduate School of Education, Faculty of Social Science, University of Southampton.

Pike, M.A. (2000b) Keen readers: adolescents and pre-twentieth century poetry', *Educational Review*, 52 (1): 13–28.

Pike, M.A. (2000c) 'Pupils poetics', *Changing English – Studies in Reading and Culture*, 7(1): 45–54.

Pike, M.A. (2000d) 'Boys, poetry and individual talent', *English in Education*, 34(3): 41–55.

Pike, M.A. (2000e) 'Spirituality, morality and poetry', *International Journal of Children 's Spirituality*, 177–91.

Pike, M.A. (2001) 'Adolescents as active readers', in NFER (ed.) *TOPIC (Practical Applications of Research in Education)* 26. Slough: NFER.

Pike, M.A. (2002a) 'Aesthetic distance and the spiritual journey: educating for morally and spiritually significant experiences across the art and literature curriculum', *International Journal of Children's Spirituality*, 5(2) 7(1): 9–21.

Pike, M.A. (2002b) 'Action research for English teaching: ideology, pedagogy and personal growth', *Educational Action Research*, 10(1) 27–44.

Pike, M.A. (2002c) 'The most wanted text in the West: Rewards offered for reading the Bible as literature', *The Use of English*, 54(1): 29–42.

Pike, M.A. (2003a) 'On being in English teaching: a time for Heidegger?', *Changing English – Studies in Reading and Culture*, 10(1): 91–99.

Pike, M.A. (2003b) 'The canon in the classroom: students' experiences of texts from other times', *Journal of Curriculum Studies*, 35(3) 355–70.

Pike, M.A. (2003c) 'The Bible and the reader 's response', *Journal of Education and Christian Belief*, 7(1): 37–51.

Pike, M.A. (2003d) 'From personal to social transaction: a model of aesthetic reading in the classroom', *Journal of Aesthetic Education*, 37(2) 61–72.

Pike, M.A. (2003e) 'Belief as an obstacle to reading: the case of the Bible?', *Journal of Beliefs and Values*, 24(2) 155–63.

Pike, M.A. (2003f) 'From the picture to the diagram? Literacy and the art of English teaching' *The Use of English* 54(3) 211–16.

Pike, M.A. (2003g) 'Aesthetic distance and the spiritual journey', in C. Ota, C. Erricker, J. Erricker, (eds) *Issues in Spiritual Education: Literary, Aesthetic and Empirical Approaches*. Brighton: Sussex Academic Publishers.

Pike, M.A. (2004) 'Aesthetic teaching', *Journal of Aesthetic Education*, 38(1).

Protherough, R. (1986) *Teaching Literature for Examinations*. Milton Keynes: Open University Press.

QCA (1998) *Can Do Better – Raising Boys' Achievement in English*. London: QCA.

QCA (1999a) *The Promotion of Pupils' Spiritual, Moral, Social and Cultural Development – the Contribution of Subject Teaching in Secondary Schools and Colleges*. London: HMSO.

QCA (1999b) *Improving Writing at Key Stages 3 and 4*. London: QCA.

QCA (2002) Changes to assessment 2003: *sample materials for Key Stage 3 English*. London: QCA.

Reimer, K.S. and Furrow, J.L. (2001) 'A qualitative exploration of relational consciousness in Christian children', *International Journal of Children 's Spirituality*, 6(1): 7–23.

Richardson, P. (1998) 'Literacy, learning and teaching', *Educational Review*, 50(2): 115–34.

Rosenblatt, L. (1968) *Literature as Exploration*. London: Heinemann.

Rosenblatt, L. (1978) *The Reader, the Text, the Poem: The Transactional Theory of the Literary Work*. Carbondale, IL: Southern Illinois University Press.

Rosenblatt, L. (1985) 'The transactional theory of the literary work: implications for research', in C. Cooper (ed.) *Researching Response to Literature and the Teaching of Literature*. Norwood, NJ: Ablex.

SCAA (1995) *Spiritual and Moral Development*. London: HMSO.

Schön, D. (1983) *The Reflective Practitioner: How Professionals Think in Action*. New York, NY: Basic Books.

Selden, R. and Widdowson, P. (1993) *A Reader's Guide to Contemporary Literary Theory*. New York, NY: Harvester Wheatsheaf.

Senior, K. (1995) 'Pupils go media mad', *The Citizen*, 23 June.

Smith, D. (1999) *Making Sense of Spiritual Development*. Nottingham: The Stapleford Centre.

Smith, D. and Shortt, J. (2002) *The Bible and the Task of Teaching*. Nottingham: The Stapleford Centre.

Stables, A., Morgan, C. and Jones, S. (1999) 'Educating for significant events: the application of Harre 's social reality matrix across the lower secondary-school curriculum', *Journal of Curriculum Studies*, 31(4): 449–61.

Stenhouse, L. (1975) *An Introduction to Curriculum Research and Development*. London: Heinemann.

Stevens, J. (2000) 'The new A levels: critical theory in the sixth form classroom: a very, very short introduction', *The Use of English*, 52(1): 1–11.

Stevens, J. (2002) 'The demands of synoptic assessment in the new English literature A level', *The Use of English*, 53(2): 97–107.

Stibbs, A. (1979) *Assessing Children 's Language – Guidelines for Teachers*. London: Ward Lock Educational/NATE.

Stibbs, A. (1991) *Reading Narrative as Literature: Signs of Life*. Milton Keynes: Open University Press.

Stibbs, A. (1996) 'The marriage of Bitzer and Sissy: is there a place for knowledge about literature in secondary teaching?', *The Use of English*, 48(1): 29–37.

Stibbs, A. (1998) 'Language in art and art in language', *Journal of Art and Design Education*, 17(2): 201–9.

Stibbs, A. (2000) 'Can you (almost) read a poem backwards and view a painting upside down? Restoring aesthetics to poetry teaching', *Journal of Aesthetic Education*, 34(2): 37–47.

Stibbs, A. (2001) 'For how long, where, and with whom: narrative time, place and company as generic distinguisher and ideological indicators', *Changing English*, 8(1): 35–42.

Taylor, C. (1993) 'Engaged agency and background in Heidegger', in C. Guignon (ed.) *The Cambridge Companion to Heidegger*. Cambridge: Cambridge University Press.

Tolstoy, L. (1997/1930) 'On art', in D.E. Cooper (ed.) *Aesthetics: The Classic Readings*. Oxford: Blackwell.

Tompkins, J. (ed.) (1980) *Reader-Response Criticism*. Baltimore, MD: Johns Hopkins University Press.

Trelawny-Ross, D. (1998) 'The forum: helping students respond meaningfully to poetry as well as pass exams', *English in Education*, 32(1): 45–54.

Trotman, J. and Kerr, T. (2001). 'Making the personal professional: pre-service teacher education and personal histories', *Teachers and Teaching: Theory and Practice*, 7(1): 157–71.

TTA (2000) *Supporting Assessment for the Award of Qualified Teacher Status: Secondary English* (A4 booklet and video tape).

References

TTA (2002) *Qualifying to Teach: Professional Standards for Qualified Teacher Status and Requirements for Initial Teacher Training*. London: TTA.

Vygotsky, L. (1978) *Mind in Society*. Cambridge, MA: MIT Press.

Vygotsky, L. (1986) *Thought and Language*. Cambridge, MA: MIT Press.

Wade, B. and Ball, M. (1983) 'Advanced level literature: a consumer report', *Journal of Research in Reading*, 6: 7–18.

Wade, B. and Reed, M. (1987) 'Students' experiences of their literature courses: a comparative study', *Educational Review*, 39(1): 55–64.

Webb, E. (1992) *Literature in Education – Encounter and Experience*. London: Falmer Press.

Winston, J. (1999) 'Theorising drama as moral education', *Journal of Moral Education*, 28(4): 459–71.

Winter, R., Buck, A. and Sobiechowska, P. (1999) *Professional Experience and the Investigative Imagination: the Art of Reflective Writing*. London and New York, NY: Routledge.

Yates, C. (1999) *Jumpstart: Poetry in the Secondary School*. London: The Poetry Society.

Author Index

Subject Index